ALSO BY MARK OPPENHEIMER

Knocking on Heaven's Door:
American Religion in the Age of Counterculture

Thirteen and a Day

AND A DAY

The Bar and Bat Mitzvah
Across America

MARK OPPENHEIMER

FARRAR, STRAUS AND GIROUX

NEW YORK

296.4424
Oppenheimer

Farrar, Straus and Giroux
19 Union Square West, New York 10003

Copyright © 2005 by Mark Oppenheimer
All rights reserved
Distributed in Canada by Douglas & McIntyre Ltd.
Printed in the United States of America
First edition, 2005

Library of Congress Cataloging-in-Publication Data
Oppenheimer, Mark, 1974–
    Thirteen and a day : the bar and bat mitzvah across America /
Mark Oppenheimer.— 1st ed.
        p.   cm.
Includes bibliographical references.
ISBN-13: 978-0-374-10665-2
ISBN-10: 0-374-10665-7 (hardcover : alk. paper)
    1. Bar mitzvah.   2. Bat mitzvah.   3. Jews—United States—Social life
and customs.   I. Title.

BM707.O67 2005
296.4'424—dc22

                                                    2004016793

Designed by Debbie Glasserman

www.fsgbooks.com

1   3   5   7   9   10   8   6   4   2

IN MEMORY OF
REBEKAH MULLER KIRSCHNER
(1907–1990)

I certainly wasn't an adult in the legal sense. I couldn't go out and live life on my own now. I couldn't support myself. So what then? It meant I had a responsibility, now, to go to services and try to get something from them. Now I could truly feel guilty for sneaking out of Rosh Hashanah services to sit in the hall and play cards.

—DAN LAZEWATSKY, AGE SIXTEEN

I have not been to a bar mitzvah, but from what I have heard, a bar mitzvah is like a birthday party, except there is a long ceremony before the party actually begins.

—THEEDA LONG, AGE SIXTEEN

As I crossed the floor to the bimah, I realized that the way in which I was becoming an adult in the Jewish community was that nobody who didn't speak Hebrew would understand what I was about to sing and I would be able to explain it to them and to teach them. With the ability to teach came the greatest power and responsibility.

—SIMONE WEISMAN, AGE SIXTEEN

Contents

Author's Note

Many Jewish words have two versions or pronunciations, and consequently two spellings: a Hebrew or Sephardic form, which has become popular because it is used in modern Israel, and a Yiddish or Ashkenazic form, common to most European Jews but used less as time goes on. Thus, what was once a bas mitzvah is now generally a bat mitzvah; Shabbos, the Sabbath, is more often Shabbat; and a tallis, or prayer shawl, has become a tallit. In this book, I let people speak as they wish. When not quoting others, I use both pronunciations and various spellings as they seem appropriate to the town, synagogue, or family, or just as they sound right to me.

Thirteen and a Day

Introduction:
The American Rite

*T*he typical bar or bat mitzvah ceremony—the religious part, anyway—is quite simple. A boy of about thirteen, or a girl of twelve or thirteen, leads a portion of the traditional Jewish Sabbath service and reads aloud some of the Bible portions assigned to that week. The event is supposed to mark the moment when a young Jew assumes the responsibilities of religious adulthood.

In the United States, however, when most people hear the term "bar mitzvah," "bat mitzvah," or the plural, "b'nai mitzvah," they think of the party that follows the religious ceremony. The language we use is telling: while one really *becomes* a bar or bat mitzvah, a son or daughter of the commandment, Americans speak of "having" a bar mitzvah, the way one "has" a wedding. Even for traditional, observant Jews who take the religious aspect seriously, a bar or bat mitzvah is as much an event as it is a person; for irreligious Jews, it's one of the very few events, along with yearly celebrations of Hanukkah and Passover, that may mark them as Jewish.

For several centuries after the bar mitzvah's beginning in medieval times, the ritual was, as far as scholars can tell, only a rite of passage from Jewish youth to manhood, not a grand feast. We don't even know if parties for the bar mitzvah existed before the sixteenth century. But now the party is often a social coming-out, a boy's or girl's first big day, analogous to a debutante's ball. Once, the best-known visual image of a bar mitzvah was the German painter Moritz Oppenheim's 1869 painting of a bar mitzvah boy delivering his speech; today, far more people would recognize Lauren Greenfield's famous photograph, from her book *Fast Forward*, of thirteen-year-old Adam dancing at a bar mitzvah in Los Angeles, his face level with a hired dancer's breasts.

A century ago, the bar mitzvah was not an important part of Jewish American social life. Reform Jews did not practice the bar mitzvah, and few Orthodox Jews could afford lavish balls in their children's honor. When there was a party, it was for relatives and for parents' friends, only incidentally for other teenagers. The bar mitzvah boy was discharging a religious duty, and for his learning, for his successful completion of the task, he would get his parents' pride, some small gifts— a wallet, a money clip, a fountain pen—and maybe a little money, to be put in his first savings account. Only fifty years ago, it would not have seemed possible that the bar mitzvah would become common in every branch of Judaism and the bat mitzvah nearly ubiquitous too. Nobody foresaw the parties for hundreds, with deejays and professional dancers and decorations costing thousands of dollars or even more. But b'nai mitzvah became so popular, so swiftly, that now it's hard to imagine a time when they were not such a big deal.

There was such a time once, a time when many faithful Jewish boys and girls gave only a thought to the ceremony and even less consideration to the party afterward. But today, if a family goes to synagogue at all—and often even if they don't go—the children celebrate b'nai mitzvah. How they celebrate them, what those celebrations look like, and what they mean have become a problem for contemporary Judaism, with the power to pervert religion into neurosis, joy into anxiety.

Worried rabbis and parents try to focus their children on the spiritual, rather than the material or sensual, significance of b'nai mitzvah, but success has been fitful. Particularly in areas with big Jewish populations, the lavish bar or bat mitzvah party is not just a rite but a right: in Great Neck or Beverly Hills, to have parents who won't throw a big bar mitzvah party is like having parents who won't allow television; to have the religious ceremony with no grand festivity afterward would be like Hanukkah without the presents. It's not that a bar mitzvah can't be a simple affair, but in these towns the simple affair is the unusual one, and the low-key bar mitzvah is left to self-styled bohemians and counterculturalists.

There is a lot of angst about these parties. Not only can they be elaborate and expensive, but they can be depressingly similar. They are time-consuming. They are repetitive. In towns with large Jewish populations, junior-high-schoolers may be invited to a bar or bat mitzvah every weekend of the school year: endless carpooling for parents, dozens of party dresses for girls, a thousand dollars in gifts. And yet these festivities are one of American Jews' gifts to the world.

I am Jewish, but I had no bar mitzvah. I would not say that my parents are against religion, but they were not raised to think that religious rituals are very important. My mother's parents were communist, atheist schoolteachers. As a young girl, struck by a brief case of religiosity, she convinced them to take her to a Reform temple. But soon it passed. Her two older brothers, of course, never had b'nai mitzvah. My father was raised by irreligious German-American Jews, of an old Pittsburgh family, and in place of b'nai mitzvah his temple celebrated confirmation, the nineteenth-century Reform Jewish ceremony modeled on the Protestant tradition. Being confirmed did not require reading from Torah, and so my father, like my mother, never learned Hebrew.

Like many Jews in the 1930s, and again in the 1960s, my parents—married by a justice of the peace, not a rabbi—practiced leftist politics instead of religion. When I was two years old, our family moved from New York City to Springfield, Massachusetts, where we joined not a synagogue but Mudpie, a child-care cooperative that met in the auditorium of an Episcopal church. Mudpie was politically correct in the late 1970s, before anyone used the term "PC," and we were taught, for example, to say not "mailman" but "letter carrier." The other parents included Robert and Ellie Meeropol, the son and daughter-in-law of Julius and Ethel Rosenberg, the communists executed for conspiring to sell atomic secrets to the Soviets. Some of the Christian families attended liberal churches, Unitarian or Congregationalist, but none of the Jewish families went to synagogue. Leftism, not Torah or Zionism, was what mattered.

I knew almost no other Jewish children in Springfield, and none from religious families. Springfield was Irish, Puerto Rican, Italian—Catholic through and through—and the only b'nai mitzvah I attended as a child were my cousins', in Chicago and Philadelphia. When I got to college at Yale, I felt as if I were meeting other Jews for the first time. I met Jews who had been to Israel, Jews who could read Hebrew, Jews who planned to be rabbis, Jews who, with a kitschy irony, still wore T-shirts received as bar mitzvah party favors. (A T-shirt given out on a bar mitzvah party cruise read, "I rocked the boat at Josh's bar mitzvah!") There were famous Jewish professors: the literary critic Harold Bloom, the poet John Hollander, the Yiddish scholar Benjamin Harshav. For the first time, I heard the ram's horn blown on the Jewish New Year, when James Ponet, the brusque, bearded Yale rabbi, barreled into the dining hall where I was eating, stood on a chair, and summoned a long, sharp wail from the shofar. It was bizarre, but intriguing. At Yale's Kosher Kitchen, I attended my first traditional Sabbath meal.

Slowly, I came to wonder about the absence of Judaism in my childhood. I began to take classes that would fill the gaps in my learning. In my junior year, I discovered Professor Harry Stout's course on religion from the Puritans to the Civil War, and it was exciting precisely because I was beginning from a place of such ignorance, whose attenuation I could feel from week to week: "So *this* is what the leftists were keeping from me," I remember thinking. A year after graduating, I returned to Yale for graduate school, six years studying American religious history—which is, given the population of the United States, mostly Christian history. Judaism was one of my "minor fields," which means that I gleaned just enough knowledge to sound reasonably informed in front of undergraduates, though in truth I was hopelessly out of my depth. I took one semester of biblical Hebrew, which I quickly forgot. I was learning about Judaism, but only in the spotty way of an amateur. I started going to synagogue occasionally.

During some time off from graduate school, I worked as a religion writer for the *Hartford Courant*, and I picked up bits of knowledge from the Jewish rabbis and scholars I met, complementing what I had learned from my professors and Jewish grad student friends. I was growing comfortable with the talk—learning to call the holidays the "chagim," to call synagogue "shul"—and with the experience of synagogue prayer.

Jews like me, who come to the tradition a little late in life, sometimes go back and try to earn some credits that they missed earlier. *Today I Am a Boy*, by the set designer David Hays, is about the author's celebrating his bar mitzvah at nearly seventy. I took a trip to Israel that was led by a young woman, Rachel Cymrot, who had celebrated her bat mitzvah while a student at Bates College. Daniel Adamson, a law student I know, son of a Jewish mother and a Gentile father, studied for months during law school for his bar mitzvah, which was followed by a small party, about thirty people, including his obviously proud parents. (I should not forget Krusty the Klown, of television's *The Simpsons*, who returned to his roots and became an adult bar mitzvah in a ceremony presided over by his father, Rabbi Hyman Krustofski, voiced by the comedian Jackie Mason.)

Jewish friends occasionally ask if I might want to celebrate an adult bar mitzvah. The answer has always been no, I think because the upbringing my parents gave me—in which I knew some Jews, liked Jews, and had no animosity toward Judaism, but lived in a Gentile city and knew little about how most Jews lived—is itself a religious heritage. It's a heritage suited less to personal piety than to cultivating a respectful curiosity about Judaism in others; and nothing is more typical of Judaism in others than the bar and bat mitzvah. It belongs to Jews liberal and ultra-Orthodox, rich and poor, urban and rural. We don't really know where it comes from, but we know it's not going anywhere.

For some Jews, the ubiquity, the totalizing nature, of the bar and bat mitzvah makes it a thing to do; for me, it made it a thing to study. B'nai mitzvah are religiously important and they are sociologically interesting; they are the Christian's baptism and the Muslim's pilgrimage to Mecca combined, rituals of initiation and of maturation. They are celebrations too: what begins in the sanctuary with piety, even solemnity, moves to the dining room, catering hall, or hotel ballroom, gaining in merriment along the way.

Jews in Israel and in Europe, where the first bar mitzvah feasts were held, have followed the American lead in making those feasts bigger and more elaborate than ever. And as Jews have moved into religiously mixed neighborhoods here in the United States, b'nai mitzvah, perfectly embodying our country's peculiar mix of piety and materialism, have begun to transcend Judaism altogether. In 2004, *People* magazine reported that adolescents in Los Angeles were celebrating "faux mitzvahs"—parties for *non*-Jews envious of their Jewish classmates. If present trends hold, the bar mitzvah might someday be more popular than Judaism itself.

And every part of me—journalist, historian, Jew—wondered how this had happened.

To investigate the wild and growing popularity of b'nai mitzvah, I traveled around the country trying every Saturday to find a bar or bat mitzvah to crash. Sometimes I invited myself ahead of time, but just as often I showed up and hoped people would talk to me afterward. That had not been my initial plan—I had not wanted, for example, to travel to Alaska in the dead of January to visit Hasidim. At first, I'd thought I could learn what I wanted to know by reading books from the library. But almost nothing was written. Then I tried to spend a year with one synagogue, studying one community deeply rather than trying to sample a whole country. But the higher ups at Westchester Reform Temple, who at first had been amenable, changed their minds and said that they didn't want me around.

That was probably just as well. I soon realized that if b'nai mitzvah were truly American, I would have to see them across America. Westchester Reform Temple's rejection of my plan sent me on an odyssey, in the true sense of the word, a trip that ends where it began. After a year of traveling, I was back in New Haven, the same person, with the same familiar, half-hearted religiosity, arguing Judaism with the same skeptical friends. The only difference was that in Alaska and Arkansas, in Florida and Louisiana and New York, I had met some very thoughtful people, young and old, who in celebrating b'nai mitzvah had practiced an aspect of Judaism that I had not. And it was no mystery to them why they had.

"Why would you want to write about *that?*" adult Jews asked, when they heard about my project. "Who would want to read about a bunch of spoiled children?"

The sentiment is regrettable, but it points to something real, the sour experience many b'nai mitzvah have. Well into my research, I asked a class of juniors at Newton North High School, in the synagogue-rich town of Newton, Massachusetts, to write short reflections on their experience with b'nai mitzvah. (Three students' replies yielded the epigraphs to this book.) About half the Jews (and non-Jews) remembered b'nai mitzvah fondly, but others looked back with complicated, or plainly negative, emotions. Hana Dembe expressed a common sentiment: "Seventh grade was a year filled with first kisses, awkward slow dancing, braces, changing voices, and scandal. Mixing these things together causes disasters known as b'nai mitzvah." Ellie Teymouri, whose family is Iranian and Muslim, wrote, "One of my close friend's bar mitzvah ended in tears for him because the girl he had a crush on hooked up with another boy, right in front of him." Britney Lai wrote about an unpopular boy who had hopefully invited all of his classmates: "No one wanted to go, and his mother had to call everyone in my school and personally ask them to come."

And yet the saddest comments I heard, when I began asking people about their b'nai mitzvah, were not from Jews who hated the experience, but from Jews who enjoyed their own b'nai mitzvah but were disdainful of others'. Such a person would assume a posture combining distaste and condescension: "My bar

mitzvah was a very nice affair. Very simple, very tasteful. Not at
all like so much of what you see today." His bar mitzvah, or her
bat mitzvah, had had nothing in common with those examples
of vulgarity and excess: "Well, I am from Scarsdale, where our
bar mitzvahs are nothing like the ones on Long Island"; "I live
in Greenwich, where we do things so much more low-key than
in Scarsdale"; "Up in Litchfield County, where I grew up, Judaism is about religion, not about parties the way it is in Greenwich." One's good taste and class apparently increase directly
with one's distance from New York City.

I was happy enough to see the conversation end there, because I came to learn where it could lead—into outright Jewish self-loathing: "That's one of the reasons I was so happy to
leave Syosset. Those were not my kind of Jews, with their
frosted hair and cars from Daddy. Total JAPs. And the bat
mitzvahs were just *absurd . . .*"

That ambivalence is everywhere in books and movies too.
There are few depictions of b'nai mitzvah in literature before the 1970s—none in Saul Bellow's novels, none in Philip
Roth's (although Alexander Portnoy in *Portnoy's Complaint*
reminisces about his bar mitzvah years after the fact, on the
analyst's couch)—but when the bar mitzvah does become a
subject for literature, it is treated as a source of discomfort,
best handled as a joke. The earliest major bar mitzvah scene
shows Duddy Kravitz, the young shyster in the Canadian
writer Mordecai Richler's 1959 novel *The Apprenticeship of
Duddy Kravitz*, making a quick buck filming young Bernie
Cohen's bar mitzvah and selling the film to Bernie's father. (It
may be that Duddy hatched this idea, now common, of filming the bar mitzvah; the practice is forbidden in traditional Judaism, which does not permit the operation of electronic
equipment on the Sabbath, and home movies were not afford-
able before the 1950s anyway.) In both the book and the

movie version, which stars a young Richard Dreyfuss as Duddy, the bar mitzvah film is a farce, a bit of ersatz art cinema that splices scenes from African tribal rites and the circumcision of Jewish newborns with Bernie's bar mitzvah.

Only much later, in the 1990s, do bar and bat mitzvah scenes become common in books or film, and still they are played for laughs. In the 1997 Woody Allen movie *Deconstructing Harry*, Donald has a *Star Wars*–themed bar mitzvah, his caterers dressed up as stormtroopers. In a 2002 episode of *Frasier*, Frasier Crane, the consummate Gentile, eager to give a speech in Hebrew at the bar mitzvah of his son, Frederick (raised Jewish by his mother, Lilith), through a series of cruel mishaps ends up delivering a speech in the *Star Trek* language of Klingon, which he thinks is Hebrew. It's all very funny— one of the funniest *Frasiers*—but it is difficult to imagine a Catholic girl's First Communion, or a Muslim's Ramadan fast, working so well as a joke.

I did find affectionate representations of b'nai mitzvah—in a poem by John Hollander, in the William Finn musical *Falsettos*, in the Adam Sandler movie *The Wedding Singer*, in John Schlesinger's 1971 movie *Sunday Bloody Sunday*—but they are exceptions. More typical is the crass party that Samantha Jones organizes for the bratty, bitchy Jenny Brier on HBO's *Sex and the City*. "My father has invited over three hundred of his most powerful friends to this event," Jenny tells Samantha. "They're not all coming. The Clintons can't make it, of course. But like I told Daddy, we'll be lucky if we can swing this for under a mil." In general, the bar mitzvah is trotted out to be mocked.*

---

*A full catalogue of major bar and bat mitzvah scenes in the arts would include television shows like *Seinfeld*, novels like Herman Wouk's *Marjorie Morningstar* and Michael Chabon's *The Amazing Adventures of Kavalier & Clay*, and movies like *Safe Men* and *Starsky & Hutch*.

B'nai mitzvah can call forth an especially poisonous form of self-loathing, a cocktail of bad childhood memories and condescending sneers that are really masking insecurity. Consider this e-mail that one powerful New York editor, a Jewish man, wrote after reading my book proposal: "I don't think I'll have the interest, or the patience, to go through the bar mitzvah process again. Once was enough."

The Torah, I was surprised to find, mentions no special ceremony to mark the onset of adult responsibilities. Nor does the legal code the Mishnah, nor the Talmud, the great commentary on the Mishnah. Many Jewish rituals are saved from obsolescence by their provenance: we have to find ways to keep them fresh, because God has told us to keep them alive, even if they seem kitschy, corny, or uncomfortable. The Passover seder might have its funny moments, like the antiquated question about why we recline to eat even as everybody is sitting up straight, but it is commanded by the Book of Exodus. Purim is a fine opportunity for public drunkenness, but it also entails a celebratory reading of the Book of Esther. That rationale, however, doesn't explain the bar mitzvah's persistence.

What is more, thirteen is not even the biblical age of majority. In Exodus 38, in the census taken during the building of the Tabernacle in the desert, only Jewish men aged twenty and up are counted (there are 603,550 of them). In Numbers 1, in the second year following the exodus from Egypt, another census is taken in Sinai, and again twenty is the age of majority—but that has nothing to do with participating in religious ceremonies; for that, it seems that a boy has only to be old enough to know what he's doing. Thirteen is first mentioned as an age of maturity in Pirkei Avot, the third-century compendium of Jewish ethical precepts; in the fifth-century commentary Genesis Rabbah, we first learn of the prayer of thanks said by a father when his son reaches thirteen, a prayer still said today in many bar mitzvah ceremonies: "Blessed is the One who has exempted me from responsibility from this one's punishment." But scholars don't know if in the fifth century this prayer was part of a larger ritual, or if the son was even present for its recitation.

Sometime in the Middle Ages, thirteen and a day became the age of Jewish majority: before then a boy was forbidden to lay tefillin or be counted in a minyan, but over thirteen he was obligated to do so. The historian Ivan Marcus suggests that once the age was set, "the moment of transition from religious childhood into adulthood was made into an increasingly elaborate rite of passage." Among some European Jews, the creation of an age of responsibility was followed by the creation of a rite to mark that responsibility. From then on, one did not just become a bar mitzvah, one also celebrated, or *had*, a bar mitzvah, some sort of ceremony. But we have no idea how widespread this rite of passage was, and Marcus concludes that in medieval times the bar mitzvah seems "to have been a relatively isolated practice of some German rabbis."*

The bar mitzvah party was first described by the Polish rabbi Shlomo ben Yehiel Luria, who in the mid-1500s wrote that when a boy reaches age thirteen, "the German Jews make a bar mitzvah feast [and] there is no greater obligatory feast

---

*And we're only talking about Europe. In Yemen, for example, where Jews kept the old tradition of teaching children to keep commandments as soon as they were able, bar mitzvah customs never developed at all. Everything we know about the early history of the bar mitzvah is summarized by Ivan Marcus in *The Jewish Life Cycle: Rites of Passage from Biblical to Modern Times* (Seattle: University of Washington Press, 2004), ch. 2.

than this." The feast is considered a se'udat mitzvah, an obligatory religious meal, and the boy "is trained to offer a Torah exposition appropriate to the occasion"—the first extant reference to the bar mitzvah speech, which has become basic to the ritual.

No mention is made of the bar mitzvah or the party in Jewish memoirs of the seventeenth and eighteenth centuries, so it would seem still not to be a common practice. Evidence from the nineteenth century is also scant. There is Moritz Oppenheim's 1869 painting, and in 1887 the Hungarian rabbi Moses Weinberger wrote, in his memoir of travels among American Jews, that although boys in New York lost religion immediately after their b'nai mitzvah, they celebrated the event "by the hundreds every year . . . amid enormous splendor and great show."*

The bar mitzvah had taken hold among observant Jews, but Reform rabbis predominated in the United States, and they were committed to a less oriental, more assimilated Judaism, embracing innovations like holding Sabbath services on Sunday, calling rabbis "Reverend," and ignoring kosher law. These rabbis replaced the bar mitzvah with confirmation, which was little more than a Hebrew school graduation, and the bar mitzvah might have become extinct but for the influx after World War II of thousands of Orthodox Jewish European refugees and the growth, at the same time, of the Conservative movement, founded as a middle path between Reform and Orthodoxy and committed to the bar mitzvah. In Reform Judaism, the bar mitzvah made a comeback in the late 1960s and 1970s, when young Jews and their rabbis, influenced by

---

*Moses Weinberger, *Jews and Judaism in New York*, originally published in 1887. Translated and edited by Jonathan Sarna and published in English as *People Walk on Their Heads* (New York: Holmes and Meier, 1982).

the ethnic pride movements of the counterculture and the resurgence of Zionism after the Six Day War, began to emphasize the study of Hebrew—and the bar mitzvah was all of a sudden a proud, desirable alternative to the deracinated, Christian-seeming confirmation.

In traditional Judaism, there was no such thing as a bat mitzvah, because the obligations of synagogue fall on men. But scholars have found evidence of girls' coming-of-age parties in Warsaw in 1843 and in Lemberg in 1902, and some Italian rabbis in the mid-nineteenth century blessed twelve-year-old girls alongside thirteen-year-old bar mitzvah boys. The modern bat mitzvah, involving the twelve- or thirteen-year-old daughter of the commandment in some part of the Sabbath service, originated on March 18, 1922, when Mordecai Kaplan, founder of the liberal Reconstructionist movement, led a ceremony for his daughter Judith at his synagogue in New York City. She was not permitted to read directly from the Torah parchment; instead, she stood at a "respectable distance from the Scroll," according to her memoir, and read from a chumash, a bound book of Torah. Kaplan called the rite a bas mitzvah, using the Ashkenazic pronunciation of *bat*; he hoped his daughter's service would become a model for Jewish girls.

The ceremony did not catch on right away. Historians know only that it began to spread among Conservative synagogues, slowly, in the 1950s. The girls' b'not mitzvah were often on Friday night, while the boys' b'nai mitzvah got prime time on Saturday mornings. When Reform Jews adopted the practice, they changed all that, permitting girls, too, to read from Torah. By the 1970s, then, Reform Judaism, which a hundred years earlier had pushed this Hebraic practice to the margins, had become the institutional home of the fully egalitarian, Hebraized bar and bat mitzvah. Conservative Judaism has also made bar and bat mitzvah identical rites, and even some Orthodox shuls now offer a ceremony for girls.*

This messy history suggests that there was no golden age of the bar mitzvah in the United States, no time when the ritual reliably inducted believing boys into a fraternity of religiously committed Jewish men. It was always a source of tension and conflict. Jewish immigration, which ensured that the bar mitzvah would live on in the United States, also gave Jews a freedom that has ill served religious observance. Here, Jews were not barred from any profession; here, they were not kept in the ghetto or in the Pale of Settlement. Here, wealth would rival erudition as a marker of manhood.

Yet the bar mitzvah, a ritual that honors a boy's encounter with Torah and his ascent to religious maturity, flourishes in a country where Jews do not take religious maturity very seriously.

Rabbis tell sad stories of families who join a synagogue two years before a boy's thirteenth birthday, enroll him in bar mitzvah training, see him through the big day, and then quit the synagogue immediately. The rabbis fume with frustration at Saturday morning services entirely given over to the bar or bat mitzvah of the week, where of the two hundred people in the pews more than half are friends and relatives of the boy or girl, or business associates of the father or mother. The regular congregants, the week-in, week-out worshipers, are perpetually a minority at their own synagogue. The rabbis preach sermons against ice sculptures and twenty-piece orchestras and invitations that cost five dollars apiece.

*See Paula E. Hyman, "The Introduction of Bat Mitzvah in Conservative Judaism in Postwar America," *YIVO Annual*, 1990, Northwestern University Press, 133–146.

But those indifferent parents who frustrate their rabbis are firmly resolved to see their children become b'nai mitzvah; when those children grow up, many of them will insist on b'nai mitzvah for their children. My parents were unusual in letting the ritual fall away. Even parents more conflicted about Judaism than mine see their children read Torah one Saturday: Noam Chomsky, secular Jew and anti-Zionist, reluctantly joined a synagogue when his daughter insisted on celebrating a bat mitzvah.

The bar and bat mitzvah must be better than their reputations, or else they would have disappeared long ago. If, as an anthropologist might have it, the bar mitzvah were just a rite of passage, a hero's trial like one of the twelve labors of Hercules, then it would be especially unsatisfying, because for most American Jews there is no trophy on the other side, no new privilege. For Orthodox Jewish boys, yes, their lives change after they become b'nai mitzvah: they are expected to uphold all 613 commandments of Torah, to pray every day, to be counted in the minyan of ten males required for prayer. But for most Jewish children and their families, the satisfaction of a bar or bat mitzvah must lie elsewhere.

The few books that I found about b'nai mitzvah could not explain why many assimilated and irreligious families keep the ritual, nor why this relatively young ceremony has been embraced by more observant Jews, who usually equate legitimacy with age. So as I traveled around the country and talked with people who produced this bit of religious culture, as I met with bar mitzvah boys and bat mitzvah girls, their parents and stepparents, their rabbis and teachers, their caterers and deejays, I tried to discern why, in a country with religious freedom, in which nobody has to do anything in church or synagogue or mosque, people take such trouble to keep this one part of their faith.

They did not always articulate their reasons plainly, but everyone involved agreed that b'nai mitzvah provide occasions to perform, *publicly*, something they considered valuable: the chanting of an ancient language, the renaissance of an old musical form, the independence of women, a convert's membership in his new religious community, the survival of Judaism in a town with few Jews, or even devotion to the simple idea that there are things worth doing just because our parents and grandparents did them.

This is not the Protestant idea of religion, which exalts the individual's relationship to Scripture and God, nor does it seem to correspond with William James's definition of religion as "experiences of individual men in their solitude." No, the bar and bat mitzvah are successful Jewish rituals because they are communal and public. They have an audience. And for Jews—battered by genocide, lax observance, intermarriage, and low birthrates—visible affirmations of their mere existence as a people are especially appealing.

I did not have to look hard to find b'nai mitzvah ceremonies and parties, even expensive ones, that still mattered, that were meaningful and moving in ways that had nothing to do with the party favors or the dessert tray. In a way, mine is a minority report. For whatever reason, the two years I spent investigating this topic coincided with more b'nai mitzvah articles than usual in the popular press, articles about the faux mitzvah and the party motivators and the limousine drivers who earn their living chauffeuring adolescents around. I wanted to resign my project in disgust after talking with Howard Szigeti, the Toronto entrepreneur who started an online b'nai mitzvah gift registry to save children from duplicate presents. I asked him how he had come up with the idea. "My daughter got three menorahs, two Lava lamps, and an Eskimo sculpture," he said. "She loved the Tiffany bracelet she got. So my wife saw the need for a gift registry, and here we are."

But a year after that interview, Szigeti's business had failed. Meanwhile, if history is any guide, the bar and bat mitzvah will persist. The public celebration of Jewish adulthood will continue; the community will always want to mark the day. How Jews mark the day is what will change. The parties might get bigger before they get smaller. New customs, unimaginable to us now, will arise, serving the needs of certain Jews in certain times and places. But as I meandered from the Northeast to the Far West, with stops in between, I was impressed by how similar the needs were: to keep it going, to say it loud, to do what's been done.

1

The Partyers

*D*oes a Jew need permission to loiter in a synagogue and chat with other Jews?

In the Old Country, the idea that any Jew—any male Jew—might not belong, might need clearance, would be absurd. But in the United States, where we "join" synagogues by paying membership dues, I knew I had to ask. When I approached the senior rabbi of Westchester Reform Temple in Scarsdale, New York, and asked if I could use his synagogue as a home base for my research, attend all its b'nai mitzvah for one year, and interview the children and their families, he said yes. A young, affable man, tall and dark and still lean from his years with a professional Jewish dance troupe, Rabbi Rick Jacobs told me that he had allowed a documentary film crew to film his son's circumcision, and he was interested in any project that helped expose people to Judaism. Not only was he eager to help teach people about b'nai mitzvah, but he hoped that his congregation might benefit by being put under my magnifying glass. Maybe by being written about, they would learn something useful about themselves.

Two months later, in August, as the year's bar mitzvah boys and bat mitzvah girls were returning from summer camp and doing their back-to-school shopping, I called again to make sure I still had his permission.

"I still have to run it by the temple board," Rabbi Jacobs said this time. "I'll know more at the end of the month."

On September 5, he sent an e-mail that began, "No decision has been made with regard to your desire to do field research here . . . I won't have a definitive answer until after the Holy Days." Three weeks later, he wrote to say that his board of directors had decided that they did not want a writer at their temple.

I was irked. Yes, I was a writer, and writers are not to be trusted. But I was also a Jew, and this was a Jewish house of worship, and I believed that I had every right to be there. I was also worried by what this episode said about my people. What were we afraid of? Why would we ever tell anybody that he couldn't come watch us worship? Christian churches take out ads in the newspaper and on billboards along the highway imploring people to come visit, but a curious Jew ran the risk of being barred from a temple. Were we Jews as clannish and scheming as the anti-Semites said we were?

That was an unfair question, of course. Even the most welcoming religious communities are more likely to welcome those who come in good faith than those with an inquisitorial agenda, paid by a publisher to find juicy material. Rabbis want to protect their congregations' families; parents want to shelter their children. Still, there was an implication that something happened on those Saturday mornings that could make Jews look bad. And whatever that was, I decided, it was not my job to protect their secret.

I was beginning to formulate my alternative plan—traveling the country, going to b'nai mitzvah in many different synagogues, in many different regions—but I was still curious about what the board of directors in Scarsdale had not wanted me to see. And even if Greater New York was not to be the focus of my research, it wouldn't do to neglect New York entirely. So, several times that fall and winter, I attended services, uninvited, at Westchester Reform Temple.

There was a bar or bat mitzvah, often two, every Saturday, so any weekend that I was home in southern Connecticut I could drop by. The morning of Saturday, December 7, 2002, was typical. At about 10:30, I parked my Ford wagon in the large lot, dotted with a few scattered cars; at about 10:45, dozens more cars began to roll in. Some let out a young boy or girl, then did three-point turns and drove away again, to return for the child after the service. Most of the cars parked, and out of them would come a boy wearing a tie and a jacket, or a girl in a skirt or dress, and two well-pressed parents.

There were two b'nai mitzvah that morning, Ethan and Lisa.* Rabbi Jacobs's predecessor had refused to do afternoon b'nai mitzvah, because so many families seemed to regard them as just a prelude to the evening party, with guests sometimes arriving in clothes inappropriately formal—girls in what looked to be prom gowns, boys in black tie and dinner jackets. But Rabbi Jacobs had caved to necessity. With so many b'nai mitzvah to get through every year, one needed the afternoons, so Ethan and Lisa would not be the day's last Torah readers. They sat on the stage, looking a little uncomfortable, as if they did not know each other. Two rabbis and one of the two cantors were present, sitting near the nervous children. When I walked in, the only remaining seats were in the back, by the door. I found on my seat a special siddur, or prayer book, printed expressly for bar and bat mitzvah services. The liturgy inside, the prayers and hymns and order of service, was short and easy, every part of it selected, it seemed, for singability,

*These are the only two names I have changed in this book.

pronounceability, and brevity. After some opening prayers, Rabbi Jacobs descended lithely from the stage and began pacing in front of the pews. He offered no sermon but instead asked the children questions, like a talk show host, or maybe an eagerly Socratic law school lecturer.

"What's important about today?" he asked.

Nobody answered, and he cajoled silently, moving his head forward and back with encouragement.

"It's Pearl Harbor Day," a boy called out.

"Yes, what else?"

"It's the last day of Hanukkah!" a girl shouted.

"Yes, that's right. And what is important about Hanukkah?"

"The Maccabees defeated the Greeks!"

"Yes, and what is another miracle?"

"The oil burned for eight days and nights!"

"Yes, yes, good," the rabbi said. "Now, can anyone think of a third miracle that we celebrate when we celebrate Hanukkah?"

A long pause, then Rabbi Jacobs answered his own question: "The miracle that the Jewish people have survived."

There were murmurs of assent, and the order of service resumed. Ethan and Lisa each read a bit of Torah, competent and brief, and Lisa chanted a short passage of the haftarah, or prophetic reading, which that week was a story of King Solomon, from 1 Kings.* They each gave a drashah, a short expository speech, and then sat down. Rabbi Jacobs stood up and faced each child, one at a time, asking them to stand in turn and receive his personal message. First, he drew

*Not all of the haftarot, or prophetic readings, are from the books named for prophets, like Jeremiah or Amos; rather, they are all from the section of the Hebrew Bible called Nevi'im—Prophets—a section that goes from Joshua to Malachi and includes history books like 1 and 2 Samuel and 1 and 2 Kings.

connections between Ethan's Torah portion, which included the story of Joseph's dream of the seven cows, and the Zionist leader Theodor Herzl's famous saying, "If you will it, it is no dream," and then Martin Luther King's "I Have a Dream" speech. It was grandiose stuff and seemed a bit of a stretch: all that Ethan, Herzl, and King had in common was the use of the word "dream," but the boy smiled, happy to take his place in the pantheon of great orators.

The rabbi next asked Lisa to stand. In her drashah, Lisa had mentioned Joseph's struggle to be honest: Joseph recognizes his brothers, but he pretends not to and sends them away. The rabbi said that her discussion of honesty had made him think of the need to be honest about one's Judaism, never to deny one's heritage. It was the day after Winona Ryder had been sentenced in court for stealing accessories from a Beverly Hills store, and the rabbi got some laughs by indicting her for a different crime, lack of Jewish pride.

"Do you know what her real name is?" he asked. "Winona *Horowitz*. And do you know what George Burns's real name was? Nathan *Birnbaum*. And Barry Manilow? Barry *Pincus*. And Tony Curtis?"

"Bernie Schwartz," an old man behind me muttered.

"Bernie *Schwartz!*" the rabbi exclaimed. "Lisa, as you go forth, remember to always be honest about your Judaism, be proud of it."

As the children sat down, the cantor led us in a closing hymn, and the old man behind me said, "Beautiful, just beautiful."

Leaving the Scarsdale synagogue, I found that it was not the lack of rigor, the watery Judaism, the shortened service, or the relative absence of Hebrew that bothered me most. One thing I was already learning in my interviews was how few adult Jews remembered a lick of Hebrew from their b'nai mitzvah. At no time in history was it usual for Jewish thirteen-year-olds to be able to declaim Hebrew or lead services with great mastery—more than now, yes, but there were always Jewish illiterates and Jewish peasants, men with calloused hands and no time for books. What saddened me about the Scarsdale b'nai mitzvah was how they had overshadowed Shabbos; by robbing the day of its central purposes, communal prayer and public Torah reading, b'nai mitzvah's heightened importance within this Jewish community actually seemed to cripple the ritual's religious potential. At Westchester Reform, the main Saturday service is not an awesome Torah reading followed by a carefully prepared rabbinic sermon, or a lively minyan of Jews davening the day's prayers, but a hall filled with dozens of guests of the special boy or girl and a rabbi and cantor who play to this ad hoc congregation, many of them Gentiles or relatively ignorant Jews. This means that the first Torah service a young man or woman takes part in is not a true Torah service at all, but a reasonable facsimile of one. Rather than have the opportunity to fail in front of a community of adult Jews, the child is guaranteed success for an invited audience of friends and relatives.

When rabbis of large congregations catch up with their old seminary classmates, at conventions or over e-mail, one of the great frustrations they talk about is how to save Shabbos from the bar mitzvah. They are not indifferent to the problem they face, and they struggle mightily to find solutions. Westchester Reform is not the only synagogue to face the problem of ever-shifting Saturday congregations with nothing in common each week except an invitation. It's a problem, rabbis know, that the Jews who just want to pray because it is their day of rest or contemplation or worship have been crowded out. At large synagogues, especially the ones that irreligious parents join to get their children "bar mitzvahed," what used to be, fifty years ago, just a young boy reading a bissel of haftarah and then taking his seat again is now a child star whose moment of celebrity trumps traditional worship. Becoming an adult is more honored than being an adult.

And this problem is amplified by the brevity of the Reform service. When the whole service has been shortened to scarcely over an hour, a child's twenty minutes or half hour dominates the morning. At B'nai Jeshurun, a Conservative synagogue on the Upper West Side of Manhattan famous for its lively music, Saturday services last close to three hours, and seven congregants chant Torah—which means that even two b'nai mitzvah celebrations take only a fraction of the day's worship time. The morning that I saw Gabrielle Baum and Jillian Roffer become b'not mitzvah, five adults also chanted; the girls each gave a five-minute speech, but the rabbi spoke for fifteen minutes. Each girl had about fifteen guests her age, sitting in the balcony (and, it must be said, talking rather loudly), but hundreds of adults prayed below.

As nearly the only adult participants in their Saturday services, the clergy at Westchester Reform have a very different task from that of Rabbis Rolando Matalon, Marcelo Bronstein, and Felicia Sol at B'nai Jeshurun. Every time I went to Westchester Reform, the rabbis and cantors did a creditable job of educating everybody, without talking down to them, and holding the attention of fidgety adolescents anticipating a party afterward, but it was clear that tradition was losing to expediency. On the day that Ethan and Lisa became a man and a woman, they did so before a room filled with other boys and girls, or newly minted men and women—but if there were old sages of the temple, or Hebrew experts, or pious folk who came to services regularly, they were hard to spot. In fact, they had probably come and gone: to create a more intimate worship experience for the temple regulars, Westchester

Reform, like Boston's largest Reform temple and many others, had started an alternative Torah service early on Saturday morning, making the later service purely a bar or bat mitzvah event. So with the regulars opting to come either on Friday night or early on Saturday, the adults best suited to mentor Jewish adolescents would not even be present for their b'nai mitzvah.

The problem was not that nobody here cared about Judaism, but that no matter how much they cared, their enthusiasm would be frustrated. These children surely could have meaningful bar and bat mitzvah experiences, and I expect that many did. Studying, showing what one has learned, and then being celebrated for it is an elating experience, not easily ruined. But this temple, if not quite one of the bar mitzvah "factories" that all rabbis accuse the *other* shul in town of being, was still a bit too mechanized. It was more Wal-Mart than family store, more state university than small college.

Yet Westchester Reform was quite cozy compared to what I found in New York City: the biggest temple of all, Congregation Emanu-El, with a membership of three thousand families.* It's a congregation easy to join, but hard to get into: I visited the massive limestone cathedral, at Fifth Avenue and Sixty-fifth Street, five times, and each time I was greeted by an outside guard and then, inside, by another guard. They were Hispanic men in their forties or fifties, wearing doormen's uniforms with handsome dark ties and well-shined

*Emanu-El's Web site says, "With a membership of over 3,000 families and 10,000 people, it is the largest congregation of Jewish worshippers in the world." But the Web site of the Stephen S. Wise Temple in Los Angeles begs to differ, insisting that it is "the largest Jewish congregation in the world," with "more than 3,500 families."

shoes. For Shabbos services, on Friday evenings and Saturday mornings, no questions were asked: the guards merely looked the crowd up and down as it passed into the giant sanctuary, the world's largest Jewish house of worship, with a seating capacity of twenty-five hundred people. Often, however, I was trying to gain admittance on a Saturday afternoon or a Sunday, when special events are held, and then the guards were more vigilant: "Are you here for the baby naming?" "Are you here for the bar mitzvah?" "Which bat mitzvah are you here for?" After twice failing to improvise a good lie, I decided that if I couldn't get to see a bar mitzvah, I could at least crash a party.

Late one Saturday afternoon, I parked my car near Fifth Avenue and Sixty-seventh Street, two blocks north of the synagogue entrance. Emanu-El faces the eastern edge of Central Park, and as I waited for the 4 p.m. bar mitzvah to let out, I gazed at the greensward across the street, trimmed and lush, God's private garden. At about 5:15, I noticed the first signs: three girls, junior-high age, stepped from the building onto the sidewalk, their mobile phones already to their ears. They were immediately followed by a rush of more boys and girls, squeezing through the double doors and then expanding onto the streetscape in billowing circles, like dye in water. The boys were in blue blazers and striped ties, the girls in high heels, black dresses with spaghetti straps, and unpracticed makeup. At a distance, parents followed, fathers in dark suits and mothers in cashmere or houndstooth. The women wore dark sunglasses, which made no sense given the late hour. One of the Hispanic guards efficiently gathered the children and led them to the southern corner of the block to wait for a green light; when it came, they crossed Fifth Avenue, where in front of the Arsenal, home to the New York City Department of Parks and Recreation, two large coach buses awaited the young passengers. I started my car and revved the engine. I waited, and waited, and when I saw the buses signal left and pull away from the curb, I started up slowly, smartly pulling into traffic behind them. As we began to descend the blocks, I prepared for a long pursuit down the East Side.

But after about two minutes the buses signaled left once more and pulled to a stop in front of the Sherry-Netherland, the swank hotel on Fifth between Fifty-ninth and Sixtieth. I had successfully tailed the bar mitzvah party six blocks to its destination. I zipped into a free parking spot almost directly in front of the hotel, then idled the engine and slouched in my seat as the parents, all of whom had walked, passed to my left on the sidewalk. Only after all the parents were inside and their sons and daughters had disembarked and followed them in did I get out of the car, straighten my tie, check the part in my hair, and enter.

"Are you here for the bar mitzvah?"

My inquisitor was a tall man with a ghoulish face and a funereal voice, wearing a black dinner jacket.

"Of course."

"This way, please."

He opened a door in the side wall to reveal a stairwell leading down. Voices came from below. I walked carefully down the narrow, winding stairs, and at the bottom I found myself in a basement catacomb, a suite of plush, carpeted rooms buzzing with children and parents, quaffing drinks and eating pizza bites and miniature egg rolls. Chandeliers hung low, walls were paneled in wood. In one room, parents crowded against a long oak bar, and in another, minors downed soda from little glass bottles. Through an open door, I could see tables set for dinner. The largest room of all was dressed up as a casino. At one station, boys and girls gathered around a roulette wheel, placing bets with fake money. There were two blackjack tables with regulation green felt tops ("BLACKJACK PAYS 3 TO 2," the felt read), and dealers were flipping cards, coaching the children to stick when the dealer shows 5 and always to split 8s.*

In the middle of the casino a table was piled high with board games—chess sets, backgammon sets, Monopoly—and other treats, like automatic card shufflers. These party favors could be purchased with the fake money won at the fake gaming tables. At a smaller table, off to the side, sat a stack of young adult novels, like *The Chocolate War* and *I Am the Cheese* by Robert Cormier and the Harry Potter books by J. K. Rowling. The books bore on their title pages blank name plates, waiting to be inscribed. A hand-lettered sign suggested that to honor the bar mitzvah boy, guests "join us in a donation to the UKARE reading room at I.S. 90." UKARE, I later learned, stands for "Uptown Kids Are Reading Everyday"; I.S. 90 is in Washington Heights, a predominantly Dominican neighborhood in northern Manhattan.

It was a relatively sedate party, notable mainly for a sophistication inappropriate to the age group. Though not particularly garish—no laser show, no celebrity impersonators—it was still not the kind of event that rabbis want their synagogues to be known for. Much stigma attaches to the parties, and rabbis often feel like the one described in the seminal article "The Coming of Age of Mark Moskowitz," by Maury Levy, which appeared in the March 1972 issue of *Philadelphia* magazine and launched one of the great Jewish legends, the bar-mitzvah-

---

*Many bar and bat mitzvah parties today have a "theme." Woody Allen's Donald has a *Star Wars* theme; my cousin Bryan had a golf theme, with balloons dimpled like golf balls; and this party was clearly a casino night. I see nothing wrong with theme nights, though one is tempted not to quarrel with my friend Rachel Tiven's mother, who, when asked what the theme of Rachel's bat mitzvah party would be, answered, "Judaism."

boy chopped-liver bust: "Across the room, the rabbi is turning green as the olives they used for eyes. The boy and his parents are admiring the wonderful likeness. They made him turn all different ways to make sure all the angles are right. 'That's my boy,' Morris Moskowitz says proudly. 'Well, time to dig in.' He picks up a fork and a plate. 'Okay, who wants the nose?' " The spending, and the gaucherie, had increased by the time of "Bash Mitzvahs!" a widely read 1998 *New York* magazine article in which Ralph Gardner Jr. wrote, "If the parties have not quite surpassed the overabundance of the eighties—when real estate tycoon Gerald Guterman rented the *QE2* for his son Jason's bar mitzvah and Ivan Boesky dropped by in his helicopter on the way to jail—they're getting there. The $250,000 bar mitzvah for boys and bas mitzvah for girls (the girls' parties are often more lavish than the boys') isn't out of the ordinary. According to bar mitzvah planner Lee Tannen, 'We get apologetic phone calls—"Hi, we're not like your other clients, we only have $50,000 to spend; we live in a rent-stabilized apartment on Central Park West." ' "

And the bar mitzvah's reputation has, if anything, gotten worse in the years since. In 1998, Gardner attributed the New York bar mitzvah party culture to, in part, the vigorous stock market, but the crash two years later did not usher in an era of restraint. Perhaps there were fewer families renting out Radio City Music Hall, but, as chronicled by *New York Times* journalist Elissa Gootman in an even more notorious article, what had been lost in cash flow could be made up for in other, no less troubling ways:

> Lorne Hughes grew up in the Virgin Islands and now lives in Los Angeles, but he regularly spends his weekends dancing with 13-year-olds in braces and formal wear at bar mitzvahs from Great Neck to TriBeCa.

There he was last Sunday night, dressed in form-fitting black clothes and smiling ecstatically as he danced to Ricky Martin and Jennifer Lopez songs with middle school students and their immaculately coiffed parents at the Toy Building in Manhattan.

He looked as if there was nowhere he would rather be, and every guest he pulled onto the dance floor looked the same. And that was precisely the point.

Mr. Hughes, known as Lonnie, is part of a profession known as party motivators. They are attractive, hard-bodied students, aspiring actors and the like, who are paid to dance at sweet 16's, corporate parties and the occasional wedding, but most of all bar mitzvahs and bat mitzvahs, where the presence of three generations of party-goers, among them dozens of 13-year-olds, creates the potential for even the most carefully engineered affair to dissolve into boredom or chaos.

The party motivators, who have been around since the 1980s but became *necessary* only in the 1990s, chat up the guests at cocktail hour, often engaging the boys and girls in flirtatious—but not too flirtatious—conversation, and then dance, dance, dance when the music starts to play. "Motivators must look young enough to enthrall a 13-year-old," Gootman writes, "yet mature enough that when they dance suggestively with the parents, everything looks legal."

As Gootman notes, the motivators now pop up at all kinds of functions, and their influence has transformed the venerable old occupation of the deejay, who is no longer just supposed to play music but now must also "get this party *started*!" as they shout, and "get *everybody* on the dance floor!" My friends and I still laugh at the memory of a deejay we saw at a Philadelphia wedding in 1999: an Adam Sandler type dressed in a subdued black blazer, he seemed mild-mannered enough, feeding one CD after another into his deck—until, that is, he stepped out from behind his console, took to the dance floor, turned his black jacket inside out to reveal quilted gold lamé, transforming himself into a party superhero, and dragged us out of our seats to shimmy with him.

I saw the motivators at b'nai mitzvah everywhere, young and attractive and well remunerated—the most popular motivators bill one thousand dollars for a night. They were in Ridgefield, Connecticut, and in suburban New Jersey. They have spread to Canada too. They take what would otherwise be a junior-high dance with some parents chaperoning and make it into a highly sexualized, very adult affair.

One could argue that the formality and sexuality of these parties does suit the occasion. If a boy has just become a man or a girl is now a woman, then it may be fitting for them to dance like adults, with adults, in the evening hours. That theory is not so workable, however, when one remembers that we no longer live in an age when being thirteen is close to being married. These boys and girls have algebra tests on Monday. What their parents are giving them is not an entree into adulthood but a one-night stand with adulthood.

This precocious fantasy is reinforced outside b'nai mitzvah, especially in New York, where teenagers often go barhopping and clubbing. Still, it is a fantasy. Most guests do not have to be paid to show up at parties. The motivators are actors, not friends or even acquaintances. And they are not even actors who are meant to look like guests—in fact, they are supposed *not* to look like guests. An outsized proportion of party motivators are black or Latino or Asian. B'nai mitzvah today, especially in and around the big cities, are often spectacles of young Jewish boys grinding up against tall Latina women in hot pants and young Jewish girls sandwiching chiseled, shaven-headed black men on the polished dance floor. Even when the motivators are white, they are not dressed in the Brooks Brothers, Polo, Laura Ashley, and Neiman Marcus that the kids wear; they come in stylized Italianate suits, sateen shirts, and shiny black shoes, collars unbuttoned and hair carefully gelled into proper formation. They are selling an experience more ethnic than any that the children's parents would allow them to experience for real. An experience more uptown, perhaps, or more downtown, like the miscegenating Greenwich Village of old, but definitely not Upper East Side.

I enjoyed sneaking into bar mitzvah parties, and soon I learned how to get into the private bar and bat mitzvah services too. On Thursday or Friday, I would look at Emanu-El's online weekly bulletin, which listed the names of that weekend's b'nai mitzvah and the times that the ceremonies began. Then, when the guard asked me what event I was there for, I could confidently bluff, "Jimmy Goldfarb's bar mitzvah." It worked every time, and as I suavely blended in with the crowd of invited guests, I would smile at my own resourcefulness. I would take a seat near the back—but not too far back—and keep my eyes down, looking at the Union Prayer Book I found in the back of the pew in front of me. If any of the bar mitzvah boy's family saw me, they would take me for a cousin from the other side of the family.

The last time I went, it was an evening affair. The bar mitzvah was to begin at 5:30 p.m. in the Beth-El Chapel, the temple's small sanctuary off to the left of the main hall, ill-lit and pleasingly Gothic; it holds 350 people and was about two-thirds full. Guests made small talk, waiting for the service to begin. Without turning around, I heard a man standing behind me and to my right, in the aisle, greeting the couple

seated behind me. The men asked one another how business
was. The man standing up said, "Who would have thought a
financial planner is also a psychotherapist? You wouldn't believe the people I have crying in my office these days. I tell
them I would help them out if I were in better shape myself."
The bar mitzvah boy's sister walked up to a woman in front of
me, on the aisle. They kissed, and the older woman asked,
"Where's your mother?" "She's right up there," the sister said,
pointing to the stage. "Oh, when did she become a blonde?"
Behind me, the posse of school friends whispered and flirted.
There were two black children and about forty white children,
and all of them were dressed as if for their first job interviews
ten years hence.

David Posner, Emanu-El's senior rabbi, assumed the pulpit.
There was no cantor and none of the pomp that accompanies
a regular Shabbos service at Emanu-El, in which the senior
rabbi, an assistant rabbi, and the cantor enter from the rear,
walk the length of the entire chapel, ascend the stairs together,
then split off—one to the pulpit, one to a seat on the left, the
third to sit down on the right. I wondered if a cantor for a private evening bar mitzvah cost extra. But Posner had authority
enough to hold the stage. Rabbi Posner is a familiar figure at
Upper East Side marriages, funerals, brises, and b'nai mitzvah.
Although he leads the congregation most identified with
Manhattan's old-money Jews, the Schiffs and Strauses and
Lehmans, he was born in Brooklyn and retains a slight outer-
borough accent. Filtered through homiletics classes, his voice
now sounds like a carnival barker's, pleasantly mellifluous, reassuring in a metallic way, gravitational.

Posner invited us to open our Union Prayer Books to the
weekday afternoon service. The old, concise, mostly English
Union Prayer Book has been abandoned by nearly all Reform
congregations for being insufficiently Jewish, but Posner

would sooner retire than see it go. He said the Sh'ma, the central prayer of Judaism, first in English and then in Hebrew. After some further preliminaries, he removed the Torah scroll from the ark behind him and unrolled it on the bimah, the lectern or table where the reading takes place. Ben, the bar mitzvah boy, read several lines of Noach, that week's parashah, the section of Genesis that tells the story of Noah and the Flood. He stumbled at places, and one could hear the rabbi prompting him, quietly. After a minute or two, when it was over, Ben recited the Hebrew prayer that concludes a reading. In his speech, he offered a short interpretation of the story.

"How did God know that Noah would have the time, be able to round up two of each animal?" Ben asked. "How did God know that Noah would be able to build the ark? How did Noah know that God would really save him from the flood? It's a story of trust between God and Noah."

At the conclusion of his speech, Ben said how grateful he was for all the people who had helped him prepare for his bar mitzvah, and as a final, lighthearted comment he added that he was grateful above all for the party about to come. After his rocky road through the Torah portion, Ben seemed to mean it.

Forty minutes after entering the chapel, we left. It had been a fine example of what scholars call Classical Reform, the old-style, German-influenced Judaism that disdains yarmulkes (which only a few of the men that day had worn, the rabbi not among them), embraces the Christian organ (traditional Judaism forbids playing instruments on Shabbos), and nearly banishes Hebrew for English. The whole effect, with the organ pipes resounding behind me as Rabbi Posner in his doctoral robes stared solemnly out at us, had all the false grandeur of a melodrama in a silent-film movie house. I thought of Susan Sontag's definition of "camp" as "a seriousness that fails."

It failed for me, anyway; it felt imitative, of what I was not sure. But everything is moving to somebody. Once, when I took a tour of a Mormon temple, I joked to a woman walking next to me that the building was decorated like a first-class businessmen's hotel. I meant it as a snide insult, but the woman shook her head slowly with a sense of awe, smiled, and said, "I know, isn't it wonderful!" Profundity is a very personal thing.

I walked out with the crowd and went straight to a tuxedoed Hispanic driver leaning against a white, midsized party bus. I asked him where he was taking the kids. "Forty-ninth and Lex," he said, and five minutes later I was parking my car a block away from the W Hotel. Inside, surrounded by the frosted glass, blond wood, and geometrically groomed plants of the W, I saw a sign directing me up one flight of stairs to the bar mitzvah party. About one hundred guests were neatly dividing between two party rooms, one on each end of a balcony overlooking the hotel bar. In the left-hand room, the dining room, adults were lubricating with whiskeys and glasses of white wine; to the right and down a small hallway, the children ate hors d'oeuvres. As the guests sorted themselves out, I stood on the balcony and looked out at dusky New York. I noticed that a small auxiliary bar had been set up right next to me. Nobody had found it yet, and there was no line. The bartender, a young, blond, gay-seeming man, looked bored.

"Drink?" he asked me.

"Gin and tonic," I said.

"Tanqueray or Bombay?"

"Bombay will be fine."

He mixed me my drink, and I asked him about the b'nai mitzvah he had worked.

"You should have seen the one they had in here last week,"

he said. "They had this photography booth, and it could either take a real photo of you or it could produce a drawing of you, like someone had done a sketch or something. You could pick which one you wanted. And they had a tattoo artist walking around painting, you know, those, what are they, temporary tattoos? And they had a glassblower blowing glass things for them. Of course, I was at a party last week at this other hotel I work at, down by Wall Street, where some Colombian businessman had a party for five hundred people that lasted until four in the morning. You should have seen the security he had."

I walked back to the kids' area. For unclear reasons, the party photographer, a woman wearing the tailored black preferred by photographers trying to be inconspicuous and by New Yorkers more generally, had on one of those headsets used by rock stars in concert and by Old Navy salesclerks. As she whirled around the room looking for good action shots, she seemed to be minding instructions coming from her earpiece. A videographer also worked through the crowd, a high-beam mounted on his camera illuminating the boys and girls at play. Unlike the casino room of two weeks earlier, which had had a unified theme, this room had an assortment of games, alike only in their intended age group: a basketball shooting alley, like the kind you see at amusement parks; a video game that played simulated NFL football or NBA basketball, depending on which switch you flipped; and, once again, a roulette wheel and two blackjack tables.

Seeing a woman who might have been the mother walk into the room, I walked toward her, pulling out my mobile phone as I walked, trying to look official. I had a plan: if questioned about who I was, I would say that I was security, and that the hotel always liked to have someone keeping an eye on its events, especially the Jewish events, in case of terrorism. In my khakis, blue blazer, and Liberty of London tie, I could definitely be preppy undercover security. I passed the woman, who did not look at me, and went back to the balcony for another free drink. Some children had migrated out with me, and they were mugging for the photographer. Their giddiness said it was still early in bar mitzvah season; by springtime, the weekly routine would wear them down. After their pictures had been snapped, they got in line at the photo station, with a stool beneath a lighting umbrella. A man took pictures, and next to him a woman inserted the instant photos into Sno-Globes. At one end of the room, against a wall, a table held a heaping tray of pigs in blankets. The photographer's assistant, a dark, heavy woman with thick hair pulled back from her face, looked at me and shrugged. "Have a pig," she said.

I went to pray at Emanu-El on a rare Saturday morning with no b'nai mitzvah scheduled. At 10:30, when services began, there were fifteen people; by the end, an hour later, there were about forty. They were mostly old, in their sixties and seventies. There was one young couple, in their mid-twenties. The man was in a blue blazer, white shirt, and rep striped bow tie, and with him was a blond woman, cute but not dainty, with a strong Jewish nose. She was wearing a light blue cashmere sweater and a string of pearls. The man was not wearing a yarmulke, as most of the men were not. There were perhaps fifteen single men, as many single women, and several couples. A disheveled man looked as if he had come in from the cold. Nobody sat near anybody else. The giant, cavernous sanctuary, with the organ playing softly, like a dirge, and with a steady drone of rain outside—there was a storm on the way, and it dropped below freezing that night—felt like a large Catholic or Episcopal church, oaken and austere, but com-

forting in its adamantine solidity, with worshipers huddled
against the elements. People were shaking out umbrellas.

Two lecterns anchored the stage. At the lectern to my left
was the cantor, a trim blond woman in her forties. To the
right were Rabbi Posner, who had led the bar mitzvah service,
and Rabbi Amy Ehrlich, the associate rabbi. The organ was
out of sight, like the choir, which was in an aerie behind and
above the stage, at about third-story level, hidden by colored
curtains above the ark embedded in the wall. As Rabbi Posner
worked through the Sabbath morning service, the choir occasionally chimed in with a chanted "A-men!" which had the effect of being God's polyphonic voice from heaven. When the
choir was not on call, you could occasionally hear the choris-
ters rustling their pages or coughing, even at one point whis-
pering.

There were thrones on either side of the stage, behind the
two lecterns. When the choir was singing, the clergy took
their seats, and when the cantor sang, the rabbis occasionally
whispered to each other. Sometimes, they looked out at us,
forty people sitting in a sanctuary built for twenty-five hundred. When it was time to take the Torah from the ark, the
rabbis and cantor got up, walked toward each other, met in
the middle, turned ninety degrees to the east, and approached
the ark together. When they got to the ark, Rabbi Posner
reached in, got it, held it aloft, and proclaimed, "This is the
Torah which God gave through Moses. These scrolls reflect
our people's history, our people's faith, and our people's
dream. So come, then, you who are the people of Israel, come
and together let us walk in the light of its truth, as we proclaim in unison the watchword of our faith: *Sh'ma Yisrael!
Adonai Eloheinu, Adonai echad!* Hear O Israel, the Lord our
God, the Lord is one!"

Five days later, I went for my appointment with Rabbi Posner. I told the guard that I was there to see the rabbi, and after he called to get clearance, he sent me up in the elevator to the eighth floor. The rabbi's secretary greeted me in his reception area and called to let him know that Mr. Oppenheimer had arrived. A minute later, Rabbi Posner came out to greet me. He took me down a short hallway to his office, invited me to sit in a large leather chair, and settled in behind his desk. We stared at each other for a moment, blinking. He was in an elegant white shirt and a purple tie. He had bright blue eyes and a firm handshake, and but for his cue-ball baldness he would have made a classic CEO.

Posner was now senior rabbi, but as a young assistant rabbi he had written Emanu-El's first guide to bar and bas mitzvah—again, the Ashkenazic, or European, pronunciation of the letter *tav*—and confirmation ceremonies. He had joined Emanu-El right from rabbinic school in 1973, the year after the bar and bas mitzvah had returned to the temple. It made sense for young Posner, with his strong background in classical Hebrew—stronger than the senior rabbi's—to write the new manual. He takes especial pride in its fidelity to proper diction.

"Since 1973," he told me, "whenever you see the temple bulletin, it says, 'So-and-so will be called to the Torah as a bar mitzvah'—you don't go to one, you don't have one, nobody 'gets bar mitzvahed'! Everybody now has become so punctilious with the language on that, and it's my fault."

Rabbi Posner was born in 1947 and became senior rabbi in 2000, after almost thirty years as an assistant. He is probably the first rabbi at Emanu-El, at least in the last century, to care as he does about proper Hebrew. It's in part an atavism, left over from a childhood very different from his congregants'.

"I came here," he said, "as a result of being a poor kid from the Brownsville section of Brooklyn with very high grades in high school. I wanted to be a rabbi since I was ten years old, I had high grades, not a wealthy family of course. So my rabbi in Brooklyn recommended to the then senior rabbi in this study, Julius Mark, that I be totally scholarshiped by Temple Emanu-El, which I was for eight years. Didn't cost my parents a dime.

"And when I finished, instead of taking a degree in Near Eastern studies—which is what I really wanted to do, but *I have no regrets whatsoever!*—they asked me to come here as an assistant rabbi, and I stayed. And I've even lived in the same building for thirty years, though I went from a one-bedroom to a two-bedroom.

"I just came here, and I worked seven days a week, and I never stopped. It's as simple as that. Marry the living, bury the dead, teach small children, do everything that the congregation asks. Do adult education. I am the music teacher in the religious school of this institution, because I did take a doctorate in the 1980s at Teachers College at Columbia in my first field of classical piano.* So I don't trust anyone else to teach music. So I do that, I teach children, I do adult education at the temple. I am teaching biblical Aramaic right now. I have taught a two-year course on the history and development of Jewish liturgy, courses in medieval Jewish philosophy, modern Jewish philosophy, early New Testament literature. I've done it all."

I asked Posner about his bar mitzvah program, and he handed me the guide the children are given, the one he wrote in 1975. He then offered his philosophy of b'nai mitzvah:

"The most important word in the religious life of this institution is not 'halakah' "—law; "it's 'rachmones'!"—compas-

---

*Dr. Posner's dissertation, completed in 1988, is titled "Reviving a Lost Art: Piano Music of Russian-Jewish Origin."

sion. "And that we have in abundance. I will not tolerate a bar and bas mitzvah program that says, quote, 'We have *standards*,' meaning the student has to read ten pesukim"— verses—"or fifteen or whatever. The only standard worthy of a synagogue's name is rachmones. That's all you have, and you can have tremendous flexibility for students with different learning styles or whatever intellectual or emotional needs.

"I've always said the child is more important than the text. Always bend the rules. There's always going to be some children who have to read in transliteration. Everybody automatically becomes a bar or bas mitzvah at this age anyway," the rabbi said, referring to the Jewish tradition that adult obligations simply begin at twelve or thirteen. "How many children during the Holocaust didn't have a chance to have a ceremony?

"Before the war, what happened? A Monday morning, his father took him to shul, he had his first aliyah"—trip to the bimah, for a Torah or haftarah reading or to say the accompanying blessings. "That was his bar mitzvah. He had a little schnapps and a piece of herring, then back home, back to the tailor shop."

I asked Rabbi Posner about confirmation, which at many synagogues has become a ceremony honoring those students who continue Jewish study into their high school years, but which at Emanu-El is folded into the bar mitzvah year.

"Now, we are the oldest confirming congregation in the United States. It began here in 1846. If anyone wants to complain about confirmation, blame it on us. The other synagogues, which do it at the end of tenth grade, have a terrible time retaining their children. So we do it at the end of the seventh grade. They have their individual bar and bas mitzvah ceremonies in the seventh grade, and then the entire class together participates in the Shavuos service on Shavuos, at the end of seventh grade. So not only have we shortened it, I moved it in 1997 from the end of ninth grade to the end of seventh grade."

The change in confirmation, moving it up by two years and offering a shorter, more intensive course of study, was a smashing success. The Hebrew school grew, and parents were thrilled.

"We have a very happy congregation as a result of that. There is no fighting with the clergy; there is no 'Why aren't you coming back? If you don't come back you broke your promise.' Nothing like that, nothing like that here."

Besides the importance of an irenic congregation, what, I asked the rabbi, did he want the children of Emanu-El to know?

"That we love them for being Jewish children, period. I never want children disciplined in this synagogue. Now, first of all, of course, the main sanctuary is enormously large. So if children are sitting in the back, the rabbis aren't going to be able to hear them anyway. They're not going to be disturbing a soul. In private services, which are held in the chapel, even if I hear a general hum in the back, I never look up. I have never disciplined a child in this temple, and I will never countenance ushers going over, disciplining them, God forbid throwing people out."

I expressed my suspicion that such a lax environment might send the wrong message, that Judaism is not to be taken all that seriously.

"I'll tell you this, there are a lot of our kids who in college take Jewish studies courses. I would love them to major in Jewish studies. Parents tell their kids they should not major in Jewish studies. I tell them I can understand where they're coming from, that if their children major in Jewish studies, they might want to become rabbis or, God forbid, Jewish ed-

ucators, and if that were the case here, the parents would
come beating down my door!"

My communist grandfather says the same thing, that there
are certainly *worse* jobs than being a rabbi, but really now,
studying Judaism is not the best use of a good head. Except
that while my grandfather is motivated by a leftist's disdain for
religion, Emanu-El parents, who, at least in Rabbi Posner's
stereotype, would come beating down his door if their children (God forbid) went to seminary, must have a different
kind of aversion. Is it just an assimilated Upper East Side aversion? Or a capitalist's aversion, the knowledge that Rabbi Posner makes a tenth of what they, his congregants, do? *A rabbi
for a son?* That kind of observance does not much interest the
Emanu-El family.

So there are concessions to fashion that Rabbi Posner must
make, and to be diplomatic he must sometimes spin or shade
the truth to make those concessions look not so bad. In his
b'nai mitzvah manual he wrote that confirmation has been
moved to coincide with bar mitzvah because the two make
sense twinned, "one ceremony stressing the importance of
each individual Jew's commitment to our faith and tradition,
and the other making explicit the allegiance that we pledge to
the totality of the Jewish people." But in person he told me
that confirmation was moved up "because nobody can continue in the eighth or ninth or especially the tenth grade. They
are all playing soccer, tennis, lacrosse." His clientele are not
terribly interested in long hours of study, and so he couches
his opposition to "standards" in terms of rachmones, compas-
sion, as if expectations were inherently cruel.

David Posner's is, of course, an impossible position. Once a
terrifically bright child, raised with a love of Jewish tradition
and a gift for Hebrew, he precociously got a prominent pulpit,
one that any rabbi would be crazy to abandon. But that pulpit

came with a congregation historically averse to seeming too Jewish, a congregation that until 1974 *forbade* the wearing of yarmulkes, a congregation theologically skeptical and inclined to value status, private schools, and "soccer, tennis, lacrosse." Posner's flock live in a city where a culture of wealth and worldliness makes for great parties but discourages contemplation and study. Manhattan, in particular, is bad for religious observance in general: dinner begins at nine, and nobody's getting up early to pray.

To judge by the numbers, material success has not proved a problem for Americans' spiritual lives. Rather, it has allowed us to build million-dollar sanctuaries, employ quarter-million-dollar preachers and rabbis, and throw half-million-dollar weddings, quinceañeras, and b'nai mitzvah. But while our money has not killed off religion, it often constricts the kind of religious experience that we have. The idea, for example, that eleven hundred families—the membership of the Scarsdale temple—would be an appropriate size for a congregation, or that the three thousand families at Emanu-El would, is influenced by the modern propensity for economies of scale. With so many families, a synagogue can have three or four rabbis, two cantors, and a passel of administrators. It can build an impressively large sanctuary and house a museum of Judaica, like the one at Emanu-El. Size means prestige, both for the clergy and for the members. How grand it is to be president of the board of directors of so large a congregation! But so large a congregation can never be a community, not in the way that a small storefront shtiebl can.

I cringed to see only thirty or forty people at Emanu-El's weekly service, but what if all ten thousand members showed up—would that be any better? Or would that simply remind people how few of their fellow congregants they really know? The larger the congregation, the smaller a percentage of it you would want to invite to your simcha, your joyous occasion. Jewish tradition recognizes that bigger is not always better, which is why the traditional prayer quorum is ten men. More are welcome, but not required. And Jewish tradition knows, too, that money can wreck as surely as it can build, which is why Jews are traditionally married in simple white robes and buried in plain linen shrouds. Ornament perverts what simplicity can sanctify.*

Hard to say which came first, the spiritual void or capitalism's rush into it. Did the bar mitzvah party industry arise to warm up an event that had already gone spiritually cold, or did the party planners and souvenir merchants corrode what had been a simpler, more earnest affair? Or does all this talk of decline presuppose a bar mitzvah heyday that never existed? It has always been perfectly possible to have a pointless, vapid bar or bat mitzvah without the help of party motivators or cruises around Manhattan (and it is possible to have a profound rite of passage celebrated with party motivators on a cruise ship).

But still, capitalism is a voracious beast, harder than ever to escape, especially in Greater New York. I attended two bar and bat mitzvah "party expos," one in Teaneck, New Jersey, the other in Greenwich, Connecticut. Like bridal expos, they were held in hotel convention centers, with rows and rows of photographers showing portfolios of their work, caterers giving away sushi rolls and crêpes prepared on the spot, and party-

---

*For an instructive comparison, see Susan Orlean's wonderful description of the *quinceañeras* in her book *Saturday Night* (New York: Random House, 1990), ch. 3. And for two good histories of American religion, each of which helps explain its relationship to markets and wealth, see Jon Butler, *Awash in a Sea of Faith* (Cambridge, Mass.: Harvard University Press, 1990), and Nathan Hatch, *The Democratization of American Christianity* (New Haven, Conn.: Yale University Press, 1989).

favor manufacturers demonstrating all the impressive things that they would do at your bar or bat mitzvah: produce movie posters based on *The Terminator*, with your guests' heads on Arnold Schwarzenegger's body; take instant photographs and transpose the pictures of your guests onto refrigerator magnets; print head shots of your guests on faux *Sports Illustrated* or *Seventeen* covers.

In Teaneck, the owner of a business called RC Entertainment was demonstrating his money booth. A girl was inside the plastic cage trying to catch Monopoly money as wind blew the bills all around her. "At the end of the night, whoever has the most fake money wins a grand prize," the man was telling her father. "We can also put real money in it, but then don't worry, nobody is able to catch more than two or four dollars. We also do bachelor parties, corporate entertainment, everything."

I sat for a tarot reading with Cindy Zweibel of Cindy Zweibel Psychic Entertainment. She was wearing colorful robes and necklaces dangling with otherworldly-looking symbols. As she laid the cards out in an H-shaped formation, she said to me, "I see you coming to a crossroads. Yes, yes. I see that it will have something to do with either money or . . . a girl. Yes, maybe money, maybe a girl. A big decision you have to make. Sometime this spring. In April, maybe a little earlier, February or March." I asked who her best clients were. "Bat mitzvahs. The twelve-year-old girls, they love it."

In the hotel men's room, I saw a middle-aged Jewish man with blond tips at the apex of his pompadour, boy-band style, wearing a gold necklace and a weird coat that looked to be made of colorful satin swatches. I recognized him as Jeff Yahney of the Yahney Entertainment Group—his ads are everywhere in the bar mitzvah party guides you can buy in suburban Barnes & Noble superstores. He was leaning close to the mirror above the washbasin, applying pancake foundation with a makeup sponge. Half an hour later, on the convention hall floor, I found his display area. He had a choice location, a double lot against the wall, decorated with lots of video screens and huge wind puppets that, attached to air hoses, somehow made popping moves as the air coursed through them: an air current would start at one of the puppet's fingertips and send a hip-hop jolt of energy through the arm, to the shoulder, and out through the other arm to the fingertip. These break-dancing puppets were about twenty feet tall. While Deejay Jeff was talking to a bald man who looked like George Costanza from *Seinfeld*, I was greeted by a cute blond woman, about eighteen years old, whose kind seemed to be employed by half the booths at this expo, whether to attract bar mitzvah boys, bat mitzvah girls, or their fathers, I cannot say. I asked her how much Deejay Jeff would cost, and she told me I would have to talk to him. When he was free, I went over to him.

"My sister is having a bat mitzvah in a couple months," I said.

"It's a beautiful thing!" he replied.

"How much?" I asked.

"Call me, we'll talk."

On the crowded showcase floor, a woman was talking to her daughter by cell phone: "See me? I'm twenty feet in front of you!"

I picked up flyers for Digital Desserts ("Who says you can't have your photo on a cake and eat it, too?"); for Miriam Jacobs, maker of custom yarmulkes; and for the Harlem Wizards, a cut-rate version of the Harlem Globetrotters that will shoot hoops with your bar mitzvah boy and his friends: "The Wizards' brand of show basketball brings the player out of every basketball fan. Opponents range from teachers and alumni to corporate CEOs and doctors. The Wizards have participated in a variety of high profile charity events playing with an A-list of celebrities which include L.A. Laker star Kobe Bryant, *All My Children*'s Susan Lucci, TV stars Luke Perry and Malcolm Jamal Warner . . ."

As one who has trouble distinguishing his own high school memories from the plot lines of *Beverly Hills, 90210*, I would grab any chance to play basketball with men who have played basketball with Luke Perry. And I see the appeal of eating a cake with my face on it. I *love* this country. Nearly everything being sold that day in Teaneck, I was buying, because life without this promiscuous silliness would be bleaker and a lot less fun.

But maybe everything has its proper time and place, and maybe one good marker of adulthood is the ability to discern them. The time and place for the Harlem Wizards and face cakes is a birthday party or a corporate retreat that sorely needs a dash of pizzazz. Nobody wants to see the Harlem Wizards at a wedding. We have few enough sacred times as it is, and it is a shame to squander opportunities to be lifted above the profane. It was difficult to see how anything for sale at the bar mitzvah expo honored the passage from boy to man, or girl to woman. On the contrary: it was all emblematic of the desire to resist adulthood, to hold tight to adolescence, to stay young at all costs.

Nothing about Greater New York requires professionally orchestrated bar and bat mitzvah parties, and in fact it is easy to name New York synagogues whose cultures militate against them: B'nai Jeshurun, the Society for the Advancement of Judaism, and the Village Temple, to name a few. Congregational cultures are themselves wildly mutable: a new rabbi preaching to a receptive audience can, within a year or two, drastically alter a community's party scene.

The saddest thing about the party culture is not that it is lavish, but that it can effect a self-perpetuating ubiquity and a sense of helplessness. A family is still free to do its own decorating, build the piñata, cook the food, and play CDs from a stereo. Many families still do. But where a spending race has, like an arms race, heated up, increasingly professional and sophisticated party choreography threatens to make homemade celebrations seem corny and juvenile. As in church and synagogue buildings, size and polish can inculcate self-doubt in those who prefer the small, handmade, and haimish. One woman, an uptown New Yorker with a hippie past and liberal politics, refused my request for an interview, saying in an e-mail that she was too embarrassed: she had finally caved and hired dancers for her son's upcoming bar mitzvah. He was afraid to have a party without them. The whole thing made her uncomfortable. She was worried that the event had spun out of control, that it would be an affair like all those she despised.

But I wonder if she didn't give herself enough credit. Her son's party might indeed have turned out to be a rote, forgettable affair, just as church services can, after a while, all look a lot alike. But sometimes it is the predictability of the liturgy that allows for individual religious experience; churchly routine can be reassuring, as the old, habitual prayers can trigger a kind of personal space for meditation. In the same way, the big parties can disappear into a kind of fog of sameness, totally forgettable—and then the most personal, memorable, enduring aspect of the day, for the boy or girl anyway, may be the actual ceremony, when all the learning and preparation, those things that have to be earned and cannot be bought, are allowed to shine. At its best, the party can be a proper adjunct to the religious ritual, but at its worst, it may be no worse than a pro forma exercise, dutifully executed. For some of the biggest partyers, I would learn, the party is not what it's all about.

2

The Girl

*B*eth El–Keser Israel, the synagogue known as "BEKI," pronounced "Becky," sits on Whalley Avenue, in New Haven,
Connecticut, across the street from the Racquet Koop, where
Yale's tennis players get their racquets strung, and the House
of Chao, a Chinese restaurant, and just up the street from
three antique shops and the local Scientology recruiting
center. Not much excitement comes to the neighborhood,
Westville, although the annual Pilot Pen ladies' tennis tourna-
ment is held a mile away (Venus Williams won every year
from 1999 to 2002), and once upon a time a local, Joe Lieberman, almost became vice president. The streets are quiet and
pleasantly gritty, and little goes on outside BEKI's doors, just
scattered Jews coming and going, often with children. The
building is made of functional white brick with an unremark-
able facade. From the outside, BEKI is clearly the beneficiary
of an impoverished but somewhat proud neglect, and the inte-
rior is worn and almost ramshackle. Only the sanctuary wears
a touch of the grand, with tall, narrow stained-glass windows
that send sashes of color onto the wooden benches.

The interesting sites at BEKI are found away from the
streetscape, on Saturday mornings, on the backs of women in
prayer. The BEKI women wear what my friend Lisa, who

teaches Hebrew to BEKI's children, calls their coats of many colors: multihued embroidered or quilted prayer shawls that unfold down their backs with pictures of sunrises, rainbows, flowers in bloom, or birds soaring. These bohemian earth-mother twists on the traditional blue-and-white cloth are common in "egalitarian" synagogues, where women may, if they choose, wear the traditional male religious garb of yarmulkes and tallisim, or prayer shawls.

The head covering for the middle-aged Hadassah set has for many years been the lacy, doily-cut cotton kerchief, pinned to the top of the head; here, however, women too wear yarmulkes, the more polychrome and nubbly, the better. At BEKI, the vibe is a mélange of Shetland-wool intellectual and post-sixties hippie; the men incline toward fezlike Middle Eastern yarmulkes and hempy, unbleached tallisim; the women, hair going naturally gray, swathe themselves in their coats of many colors and caps to match. In shul on a Saturday morning, the women pray with more vitality than their husbands, who can look like pudgy afterthoughts in pleated khakis.

On the gelid October morning I prayed at BEKI—the morning that Annie Bass became a bat mitzvah—I was seated behind Paula Hyman, who founded Ezrat Nashim, an early-1970s Jewish feminist group, and co-wrote *The Jewish Woman in America*; Matthew Lieberman, whose father, the senator, prays at the Orthodox synagogue nearby; and Rabbi Lina Grazier-Zerbarini, one of the Jewish chaplains at Yale, a lesbian with three adopted black daughters who unexpectedly dresses in the hat and long skirt of an Orthodox housewife. And then there were elderly people who have belonged to the shul for decades, young couples with children, and assorted other wandering Jews.

Unlike at some shuls, at BEKI the bar or bat mitzvah is not

central to the Saturday morning service. BEKI prays the entire Shabbos Shacharis service before the Torah is read, and morning prayers are a team effort. There is no chazan or cantor, the professional singer and prayer leader that most large synagogues employ. For centuries, in Europe and in the Americas, Saturday morning prayers have typically been led by a professional, a man who, by stereotype, has a rich baritone and an operatic mien. Until recently, he was more central to the service than the rabbi, whose main role was to be the sage and scholar of the house, not a performer. A hundred years ago, famous cantors could sell out concert halls across the United States. On Saturdays, they served a sacred purpose, glorifying the liturgy, and also a mundane purpose: like a church choir, they shepherded nervous, tone-deaf, or ignorant worshipers through the prayers. Today, Reform cantors are often folkish troubadours; Orthodox and Conservative cantors are more sober and traditional. BEKI has neither, being in that minority of Conservative shuls with enough learned members so that there are always several who can lead Shabbos services. The day of Annie's bat mitzvah, then, morning prayers were led, as always, by members of the congregation.

On this morning, nearly all of the prayer leaders were women, including Annie's mother, Carole Bass, who has a good voice, and Annie herself, who has an even better one. The rabbi had a part, as did Annie's father, Paul, so it would be a bit excessive to say that women dominated the day, but on the Saturday that Annie became a bat mitzvah, the majority of the people chanting and praying, sitting in the pews listening, and giving speeches in Annie's honor were women. The room was not quite as female as a nursing school classroom, but it was more female than, say, a law school classroom, where women are often in the majority but men do the talking. It was rather more like many English classes I have taught, a mixed-gender space where women seemed to do most of the work.

This is something new in Judaism. For most of Christian history, women could rarely be preachers, but they still had roles in the church: teaching Sunday school, cooking the pancake breakfasts, organizing the Bingo nights that paid the minister or priest—who was aided by female secretaries, teachers, and social workers, and often nuns. Above all, women were required—not just permitted—to pray. Catholic women, Lutheran women, Puritan women: like men, they were expected to be in church. But in Orthodox Judaism, when the tradition says that a Jew must do this or must do that, it can be safely assumed that the tradition is speaking of a male Jew. Until the Enlightenment, with the rise of Reform and then Conservative Judaism, women were not obligated to pray in synagogue—although they were *allowed* to pray there, segregated behind a wooden or curtained barrier, or relegated to women's galleries, so as not to distract the men at prayer. It was not important for a woman to hear the sermon, and except to teach her sons, it was not important that a woman know how to read Hebrew.*

The Jewish woman might be prized as a wife, and many Jewish wives were given economic responsibilities rare in Christendom: a woman married to a great scholar, for example, might run a business and keep the family finances, freeing her husband to study without impediment. Sara Smolinsky, the heroine of Anzia Yezierska's 1925 autobiographical novel *Bread Givers*, about immigrant Jewish poverty on Manhattan's Lower East Side, is just one of four sisters put out to work by

---

*Ann Braude explains the necessary, even dominant, role of women in American religion in her article "Women's History Is American Religious History," in Thomas Tweed, ed., *Retelling U.S. Religious History* (Berkeley: University of California Press, 1997), 87–107.

their father, a rabbi who hoards his study time like a miser. It's their duty to support him, and although they are not allowed access to Torah, they are allowed to roam New York with a freedom that most Italian or Irish immigrant girls would have envied. But higher rates of employment and literacy, both of which Jewish women have had for centuries, did not confer on them religious equality, not in the synagogue.

In the nineteenth century, the Reform movement's replacement of the bar mitzvah with a mixed-sex confirmation was fashioned, in part, as an egalitarian gesture. Women were still not invited to become rabbis or religion scholars, but the banishing of an obvious inequality certainly seemed to Jewish girls and their mothers a form of progress. But along with the sexism, the reformers excised much of the Judaism. It became impossible in many Reform synagogues, and in their Sunday schools and confirmation ceremonies, to find evidence of Torah learning or even facility with Hebrew. And this had a curious effect. In Reform communities in Germany, England, and the United States, laypeople often had such diminished knowledge of the specifics of Judaism that the only person in town who knew Judaism intimately was the rabbi and perhaps several university graduates, and these were men. Whereas the old, more traditional Jewish world contained women and girls who knew Jewish law, practice, and literature by osmosis— running Jewish households, schooling their children, overhearing their husbands' and sons' talk, living in a world saturated by Jewish practice and learning—the new, updated Reform world contained few men, and scarcely any women, with meaningful Jewish knowledge. And this meant that all religious authority resided with a few men. It remains true today that many Orthodox Jewish women speak and read better Hebrew, and know Judaism more intimately, than middling graduates, male and female, of Reform seminaries.

Reform Judaism could not, then, become the home of Jewish women's learning. (And as we might expect, the first women to craft a specifically Jewish feminist movement were, for the most part, from the Conservative movement.) Orthodox women, no matter how bright, even when given an education comparable to their brothers', could not fashion a notion of religious equality; so long as only men could publicly read Torah and only men could be counted in the minyan, the prayer quorum of ten, women simply did not count as full Jews.* It was left to Conservative Judaism to produce a generation of women who both had Jewish equality and knew what to do with it. When Conservatism began in the nineteenth century as a middle path between Reform and Orthodoxy, one that made some legal concessions to living in the modern world but still ascribed ultimate authority to the Hebrew Bible, it was not as egalitarian as Reform. But Mordecai Kaplan's invention in 1922 of the bat mitzvah, now omnipresent in Reform and Conservative Judaism, was possible only in the Conservative movement. Reform had abandoned the bar mitzvah and so had no use for a girls' equivalent, and Orthodoxy, at the time, had no egalitarian impulse.

To judge from all the boys and girls, moms and dads, and rabbis and cantors whom I interviewed, I feel confident that of the two rituals, the bat mitzvah is, in general, more meaningful. It's not just that girls of twelve, when the bat mitzvah is

---

*Recent Orthodox feminists have tried to create for themselves a feminism compatible with their faith, a feminism that takes pride in their separate but complementary sphere. I admire their intellectual industry, and they have convinced me that Orthodoxy need not be stifling for women—that it can, in the right marriage and family, exalt and honor them; for independence and dignity, a good Orthodox marriage would be better than an unhappy Reform marriage. And the learning that goes on at Drisha, the New York women's college for advanced Orthodox Jewish study, is rigorous enough to qualify them for the rabbinate, if only their tradition would allow them to become rabbis.

usually celebrated, are more mature than boys of thirteen, nor that they are a bit more likely to enjoy books and foreign languages (although this is surely true). It's also that many Jewish mothers consider themselves feminists, and for them their daughters' ascent to womanhood has an added political heft that fathers and sons do not feel. And that all mothers, feminist or not, see their daughters developing physically, changing into women and entering their childbearing years at an age when boys are lucky to have a few downy hairs on their upper lips. Woman rabbis and cantors can still seem like an exciting innovation, and if they know one of these women in the clergy, bat mitzvah girls consider them role models, even mentors—while your average American Jewish boy probably puts his rabbi far down on the list of men he admires most. Finally, at progressive shuls like BEKI, there is a palpable awareness that not so long ago Conservative Jews were still split on the question of whether women may publicly read Torah; some rabbis still considered the bat mitzvah an unnecessary contrivance, and they still sensed that on the gender question Orthodoxy might be a better guide than Reform. In 1990, my friend Lori Kauffman was still not allowed to read Torah for her bat mitzvah at a Conservative synagogue in Detroit. *Nineteen-ninety.* Until recently, it was a restricted club, and today's daughters of the commandment, the b'not mitzvah, often talk with an attitude, somewhere between giddiness and pride, that says, "We're here."

Once prayers were through at BEKI, the Torah was unfurled, and Annie Bass came to the bimah. One of Annie's schoolteachers calls her "the Wyeth girl," and when I saw Annie for the first time that morning it was apparent that the nickname owed less to her blue-eyed, long-haired appeal than to her carefree indifference to it. That week's parashah was Vayera, the section of Genesis that includes the birth of Ishmael to Abraham's handmaid, Hagar, and the sacrifice of Isaac on Mount Moriah. All seven sections were read, the first and the last by Annie. I could hear her chanting, but all I could see was her back, draped with her tallis, a sheet of purple satin with orange butterflies stitched on it, handmade by Annie and two of her friends. Before and after each section, a relative or friend of the Basses was called to the Torah to intone the prayers that bracket a Torah reading. Afterward, Annie chanted the entire haftarah, the selection from the prophetic writings, which that week was 2 Kings 4:1–37, the good works of Elisha. When it was over, Annie carried the Torah up and down the aisles of BEKI, escorted by her rabbi and her parents. Covered from shoulders to waist by her tallis, her head capped by a yarmulke and her arms weighted down by the enormous Torah scroll, Annie was, as she led the procession through the sanctuary, very hard to glimpse. She went up and down the aisles slowly, giving every worshiper a chance to reach out and touch the Torah with a prayer book or the fringed ends of a tallis, which was then kissed in devotion to the word of God. A swell of hands and prayer books descended on her every step of the procession, as if she were a celebrity stopping to sign autographs every few steps on a city street, needing half an hour to walk a block. From my seat, across the room and away from the aisle, I lost sight of her; I could see only the energetic hands and arms, draped in prayer shawls—some white and blue, some multicolored and appliquéd—surrounding her, and this inaccessibility lent a mysterious and awesome air to the march. With the sacred palimpsest in her little arms, and with all these adults adoring her and the scroll she carried and collapsing in on her, Annie appeared, when I finally saw her and touched the Torah in her arms, dwarfed and meek and a little scared. She was smiling shyly, daunted by the attention, daunted as well by the responsibility, carrying the Torah for the first time, flushed with the success of the reading, which she had carried off with aplomb. She was exhausted but hoped the feeling would never end.

When she was back at the bimah and people had taken their seats again, Annie began her drashah, her bat mitzvah speech.

"Shabbat Shalom!" she said. "This week's Torah portion is called Vayera. In the beginning of the portion, three angels come to Abraham right after he has circumcised himself. They tell Abraham that he and Sarah will have a child in a year. After the angels leave, God tells Abraham that he is about to destroy the city of Sodom because the people there are evil. Abraham argues on behalf of the people in the city, and God agrees that if he can find ten good people in the city, he will not destroy it. But the only good person found in Sodom is Lot, Abraham's nephew. Lot is tipped off in advance and leaves Sodom in the morning, before the city is destroyed."

Annie paraphrased the story that had just been read aloud in Hebrew, taking the audience through the birth of Isaac, the tensions between Sarah and Hagar, and the binding of Isaac, the story known as the Akedah.

"When God commands Abraham to sacrifice Isaac in Genesis 22:2," Annie said, "God uses the words '*Kakh na et bin'kha, et yehid'kha, asher ahavta, et Yitzchak, ve-lekh l'kha el eretz ha-Moriyah*—'Please take your son, your only son, the one you love, Isaac, and go forth to the land of Moriyah.' When I read this line, I realized that the words *lekh l'kha*—'go forth'—are used in the Torah portion before Vayera as well. In that portion, in Genesis 12:1, God tells Abraham, '*Lekh l'kha me-artzekha, umi-moladtekha, umi-beit avikha*'—'Go forth from your land, your birthplace, and your father's house.'"

These are the only two times that the phrase *lekh l'kha* is used in the entire Torah, Annie said, and she believed there was a connection between the two instances. Each time the phrase is uttered, there follows a list of what Abraham has to leave and give up. The first time, Abraham is told to give up his land, his birthplace, his father's house; in the second case, he is told to take his son, his only son, the one he loves, Isaac. And each time, Abraham is sent on a journey.

What else can we learn by comparing the two *lekh l'khas*? Annie asked. To help her study this question, she had consulted the writings of the late Nehama Leibowitz, who has achieved a mild cult status as a famous female Torah scholar:

"Nehama Leibowitz notices that in each *lekh l'kha*, God asks Abraham to forsake something. But in each instance, that something is different. In the first *lekh l'kha*, God asks Abraham to forsake his past by asking him to leave everything he knows and has grown up with. In the second *lekh l'kha*, God asks him to forsake his future by asking him to sacrifice his son and kill off the line of descendants God promised him."

Each sacrifice, Annie said, drawing on the work of another rabbi, Yossi Lew, is a *mesirat nefesh*, "a true sacrifice." But in Annie's mind, one question still went unanswered: Did the fact that these were true, selfless sacrifices make them okay—even if one of the sacrifices would be the murder of his son?

No, Annie concluded:

> In both cases of *lekh l'kha*, Abraham is given blessings from God, but they are given at different times in each circumstance. In the first *lekh l'kha*, Abraham's blessings are given directly after the command "*Lekh l'kha*" is is-

sued. In the second *lekh l'kha*, the blessings are not given until Abraham is about to sacrifice Isaac. At that point, an angel comes to Abraham and tells him not to sacrifice his son. The angel gives Abraham the blessings right after that.

I think that in the first *lekh l'kha*, the blessings are encouragement. God really wants Abraham to follow that commandment. God really wants Abraham to leave, so he gives Abraham more reason to forsake his past and become God's servant.

But in the second *lekh l'kha*, I don't think that God really wanted Abraham to follow that commandment and sacrifice his son. I think so because Abraham does not receive his blessings until he is about to actually stick his knife into Isaac. To me, this seems to say that God wanted Abraham to argue . . . Abraham argued with God on behalf of an entire city earlier in this portion, so God wanted to see if he would argue on behalf of his own son.

Annie continued in this vein, adducing more reasons that the two *lekh l'khas*, the two "go forth"s, are different in intent: the first a call to obedience, the second a call to righteous argument. Even were it not delivered by a girl four years shy of her driver's license, this speech would be a memorable example of the Jewish critical method of drawing conclusions by comparing two different contexts in which one word or phrase of Torah arises. (Christians transformed this method into what they call typology, the search for Old Testament predictors of New Testament events.) Annie did not employ the easy homiletic strategy of relating her portion to an ethical precept, a lesson for life. That is, she did not use the story of Abraham to discuss respecting one's parents, as many b'nai mitzvah use the exodus from Egypt to talk about how to treat strangers in one's midst, like immigrants or exchange students or au pairs, or as other b'nai mitzvah might use the laws of niddah, sexual purity, to talk about respect for the opposite sex at junior high school dances.

The typical bar or bat mitzvah speech, like most sermons these days, begins with the Bible and then relates it to an ethical issue we are familiar with, in life as we live it, external to the Book. There is nothing wrong with this strategy; inferring from Torah some rules for daily behavior is a central task of Judaism. But that method can quickly reduce to a kind of narcissism, as if one's most quotidian worries—whether to wear makeup, which sneakers to buy—were of great interest to God. It is more challenging to examine how the Torah, in its various parts, relates internally to itself.

Annie did hint at an ethical maxim, of course. She was endorsing dissent as a virtue. A religious virtue, certainly, but probably more: coming from a girl who wears a yarmulke and tallis and lays tefillin, habits that we associate with men, the idea that Abraham ought to have quarreled with God was likely to be more than just a scriptural gloss. Annie was saying that unquestioning obedience to God's literal word is not always right, that even traditional authority, or the authority of tradition, must be questioned, and that sometimes wisdom inheres in thinking for oneself.

And yet, in the season of her bat mitzvah, Annie Bass chose to obey religious strictures, dated and premodern, that most of us would find onerous. Annie was raised not to do homework on Shabbos, not to write on Shabbos, not to watch television or check e-mail on Shabbos. Those were her parents' rules, but it was her own decision to begin praying every day while wearing tefillin, the small black boxes containing scraps of Hebrew that are traditionally worn only by Jewish men at prayer. Tefillin, in particular, were simultaneously an example of Annie's independent thinking and of her willingness to suspend independent thought. With this religious devotion, she was choosing to accept that there are things one does not choose.

I learned about Annie's religious life during the two months after she had become a bat mitzvah. I knew of her parents, Paul and Carole Bass, the married couple who constitute one-third of the writing staff of the *New Haven Advocate*, a left-leaning alternative weekly newspaper, New Haven's answer to the *Village Voice* or the *Boston Phoenix*. Paul is the local Upton Sinclair, a fiercely fair muckraking journalist whose weekly column, "Hit and Run," has brought down a dozen corrupt local officials over the years. That he was a Yale graduate (class of 1982) who was unsparing in his criticism of the university was intriguing, but to make it an even better story, there was a rumor that Paul was a wayward member of *the* Bass family: Perry, the Texas oil billionaire, and his sons Edward, Lee, Robert, and Sid, who together had given tens of millions of dollars to Yale, and who, taken together, were the fifth-highest donors to George W. Bush over the course of his political career. If Paul Bass, the iconoclastic liberal who lived in a small colonial house and fought valiantly to check Yale's power, were related to *those* Basses, he would be a prodigal son of literary proportions.

He was not, I was disappointed to learn, one of those Basses, but in a different way he was still quite interesting. He was a Jew from Westchester County, a fairly religious Jew, I heard, and religious Jews are scarce in the world of activist *Nation*-style journalism. Knowing a little of the Basses' religious biography and a lot of their journalism, I had guessed that Paul and Carole would have a thoughtful daughter, one whose bat mitzvah might be something more than perfunc-

tory—a counterpoint, in other words, to much of what I had
seen in New York. It had been as I expected, and now I
wanted to meet the family that had made it so.

We met in the Basses' kitchen, a typical nuclear-family
command center, the most lived-in room in the house,
brighter and more inviting than the living room or the dining
room. The kitchen was small, with a cooking area, a table, and
some cabinets around the perimeter; on top of the cabinets,
between the cabinet tops and the ceiling, were Hanukkah
menorahs, Shabbos candleholders, and other bits of Judaica.
Just back from school, Annie, in a white turtleneck shirt and a
blue yarmulke, was sipping herbal tea that her mother had
just brewed and slowly peeling an orange. Paul was still at
work. Annie's younger sister, Sarah, nine years old, was playing with a friend in the living room and intermittently practicing the flute. Carole was with us in the kitchen, grating
cheese into a bowl.

I asked Annie how she had studied for her bat mitzvah.

"Mom and I read the passage together," she said. "We
translated it from the Hebrew together, a line or two every
night. A lot of kids prepare with a tutor for their speech, but I
did it with Mom. I was going to do something else, because
everybody does the Akedah. What I wrote about, the two *lekh
l'kha*s, was the only way I could explain it to myself. We read
a few pesukim a night. We translated it from the Hebrew as
we went along. I wrote out a summary.

"When we had decided on what to talk about in my
drashah, we read it through again. We had just started—we
read it before dinner—and I said, 'How many times does it
say *lekh l'kha?*' I wondered, because there are some phrases
that pop up again and again. Dad called Rabbi Whitman"—a
local Orthodox rabbi—"and he sent over a drashah he had
just written on the phrase, which it turns out is only used

twice in the whole Bible. Then I went online and found some more stuff, by Rabbi Lew and Nehama Leibowitz. She made aliyah and was a great teacher. One thing she did that was unique was, she collected other commentaries and ideas and edited her own ideas into them."

Annie did not say, "I studied with my mom." Rather, she said, "I studied with Mom," and she maintained this intimate affect even when speaking to a stranger. When I told Annie that I had taught high school English, her eyes widened and she said, "Oh, cool!" I asked her what she had been reading in English class, and instead of answering, she went over and whispered something in her mother's ear. "Sure, that would be fine," her mother said. Annie turned to me and said, "Do you want to see my bookshelf?" I told her I would love that, and she took me upstairs.

Before getting to her room, Annie politely pointed to her parents' room, Sarah's room, and the guest room, as if to acclimate me to my surroundings, or perhaps to lend her room a certain drama, as if coming at the end of a drumroll. When we entered her room, a small rectangle, she led me straight to the two large bookshelves across from her bed.

"This one is by Tamora Pierce," Annie said, pulling a book from the shelf. "It's about a female knight in a land based on medieval Europe. These three are by Orson Scott Card—do you know *Ender's Game*?" I told her that I didn't, but that my brother, a science fiction and fantasy novel reader, had good things to say about Card. "This is by Patricia Wrede," she said. "*Searching for Dragons.*"

All of the fantasy books were on one shelf, and Annie made a point of telling me, as fantasy fans do, that these were fantasy, *not* sci-fi. Above the fantasy books were the Judaica, including a book by Nehama Leibowitz; two siddurim, the Conservative movement's prayer book *Siddur Sim Shalon*, and the *Artscroll Siddur*, popular with the Orthodox; Nathan Ausubel's *Treasury of Jewish Folklore*; *The Norton Anthology of Jewish American Literature*; Isaac Klein's *Guide to Jewish Religious Practice*; Bill Moyers's *Genesis*; the edition of the Torah published by the Reform movement; and a book by Abraham Twerski, M.D., which Annie sardonically referred to as "*My Values Preached for Money.*"

After we had examined her bookshelves, Annie dove under her bed and took out a small toy chest filled with clay figurines. "Here's one of my squirrel dudes," she said, showing me a small clay squirrel. "I bake them in clay"—here her voice dropped to a confidential whisper—"*sometimes on Shabbos, which I'm not supposed to do.*" Annie showed me another figurine, which she described as a water vole, which I had not even known was a kind of animal. She showed me an envelope that held cards from a role-playing game she had invented, a kind of cousin, I guessed, to Dungeons and Dragons. On one side of each card was a picture of a sorceress or some other powerful being, and on the reverse side was a description of the powers that the being possessed.

"I can make them morph, because I have special powers," Annie said.

It occurred to me that these books, clay dolls, and games were not just the normal implements of childhood. For a child who observed the Sabbath, they were something more, an inventory of permissible Saturday fun. I asked Annie if any of her friends kept the Sabbath. "Only one or two of my friends from school are shomer Shabbos," she said, "but a bunch of my friends from shul are." This meant that on Saturdays, when her family does not drive, Annie always had friends within walking distance: friends from her shul, or synagogue, who also kept Shabbos had to live close enough to walk to BEKI, which meant they lived near the Basses.

"I like keeping Shabbos," Annie said. "It feels weird if I don't. On Shabbos, it feels weird when I turn on the lights by accident. I have to follow some rules"—the ones her parents enforce—"and I choose to follow others. I just stopped writing and it feels better. It feels cleaner. I read, we talk, we play on Saturdays instead. I do play instruments on Shabbos still"—guitar and viola, she told me. "I play music, which some of my friends don't."

Annie's explanation of why she had given up writing on Shabbos—"It feels cleaner"—is unusual for a girl so young. We tend to think of budding adults as eager to leave behind some of the insistent cleanness of early childhood, to trade innocence for something grittier—we might even say dirtier. And Annie still might turn to the dark side—rather, she *will* turn to the dark side, in that even the most childlike do grow worldlier. Someday Annie will drink, someday she will have sex—and even if she does not drink until she is twenty-one, even if she does not have sex until she is married, she will have lost the evanescent purity of childhood. We all do. Just as we all reach a moment, no matter how hard we fight it, when we find ourselves studying for a test not because we love to learn but because acing it will help us get a job. Life slaps epaulettes on our shoulders and forces us to march into the land of the grown-ups. What was unusual about Annie's response to Shabbos was her preternatural sense that cleanness is to be held on to, a precious commodity whose scarceness she will mourn when she is an adult and the world is too much with her. A day without commerce, technology, or work is a gift of childhood as well as of Shabbos, and Annie was not keen to relinquish either.

Annie's endorsement of simplicity was consonant with the bat mitzvah she had designed for herself.

"I liked my bat mitzvah because it wasn't a party. A lot of

kids give out scarves and sweatshirts and stuff. I didn't want to do that. It's not about that. We had people over after the morning service, then forty people came back for Mincha and Ma'ariv. Then we had an erev shir, an evening of song, at our house."

Annie's spare approach to partying is becoming more common as rabbis and families react to the perceived excesses of recent decades. More unusual was Annie's choice to begin wearing tefillin for morning prayer, as very observant boys do once they have become b'nai mitzvah. I expected her to say that it was the norm for girls at her Jewish day school, Ezra Academy, a rather liberal place. Instead, she told me that she and Rabbi Amanda Brodie, the school's assistant principal, were the only females who laid tefillin, and that religious observance in general was a matter of contention at Ezra.

"Last year," she said, "a lot of the eighth-graders were atheists, and they talked about it in their graduation speeches. It's an issue in tefillah"—prayer in a generic sense, not to be confused with "tefillin."

"Are you in the atheist camp?" I asked.

"No—I don't know. I participate in tefillah because other people are asking me to and because it's pretty and it's meaningful. I don't know what it means, but it's meaningful."

I had heard other religious people defiantly refuse to interrogate their religious practice. "I pray because it's beautiful," they say. "I was raised with it." Or simply, "It seems meaningful." But almost always, these had been the words of Christians. Catholics, especially, seem comfortable with this sense of mystery, with not knowing exactly why they pray but praying nonetheless. I have heard old Jews, too, perhaps Jews who say an annual Kaddish for a dead spouse, or who are afflicted by a late-life nostalgia for childhood piety, say that they go to shul just because they feel like it. Most Jews, however, seem uncomfortable with that kind of naked, inexplicable devotion. If they are not devout believers—and atheism runs high among adult Jews—they want to explain their synagogue attendance more rationally: the synagogue is a place to teach their children values, or to find a nurturing community, or to rebuke Hitler's ghost. Annie's formulation—"I don't know what it means, but it's meaningful"—would seem to many Jews a kind of willing know-nothingism, an abdication of intellectual responsibility, a return to the psychic ghetto.

Praying "because it's pretty and it's meaningful," even though she cannot say exactly how it's meaningful, seemed akin to Annie's willingness to keep Shabbos. In each case, there is an admission of weakness. Some keep the laws of Shabbos because they believe that God commands them to, and that is one form of humbling. Many others, like Annie, appreciate the sense of sacredness or slowness or "cleanness" that comes from the weekly pause; in that appreciation is a recognition that we are not capable, by ourselves, of sanctifying our days, and that even the holiest among us must subordinate themselves to certain rules. To pray just because it feels meaningful is also to admit a kind of powerlessness before the awesome experience of religion. There is humility in saying that we don't know why we do what we do, but we feel duty-bound to continue.

Those of us with the best schooling, the kind that Annie is getting, are taught to be critical thinkers: skeptical of politicians, leery of dogma, resistant to advertisers. Superstition is suspect. One does not knock on wood for good luck. Television psychics are charlatans, and Nancy Reagan was a fool for consulting an astrologer. Religion might be defensible as a force for social cohesion, or as a medium for passing on the love of Yiddish literature, Woody Allen, and lox. It might even be useful in trying times, as when one sits shivah for a dead parent. There is comfort in tradition. But prayer as an unfathomable end unto itself is weird and best avoided.

Annie Bass prays anyway. Her philosophical explanation of that choice is smart, but in its simplicity and self-assurance it fails to capture the eccentricity of her decision. At home, she lays tefillin with her father and, at school, with the boys. Annie wears a yarmulke to school, an unusual act for a girl at Ezra Academy. "Ezra Academy is an egalitarian school," the catalogue reads. "Boys and girls are given the same opportunities in the classroom, in the gym, on the playing field and in the sanctuary. Our teachers are aware of issues of gender bias and have attended workshops on the subject. The one area where boys and girls are treated differently concerns headcoverings. Boys must cover their heads while at Ezra Academy; girls may choose to do so."

Laying tefillin and covering her head allow Annie to define herself in several ways: as a student, with habits that many of her classmates do not share; as a female, assuming responsibilities more traditionally reserved for males; and as an adult, a woman and no longer a girl.

Annie and her parents agreed that she was the one who had brought them to religion, but they disagreed on how.

"I was like three, the way I remember it," Annie said. "There are two different stories. The way I remember it, I have this Hanukkah book, and I kept asking to read it again and again. I wanted to learn more about it, so Daddy, who had grown up lighting Shabbos candles but had stopped doing anything Jewish when his mother died, he remembered, and he was like, 'Do you want to light candles more often?'

"The way Daddy and Mommy remember it, I was sick and had a fever during the family Hanukkah party, so Grandpa sent a menorah, and when Daddy and I lit the candles, Mommy was so amazed to see the looks on me and Daddy's faces, and I enjoyed it so much, that he said, 'Do you want to light candles every week?' "

I visited Paul and Carole—Daddy and Mommy—at the *New Haven Advocate's* offices at Long Wharf, by the Long Island Sound. They invited me into the lunchroom, and Carole sat down with me while Paul heated up their home-prepared lunches in a microwave. They were eating something vegan, which Paul offered to share with me. Paul was wearing wrinkled pants and a button-down shirt, and Carole was in plain, untailored clothing. I had a strong sense of déjà vu, which I quickly traced to my early years in a day-care co-op. In the late 1970s, I had regularly eaten wholesome food with plainly dressed people, though none of them had worn a yarmulke like Paul. I asked Paul and Carole how they had become religious.

"Annie's the one who got us shomer Shabbos," Paul said. "She's the one who got us to keep kosher. She wasn't born Jewish. I liked religion and everything, but I wasn't sure which religion. I had tried others. I grew up in Temple Israel in White Plains. My family always had a holiday party"—which is to say, not a Hanukkah party specifically.

In the early years of their marriage, Carole had been to these parties. "There was never a tree," she said, "but it was always the last Saturday in December, and there were always presents. It was as close to a Jewish Christmas party as you could get. But this one year—it must have been '93, because I had a baby—and this other branch of the family, they mailed us a menorah. It wasn't Hanukkah, but what did we care? So Paul set it up with all the candles, and Paul and Annie lit the candles."

"And I chanted the prayer," Paul said.

"And there was something there," Carole said, picking up her story. "In the way they looked at each other. And Paul said, 'Do you want to light candles every week?' And Annie nodded. So they went out looking for Shabbos candles."

Paul said that for some time he had been looking for a way to reconnect with his Jewish heritage. He had been only eight when his mother, the keeper of Jewish tradition in the Bass family, died, and the annual holiday party was all that was left behind. "Over all the years, I had wanted to go to High Holidays," Paul said, "and I hated the fact that you had to pay to go to High Holidays. I thought that was sick." He was referring to the practice of collecting synagogue membership dues in the fall, just before Rosh Hashanah and Yom Kippur, the Jewish New Year and the Day of Atonement. Synagogues do not pass collection plates, as the exchange of money is forbidden on the Sabbath; instead, they charge an annual membership fee and allow only members to attend the High Holiday services, the most important of the Jewish liturgical year. Most synagogues offer financial aid to poorer families, but there remains the fact that your financial account must be settled up before you may pray. For many Jews, especially for those who believe that Judaism has become too materialistic, the dues, often structured as the selling of High Holiday tickets, are a contentious issue.

At about the time that they began lighting candles, Paul and Carole became friendly with the rabbi at BEKI, Jon-Jay Tilsen, and his wife, Miriam Benson. It seemed like an auspicious time for Paul to return to shul, this time with his daughter, but he was not sure how his wife would feel.

"I was a little nervous about Carole, because she was a Christian," Paul said.

"I was a Catholic," Carole said, "and I left the church. There were times when I was aware I was looking for some kind of spiritual connection. I guess one of the first things that really attracted me to Judaism, as I started to get to know it, was the intellectual exercise as a way of life. The idea that there's nothing that you have to believe, that you challenge the basic tenets of Judaism constantly and probe and test it, and realizing there's this whole tradition of wrestling with every question that I could ever possibly have about religion and the Bible and life and what it's all about, plus all the questions I'd never thought of—this tradition of all these great minds wrestling with a question, even if the answers wouldn't necessarily work for me, but there it is! And all I have to do is ask and somebody will tell me about it.

"If I had been able to figure that out when I was eighteen, maybe I would have remained a Christian; maybe I would be a Christian today. I don't know. A lot of it had to do with my own lack of maturity. I was able to, I guess, ask questions and connect with people in my thirties in a way I was never able to do when I was eighteen. It was so much the atmosphere I stepped into at BEKI, and it was so much the atmosphere I had grown up in in the church. Even though, as I said, I had grown up in a liberal Catholic family. My parents are questioners."

Paul and Annie started attending BEKI, and at first Carole stayed home with Sarah, still a toddler. But as Sarah got older, Carole began taking her to the children's room at BEKI on Saturday mornings. Until then, Carole's exposure to Judaism had been limited, but positive.

"I'd been to two different Passover seders, Workmen's Circle–type things. So it was cool, a lot of fun. It was very spirited, and it was political. It wasn't religious in any way. And then we also used to go sometimes to Paul's family seders, where nobody has any interest in the ritual at all—"

"Except you!" Paul interjected.

"—and everybody would sit there and complain about when do we eat. The whole shtick. So my real introduction to Judaism was in the children's room at BEKI on Shabbat morning, where I would go and sit with the preschoolers and learn. Which was actually a great way to start learning, because it was very friendly; it was low-key."

Carole converted in 1996, and she can now read Hebrew and chant Torah, as I saw at Annie's bat mitzvah. When she and Paul sold their house in 1994, they moved to Westville to be close to BEKI. They walk to synagogue, and their friends now come mostly from the synagogue membership. Old friends and family have accommodated the Basses' new religiosity, but it took time. The first time you see an old friend wearing a yarmulke is a bit of a shock, although it's one that wears off by the fourth or fifth time. A family that keeps Shabbos can no longer drive to Friday night parties, or to birthday parties on Saturday afternoons. They can't catch up with friends over a Saturday telephone call. This was as much of a change for Paul, the born Jew, as it was for Carole, the convert.

"I grew up Conservative, but totally nonreligious," he said.

I asked what his family made of his turn toward Judaism.

"Most of my relatives thought I was nuts. But my father, he totally dug it, he got so excited. He got very close to Annie and Carole and Sarah through this."

Carole nodded. "His uncle Marvin, whom I mentioned before hosting seders in New Jersey, was at the bat mitzvah and had such a great time. He said, 'I could tell that everybody meant it, and even the people sitting around me, they really meant it, and it's not just Yom Kippur—they really *live* this way, it's a way of life.' I said, 'Yeah, it is.' "

Just then, Josh Mamis, the editor of the *Advocate*, walked into the lunchroom.

"Ask him," Paul said, gesturing with his thumb in Josh's direction. "He's Jewish, but he thinks we're nuts."

Josh grinned and said, "They're nuts."

To prove how nuts Josh thinks they are, Paul said, "Josh thought I was serious when I said the Shubert Theater was anti-Semitic for having John Prine on a Friday night." Josh shrugged with a kind of helpless agreement, as if to say, "Well, when they're that nuts, who's to say when they're being serious?" And to someone who's not religious, it does seem crazy to skip a terrific folk concert just because of some ancient laws about the Sabbath; if Paul could pass up John Prine, why couldn't he harbor conspiracy theories about anti-Semitic concert promoters?

I asked Carole if her family thought she was nuts.

"I think my mother does," she said. "She would never say it. But yeah. Not for being Jewish, but the level of observance. Most of the Shabbat restrictions—she thinks that's nuts. I mean, she said one time something about she sees it from her perspective. Her perspective is—a couple of specific things she said. One was that when she was a kid, on Sundays she had to go to church in dress clothes, and then they would go and visit relatives and spend the afternoon with relatives. And they had to keep their dress clothes on, so they couldn't play. They just had to sit around and be quiet.

"The other thing was she could sort of see how if you're working all week, a day of rest could be a useful thing.

"Whose phrase was it about Judaism: 'an old man saying no'?* She's someone who, when she got married and had kids, she quit work and stayed home. She did volunteer stuff, but

---

*I could not find out who first called Judaism "an old man saying no," but the expression did put me in mind of H. L. Mencken's famous definition of Puritanism: "The haunting fear that someone, somewhere, may be happy."

she was a full-time mom. So if you thought about what her
weeks were like, she was home with the kids. So when the
weekend came and my dad was home, no way did she want to
be cooped up. No way did she want her Saturdays to be con-
fined to the house and wherever she could walk and not using
the phone. She needed contact with the rest of the world.

"And also, I mean, our Shabbat revolves so much around
our Shabbat community. The times when we're away or not
in, when we're spending Shabbat someplace where nobody
else is observing Shabbat, it's very isolating."

Given the sacrifices the Basses now make for Judaism, I was
surprised that Paul had been so irreligious a child. His bar
mitzvah, he told me, had meant nothing to him. I asked if it
could have been done differently, made more meaningful.
There was this disconnect between the Jewish selves of his
childhood and adulthood, and I wondered if they could have
been more seamless.

"If my mother hadn't died when I was eight, it could have
been . . ." He thought for a moment. "I'm not upset about it.
I feel I missed out on some stuff, but I explored a lot of other
things, not just in the Jewish world. I didn't join other religions, but I studied other religions."

With no good template from Paul's own childhood—and
none from Carole's—how had the parents planned for their
daughter's bat mitzvah?

"It was important to our daughter and us that it not be one
of those materialistic b'nai mitzvah celebrations," Paul said.
"We were very much reacting against that. But it was very fun
for her planning the ritual. We know somebody who had a bar
mitzvah in Israel and just read Torah and then there was a kiddush"—a gathering in which wine is blessed (and where treats
may be consumed).

"We didn't even know it was a bar mitzvah," Carole said.

"We had no idea there was a simcha happening on this Shabbat until the kiddush was over and they said, 'Mazel tov!' And I thought, Oh, that kid in the flannel shirt?"

Instead of having a big party the evening after the bat mitzvah, the Basses had a small dinner the night before.

"We did a Friday thing," Paul said. "We have kind of a chevrah"—a community, a group of friends—"in Westville for shomer Shabbos people. We love to sing and dance and all that stuff. So we had a potluck for like twenty people. We didn't get dressed up. I didn't wear a tie or anything."

On Saturday morning, after Annie Bass had read from the Torah, prayed the Musaf service, and given her speech, people stayed afterward for lunch, the Basses' treat. Then friends and relatives walked to the Basses' house to relax for the afternoon, returning to BEKI that evening for Havdalah, the candle lighting that ends Shabbos.

"Havdalah was the best," Paul said. "I mean, that was just so great. It was really special when Carole led that."

Sometime during the day, Annie, or somebody, collected Annie's bat mitzvah gifts: books, cash, checks. The gifts are one aspect of a bat mitzvah that the girl's family cannot control, for even at a modest party, eager and generous relatives can make the day quite lucrative. And no matter how earnestly a girl wants her day to be about religion, a windfall of five or ten thousand dollars may be what she remembers most. Annie's solution was to decide in advance that all checks would go to her parents.

"I remember her telling us about one of her best friends at school," Carole said. "Annie had mentioned to us several times that Sasha's deal with her parents—it wasn't a deal, it was the rule laid out by her parents—was she'd get the cash, and the checks were going into a savings account for her college education. And Annie mentioned that several times in a way that made it clear that she expected that we would do that."

She didn't get much cash, Paul said. She was much more excited about her tefillin, which she'd received a couple of weeks before.

The buffet lunch at the synagogue was the only real expenditure. The design and printing of the invitations, so expensive when done by a fancy stationer, cost Paul and Carole five dollars. Because the Bass family computer has no Hebrew fonts, Annie drew the letters for "Vayera" by hand and scanned it into a word-processing document, then surrounded it with the date and location, and that was her bat mitzvah invitation. Paul went to Staples to buy nice paper, then to the copy shop to have the photocopying done. I marveled at the honesty of a man who would not use his office photocopier to run off one hundred bat mitzvah invitations for his daughter, but Paul is a little bit compulsive in his austerity. With all the running around to get the invitations out, "it was more involved than I had wished," he told me, a bit plaintively—even though, he admitted, the postage was his greatest expense.

It is difficult to disentangle what Judaism gave the Bass family from what was already inside them. Paul and Carole were antimaterialists before they were observant Jews; in fact, it was Paul's aversion to money worship that had soured him on the Judaism he'd seen as a child. He did not have to become a religious Jew to find a simple way to live, or to find like-minded friends. The Basses did not need BEKI to give them something to do with their Saturdays. So they may have become Jews because they enjoyed the ritual, or because they believed that the commandments, such as keeping the Sabbath, would structure their lives in rich, rewarding ways. Paul may have felt called by God; Carole, it seemed to me, was a bit too much of a rationalist for that.

When I asked them, though, Paul and Carole said that what brought them to Judaism was their daughter. Since they'd become more observant, the most notable change in their lives was how they spent time with their daughters, in shul and around the neighborhood on Saturdays. Their greatest new extravagance was their two daughters' tuition at a private Jewish school. If Annie's bat mitzvah affirmed her love of learning, her aversion to materialism, and her devotion to unhurried time with family, then in some rather evident ways it was a celebration of becoming an adult Bass, her parents' peer.

Gila Reinstein, a pleasant and slightly zaftig woman in her fifties who works in the public relations office of Yale University, was the president of BEKI that year. She was at shul every Saturday, and she knew all the bar mitzvah boys and bat mitzvah girls. I had heard her give a moving talk at Annie's bat mitzvah, and I wanted to ask her both about the Basses and about b'nai mitzvah more generally. I was curious how typical Annie's bat mitzvah was, for this synagogue anyway.

"We'd have no objection to a bar or bat mitzvah every Shabbat if we had enough kids," Gila ("pronounced like the monster") said, as we sipped beers in the garden behind her ground floor apartment in a townhouse on Bradley Street. She had placed among her plants a small waterfall, which gurgled softly in the background. "But with no simcha, virtually all the regulars come anyway."

In other words, the big crowd at Annie's bat mitzvah was typical of any Saturday, not just a Saturday with a simcha. Although some of the worshipers that morning were friends or relatives who had come just for Annie, the Basses' community is, to a great extent, the BEKI community, and the BEKI community goes to synagogue, often. Rabbis have a rule of thumb that a large synagogue can expect to get one person on Shabbat for every ten "member units," families or single adults. That is, if 500 families belong to the shul, about 50 people will be there on Saturday morning. According to that rule, BEKI, with about 260 member families, should get about 26 people. It gets about 150. A bar or bat mitzvah pushes the number to about 200—an increase, but not one so great as to affect the feel of services. Unlike at the Westchester synagogue, a bat mitzvah at BEKI does not summon an improvised religious community, with weekend guests outnumbering the usual congregants. Annie Bass was reading Torah in front of her religious family, not some one-time assemblage of well-wishers.

Annie's party, too, was standard for BEKI: lunch after services, then some people retiring to the host family's house. "Families are expected to sponsor the kiddush, and to invite everyone," Gila told me. "There are no special guests going upstairs for the herring. The expectation is that everyone who's there that morning is invited."

"So there's a lot of schnorrers!" interjected Gila's brother, Stephen Steinlight, a houseguest that day who had wandered into the backyard to join us. "Schnorrer" is Yiddish for a moocher or a grubber.

Gila, his big sister, looked at him reproachfully.

"They're called *congregants*. They're the people who will still be there next week, when you're long gone."

I asked Gila how significant the bar and bat mitzvah were for BEKI's children. It depends, she said, on the child.

"For somebody like Annie," Gila said, "she is now going to take on the absolute rigors of fasting on Yom Kippur, and other obligations, practicing them and building on them. We'll put her in rotation to keep reading on Shabbat. You can't be a shliach tsibbur"—a prayer leader—"until you have reached bat mitzvah age, and now she has.

"But what does it mean? I don't think this is a major change in her life. The Basses are observant; they come every Saturday they're in town. In many ways, bar mitzvah is more of a milestone for the kids who are not observant, especially if they have a good experience. The parents may start coming to shul to help them along. The kids in their year develop a team spirit."

At BEKI, many children have a good experience, one that enhances their commitment to Judaism. Gila compared their experience to what happens to some mourners: "People say the same things about losing a parent or, God forbid, a spouse or a child. They start coming to daily minyan to say Kaddish. I've heard them say that it recentered their whole lives. They started the day with a moment of holiness and comradeship with others. And after that, when the eleven months of saying Kaddish daily was up, they became regulars, not every day, but once a week."

Get people to shul often enough, and it may stick. Many children draw close to their rabbi and congregation as they prepare to become b'nai mitzvah. But Annie had been preparing for half her life, Gila explained. This was one Jewish moment of thousands for the Basses: walking to shul on Shabbos, building a sukkah on the holiday of Sukkos, dancing on Simchas Torah, father and daughter praying together in the morning before heading off to work and school.

"The Basses are good people, loving and respectful," Gila said. But they were not typical. "They're certainly, in any community, including BEKI, on the extreme. Paul is vegan; he doesn't wear leather. He's as consistent as a person can be, but he wasn't always. He was not always vegetarian; he was not always observant." But now, Gila said, his life was unimaginable without the strictures of Shabbos. "When Shabbat comes, the outside world is finished. There is no phone. They put on a big thing of water on a low flame; they turn off the lights and put on some light timers. They're normal people—they read Harry Potter, sci-fi; they talk politics. But come Shabbat, they create this space around themselves. Other people will come by, stop by, have tea with them. They sing Shabbat songs, do the whole grace after meals. They build a sukkah. They have a whole community on Shabbat. If I lived in Westville, I'd also be a walker. You see people streaming in, pushing baby carriages.

"Annie's well-read beyond her years, quirky in a lovely way. One Simchat Torah—we do a lot of dancing on Simchat Torah—that's when I got to know the Basses. I knew who Paul was, of course. But Annie came up to me, slipped her little hand in mine, and wanted to dance with me. She talked her parents into inviting me for Shabbat dinner, and I have now been several times. I can't reciprocate on Shabbat, because it's too far for them to walk, but I have reciprocated on other occasions.

"She is bright, gentle, and shy. My recollection of her bat mitzvah is, she was almost embarrassed to be the center of attention."

Gila was right: Annie had seemed embarrassed that morning. After she had read Torah and the ceremonial portion of the morning was concluded, she had stood at the bimah for fifteen minutes while all the adults in her life conferred on her the kind of praise that is rarely sought by those who most deserve it. Jon-Jay Tilsen, BEKI's rabbi, praised Annie, sounding more like an uncle, even a friend, than like a clergyman. Tilsen seemed almost pained by the spotlight, and I guessed that he saw Annie as a kindred spirit. Paul thanked his daughter for bringing the family to Judaism, then yielded to his wife, who gave the longest speech of the morning. Annie's teachers praised her. Gila Reinstein praised her.

These direct addresses to the bar or bat mitzvah would over the year become my favorite part of the services I saw. Most parents say "I love you" to their children, but it's unusual to see a mother or father saying it so intently, and in public too. The congratulations on their becoming a bar or bat mitzvah will be the most articulate expressions of love that many children will hear from their parents, as well as the most public and perhaps the last: it's easy to tell a five- or ten-year-old how perfect and adorable she is, but teenagers grow distant, parents become inhibited, and the relationship becomes less affectionate. Adults are paradoxically less capable than children of expressing adult emotions, which means that the bar or bat mitzvah, in the first days of adulthood, may be the last time parents bring themselves to say how proud they are of their children.

While Annie suffered one kind of discomfort, I was suffering another. It was apparent, even then, before I knew the Basses or their synagogue friends, that this was not the usual bat mitzvah. This girl was very special; the adults were not shy about saying so. She was venerated for being the kind of young Jew rabbis and teachers and parents hope for, spiritually committed and spiritually gifted. Her bat mitzvah was the antidote to Scarsdale. For all these Jews who had joined BEKI because it was low-key and haimish, not materialistic or trendy, she was proof that their community could raise a different kind of Jew. They were glad to have found her; *I* was glad to have found her. It could make my book different from what I had feared, more redemptive. And I felt slightly ashamed of the burden that, unbeknownst to Annie, I was placing on her.

Rabbi Amanda Brodie, the diminutive and cheery Englishwoman who is the assistant principal of Annie's school, admonished me that "it would be a mistake to take Annie as a typical bat mitzvah. She's the only girl in the seventh grade who wears tefillin. She gets frustrated at the other kids' apathy toward tefillah. She's a very spiritual kid. She also has found for herself important spiritual leaders that she seeks out. It wasn't two days after I got here that she found me. She told me about the other female rabbi in her life. She appreciates the fact that I'm a female rabbi. She can talk to me about girl stuff."

The obvious pride that Rabbi Brodie took in Annie owed something to the frustration she felt with other students. Even at Jewish schools—perhaps especially at Jewish schools—it is considered uncool to be too enthusiastic about Judaism. During Annie's seventh-grade year, Rabbi Brodie led a Torah study group one day a week, during recess. There were five regular attendants, all of them girls. Not so few, but not so many, either. Her excitement about Annie would have to serve, then, as a reminder. The religious gift, like the athletic gift or the mathematical gift, is rare: when coaches or teachers spot a potential star, they get giddy, and they want to begin grooming. When I asked the rabbi if she thought Annie might be a rabbi someday, she smiled, was about to speak, and then just smiled again. The thought had crossed her mind.

The people of BEKI did not make Annie. Her youthful fascination with the lighting of candles, like her forceful decisions to keep Shabbos and to lay tefillin, come from someplace we cannot know for sure. Her genetic endowment? Her parents' unique nurturance? God? The Basses were blessed, however, to be in the right place and to find some very fine people with whom to practice their kind of Judaism. After our last interview, I saw Annie two more times. The first was on the New Haven Green during a free music concert on a Sunday, Father's Day. The whole family was sitting on a blanket, listening to a bluegrass band playing on a stage at the far end of the lawn. I walked over to say hello, and Paul introduced me to a bearded man wearing a tie-dyed yarmulke, a friend from synagogue. Two weeks later, I walked into Miya's, the sushi restaurant on Howe Street, just as the Basses were leaving. There was a fifth member of their crew, a teenage boy in a yarmulke. Paul introduced him as Sandy Johnston, the son of Robert Johnston, one of three Yale professors I knew who had converted to Judaism, two of whom worshiped with their families at BEKI.

I continue to see Paul, often at Claire's, the only kosher restaurant in downtown New Haven. His life and the lives of his wife and daughters are flavored by Judaism, but more to the point, they are flavored by other Jews. In Paul's neighborhood, in his congregation, and in his city, Jewish friends are everywhere, and while they did not determine the kind of bat mitzvah his daughter would have, they made it possible. B'nai mitzvah, I realized in New Haven, are inherently communal, like other Jewish celebrations: Jewish weddings require witnesses, brises are parties, and even in mourning one receives visitors. Wherever a few Jews gather, they form a new small society.

This variety among Jews, so apparent once I had made the trip from Greater New York to New Haven, reminded me that the party expos and big-city magazine articles were the worst way to understand the range of bar and bat mitzvah experiences. Annie's experience was urban, middle-class, and prayerful, which meant that she could walk to shul and live near others who did; the households of those around her were mostly free of material excess; and the impulse to worship, seriously and at length, was nurtured. Change any of these factors—move the Basses to a suburb or a farm, quadruple their income and their friends', give them a rabbi who prefers short, snappy services—and her bat mitzvah would have been so, so different.

As I traveled the country asking people why they chose to enact this ritual, answers varied from family to family, but there were noticeable patterns, depending on the town and the particular synagogue. Every small Jewish society has its own culture—BEKI is definitely not Westchester Reform—so even the most unusual child owes some of her prowess to the adults and children around her. The Passover story tells of four children: the wise, the wicked, the simple, and "the one who doesn't know how to ask." There is a temptation to see Annie as the wise, her less studious classmates as the simple, and the boys gambling Monopoly money in the Sherry-Netherland Hotel as the wicked. But Judaism teaches the unity of *Am Yisrael,* the Jewish people; according to Jewish theology, all Jews are related, literally. Which means that just as every bar or bat mitzvah owes something to other members of the synagogue, all synagogues owe something to the others. This is particularly true in the United States: Hasidim are winning converts from Reform, while feminism is moving from its roots in Reform and Conservatism into Orthodoxy. There is no "high" Judaism or "low" Judaism, and "progressives" cannot pretend they have no relation to the right wing. Some congregants may seem wise, others simple or wicked, but in Judaism they are all set a place at the table. The excess of certain New York synagogues and the pious simplicity of BEKI in New Haven were two extremes—convenient stereotypes and terrific stories, but hardly the last word.

3

The Tutor

*A*my Krisher, a twelve-year-old with long brown hair, glasses, and an outside prayer of reaching five feet tall, is sitting in the kitchen of Judi Gannon, her Torah tutor, and practicing the prayer for Rosh Hodesh, the new month, which she will chant less than two months later, the morning she becomes a bat mitzvah. She is having trouble with her pronunciation, and Judi tries to head off her frustration before it builds to a fury.

"Okay, now slow it down. We like this! Have fun with it! It's real fun!" Judi bounces her helmet of frosted hair back and forth and side to side, wearing an intentionally silly grin.

Amy is having none of this perkiness. "I can't do it," she says. "My braces were tightened yesterday. My mouth hurts." Amy's mother, Jamie, rummages through her purse and slides two Tylenols across the kitchen table.

Judi opens her own mouth and pulls back her lower lip, like a horse being readied for inspection on the auction block. "They didn't give me braces on the bottom," she says. "My parents didn't have the money. You know what the dentist said to me? 'Don't worry, you'll get married anyway.' I didn't like that comment. But I got married three times. So imagine if he'd straightened my teeth—I'd be on my tenth wedding!"

She laughs a throaty Bea Arthur laugh. Judi now smokes one or two cigarettes a day, she says, no more than three, "and never inside the house." She and her husband, Tom, go to the back patio for their smokes. She was forced to cut down when construction was going on in her backyard. She was afraid for her safety with all the construction workers around, and that helped her smoke less. Tom's two strokes, which he had around the same time, helped him smoke less, and now they don't smoke much at all, and never when a student is in the kitchen studying Torah.

Judi already guessed that braces were the problem. "I know immediately when the teeth hurt"—one of many things that Judi, Tampa's leading Torah tutor, knows about twelve- and thirteen-year-olds. In addition to divining her kids' orthodontic struggles, Judi can tell when the girls are sore from dance practice and when the boys are nursing bruises from soccer. She can tell when their mothers are lying on the phone, inventing pretexts for canceling a tutorial. She can tell by the way mothers and fathers call to their children from the car window which parents are emotionally abusive, which parents really love their children, and which fathers drink. Judi knows which mothers, on the Friday before the bat mitzvah, when the girls usually want one final lesson to make sure they have Noach or Toldot down just right, persuade their daughters that it's more important to have a manicure. And Judi knows which mothers patiently come with their daughters, to sit with them during that stressful final lesson.

Amy Krisher's hour is up—or rather, Amy and Jamie Krisher's hour is up. Determined to read Torah alongside her daughter at the bat mitzvah, Jamie has been taking the last ten minutes of Amy's lessons. She is not as musically gifted as Amy, but what Jamie lacks in ear, she almost makes up for in motherly perseverance. Her small Torah portion has a plethora of syllables marked with a revi'i, a diamond-shaped symbol that is one of the millennium-old cantillation marks that tell Jews how to chant the words of Torah. Jamie tries again and again to chant the notes of the revi'i, then finally decides that she has had enough for the week. As Amy and Jamie pack up their s'farim, Hebrew books, Judi has a final smile for Jamie and tries to find some comments for Amy, but Amy's pronunciation is nearly perfect, and Judi has to strain visibly to find constructive advice. "You could afford to slow down a little," she says. "Your syllables are a little garbled. Maybe by next week your teeth will feel better. You're doing great."

With the Krishers gone, Judi exhales, flops back into her kitchen chair, and begins one of the monologues that will characterize my time with her.

"It's Jamie's revi'i that's driving me to take my first-ever sabbatical," she says. "It's technically a revi'i, which means four, and she's giving it four tones, but they're the wrong ones! After Rachel"—Rachel Schonwetter, another one of her current students—"and Amy, that's it. I mean, I plan to come back, but I have to have Judi time first. Judi has to have Judi time! You saw my book, you saw how busy I was! I need Judi time! Now, if they build that shul on the other side of Tampa and want to make me their cantorial soloist, which they keep talking about doing, well then, I would come back for that. But will that shul ever be built? You tell me. They keep talking. They want to have the membership before they build the shul. But if you build it, they will come. You have to have the shul sometimes first. And they're all doctors over there. They could afford it. The richer they are, the cheaper. When I raised my rate, one client dropped me—right before she bought her $28,000 convertible."

.   .   .

Judi intimately sensed the hierarchy of which she was a part. The production of religion, in the United States anyway, involves hired labor. An irony: the Sabbath is not restful for the rabbi. In some very observant communities, where all the adult men are capable of leading prayers, the hired rabbi may play just a small role in Saturday services; but at most synagogues, it's his or her day to work, and the rabbi's obedience to Shabbos mitzvot, like not driving, writing, or kindling a flame, commandments meant to mark the day as restful, entails a useful fiction—useful because it reminds even the clergy that the day has special meaning, but a fiction because Saturday is stressful, the day when the new sermon will either succeed or fall flat, the day whose performance can determine next year's paycheck or contract extension. On Saturday, the cantor worries that his voice might crack, and the Torah tutor worries that her student, this young boy or girl, might after a year of practice freeze in front of all those guests, flown in from all over to hear Torah chanted well.

In New York City and Scarsdale, where money was so much in evidence, I had not thought to ask many questions about it: everybody involved seemed so well compensated. The photographer wore Prada. The farther I got from these centers of industry and affluence, the more I met people whose religious and professional identities shared the same space, willingly but uncomfortably, like roommates in a cramped apartment. Judi Gannon was able to teach Torah because she had always loved and studied Judaism—but she needed to teach Torah because it was how she paid the bills. On my last day in Tampa, I met the man who had videotaped Rachel Schonwetter's bat mitzvah: he worked Monday through Friday as a photographer for a local television station, and on Saturday, his day of rest, he earned extra cash, money that helped him pay the annual dues at his synagogue across town, where, surrounded by lawyers and doctors, he was one of the poorest members.

Jews are known for valuing scholars, not compensating them. At the biggest and richest synagogues, rabbis make out nicely: David Wolpe, rabbi of Los Angeles's Temple Sinai, makes over $200,000 a year, which he reminded me "is fairly typical for a rabbi in a major American city"; Rabbi Posner at Congregation Emanu-El, a larger congregation in a richer census tract, may do even better. But the Rabbinic Assembly, the organization of Conservative rabbis, estimates that the total compensation packages of its members range from about $55,000 to $235,000, and most rabbis surely fall at the lower end of that range. Smaller synagogues pay lower salaries, so Orthodox rabbis get less for knowing more. And some very fine cantors, chanters, and tutors are paid less still.

Judi's rate is twenty-five dollars an hour, half of what she could get in Boston, a third of what she could get in New York. It is a living, not a splendid one. B'nai mitzvah thrive because of eager parents and committed students, but also because there are men and women like Judi whose livelihoods depend on this ritual. There are caterers, florists, party planners, deejays, stationers, and rock bands whose thin profit margins would vanish entirely but for the bar and bat mitzvah. At any synagogue with more than twenty b'nai mitzvah a year, the chances are good that much of the children's preparation is supervised by part-time wage workers, often graduate students or retired ladies, who supplement small fixed incomes by doing the teaching for which rabbis have little time. At Kol Ami in Tampa, there were two of these part-time tutors, including Isaac Weiner, a recent college graduate from suburban Boston whose full-time job, until he left the next year to go to graduate school in North Carolina, was teaching at a local private high school; and then there was the full-time tutor, Judi. Women like Judi did not create the market for their services, but in the modern Jewish division of labor they have become necessary, and if they disappeared tomorrow, there would be fewer bar and bat mitzvah services, and far fewer good ones.

What Judi Gannon teaches is the cantillation, or chanting, of Torah. Chanting is not practiced in all synagogues. Reform Jews, especially, often read Torah in plain spoken Hebrew or English. But Orthodox, Conservative, and many Reform synagogues have held to the tradition of cantillation, or leyning, as it is called in Yiddish. A bar mitzvah boy who is called to the Torah in October, at the beginning of the annual Torah-reading cycle, is called not just to read from Genesis, but to chant his portion according to a musical system comprising series of stops, disjunctions, and relative pitch changes. Unlike Western music, which is marked by absolute pitch—Haydn asks you to play a C above middle C, so you play that C—words and phrases of the Torah are assigned pitch changes: for a given word, you may start in any key, and you may even improvise the starting note, but tradition will tell you whether, for that particular word in that particular verse of the Bible, you hold that note, go up, go down, go up and then down, or some other combination.

Boys and girls struggle more with these musical accents than with any other aspect of their preparation, but it's their struggles that ensure the survival of the art. Even if most b'nai mitzvah soon forget cantillation, the ones who remember will become its practitioners and its teachers. Like Latin and Ancient Greek, cantillation will never be the province of the masses, but it will stay alive as a classical language and music and as a form of connoisseurship.

In American Judaism, the educational expectations for a
bar or bat mitzvah are higher than they were fifty or a hundred years ago. Then, Reform Jews were expected to know at
most several lines of Hebrew, Conservative b'nai mitzvah
chanted a small bit of the morning service or perhaps some of
the short haftarah, and Orthodoxy had yet to be affected by
the arrival of ultra-Orthodox refugees who preferred for their
children's education a more strictly religious curriculum, one
that tends to eschew science, math, and English in favor of
more Torah. In any American synagogue, a boy or girl today is
more likely than fifty years ago to chant Torah, and at length.
This new rigor is due to immigration trends, a Zionist emphasis on Hebrew proficiency, the proliferation of Jewish day
schools, the disenchantment with assimilation, and many
other factors, one of which is the guild of professionals that
has arisen to uphold these standards. Like the best party favors, video recording, and floral arrangement, a good Torah
tutor is difficult to find but essential to have. Unlike the in-
structors at the old talmud torah, or religious school, often remembered by old men as bitter, bearded curs who enforced
discipline with a ruler, today's tutor is well versed in sensitive
pedagogy—how to know when a boy needs his Ritalin, when
to concede defeat to soccer practice and play rehearsals. Judi
knows when the braces hurt.

All Eastern religions of the premodern world seem to have
chanted, not read or sung, their scriptures. Vedic recitation in
India and Buddhist recitation in Japan, for example, were both
chanted traditions. Chanting mostly disappeared from the Ro-
mance languages, persisting only in the Catholic Mass, but cantillation survived in Hebrew Torah reading. In its early years,
cantillation was communicated by chironomy, systems of hand

signals representing the musical changes. A chironomist would stand alongside the Torah reader, signaling to remind him of the cantillation. In the Talmud, fourth-century rabbi Nachman ben Isaac says that the right hand must be kept clean because it is the hand used to signal cantillation: "Why should one wipe with the left hand and not with the right? . . . Rabbi Nachman b. Isaac said: Because he uses it to show the te'amim"—cantillation, accents—"of the Torah."*

By the eleventh century, cantillation was becoming known as "trop," a word that made its way into the various Yiddish dialects of Europe (and is now generally pronounced "trope"). "Trop" probably comes from the Greek *tropos*, via the Latin *tropus*, referring to an extended melody or mode in church music of the Middle Ages. The word is first found in the writings of Rabbi Shlomo ben Yitzhak, the eleventh-century rabbi known as Rashi, who referred to "the sweetened chant which is called 'trop.' "

As the hand signals died out, the future of trop lay in the written notation codified by Aharon ben Asher, a tenth-century scribe from Tiberius. Around 930, he finished an annotated Bible that included Hebrew vowels—an innovation for the time—as well as written notations of all the te'amim, or trop accents. Aharon's manuscript became the template for the Leningrad Codex of 1009 or 1010, the main source of today's Hebrew Bible, or Old Testament. Aharon's written trop notations have been standard since the eleventh century.†

While all Jewish communities use Aharon's written accents

---

*From tractate B'rachot 62a, in the Babylonian Talmud.
†Although he helped bring about chironomy's demise, Aharon also wrote one of the only extant descriptions of it, which can be found in his Sefer Dikdukey Ha-te'amim, written in the early tenth century. The best book about the history and practice of trop is Joshua R. Jacobson's *Chanting the Hebrew Bible: The Art of Cantillation* (Philadelphia: Jewish Publication Society, 2002).

to chant Torah, those accents are interpreted differently across the world. Just as not every system of mathematics is base-ten, and not every Western musical system is based on the eight-tone scale, not every Jewish community chants according to the same trop. For example, one of Aharon's cantillation marks, the tevir, which looks like a comma with a dot sitting in its curve, is chanted differently in the Lithuanian, German, Iraqi, Dutch, Syrian, Italian, and French customs. The same verse of Torah, notated with exactly the same markings, could even be chanted differently from one village to the next. To make matters more complicated, the trop accents can change meaning depending on the occasion. Within the Lithuanian community, to know how to chant the tevir properly one would first have to know if one was chanting Torah on a normal Sabbath, haftarah on a normal Sabbath, the Book of Esther on the holiday of Purim, the Book of Lamentations on the holiday Tisha b'Av, the Song of Songs on Pesach, the Book of Ruth on Shavuos, Ecclesiastes on Sukkos, or any Torah on Rosh Hashanah or Yom Kippur. A Muscovite or a Yemenite could have just as many different interpretations of Aharon's trop markings. Each community—each person, really—may put his own spin on the trop. While mispronouncing a word is forbidden, pronouncing it in an unusually flavored trop may be permissible.

In the United States today, boys and girls learn at most two trops, Torah and haftarah. The first trop is for the reading from one of the first five books of the Old Testament; the second, in a mournful, minor key, is for the week's prophetic reading, from a book such as Ezekiel or Jeremiah. And although American Jews are descended from all the Jewish communities of the world, they are usually taught "Binder trop," a system, based on Eastern European Ashkenazic traditions, codified by Abraham Binder in his 1959 book *Biblical Chant*.

Some elderly trop teachers continue to pass on the trop they learned in Germany or in the Netherlands, or the trop they learned from immigrant teachers, but Binder has become the norm.

In centuries past, before most b'nai mitzvah chanted Torah, the Torah reading was typically done by a congregant who functioned as the ba'al k'riyah, "master of reading," an unusually learned man who knew the trop by heart, could chant any passage of Torah on sight, and (one hoped) had a tuneful, mellifluous voice. Because Torah chant is an example of hiddur mitzvah, or beautification of the commandment; because the trop is not random but was written to dramatize and enhance the text; because the chanting of Torah helps separate the sacred from the profane, reminding the listener that these are special words and special stories; because a well-chanted bit of Torah carries better and thus is an aid to worship; and because the Talmud says that Torah must be chanted, the ideal chanter was both a good singer and a man of strong character, someone worthy of such intimacy with the word of God. In the Sha'arei Efrayim, an anonymous seventeenth-century commentary on the important sixteenth-century legal code the Shulchan Aruch, the author describes the ideal Torah reader. He must be

> a decent man; he knows the law; he is a moral person; he has a pleasant voice, he is an expert in the proper rendition of the words, the melodies, and the accents; he also has some knowledge of grammar, so he won't put a dagesh where it doesn't belong and vice versa, and he won't slur over a vocal sh'va nor vocalize a silent sh'va, lest even one letter from the punctuation and vocalization that were given at Sinai be altered, lest an erroneous reading cause a change in the meaning of even one

word . . . He should read in a loud voice, not too fast or
too slow, so as not to inconvenience the congregation,
but rather in a moderate way. Nor should he show off
with elaborate vocalization that might confuse the listen-
ers. Rather let him read with clear pronunciation and
with the sacred melody to attract the attention of the
congregation and induce them to listen.

So until the twentieth century a Jewish boy would learn
some rudimentary Torah skills, perhaps do a little chant on
the day he became a bar mitzvah, and then spend many more
Saturdays, should he grow up to be a religious man, listening
to a Jew more musical and learned than he chant Torah. Occasionally, he might receive an aliyah, be called to the bimah to
take the Torah from the ark or to say one of the prayers that
bracket the reading of a Torah excerpt—and the aliyah would
be an honor, perhaps bestowed the week of his wedding or in
recognition of a large contribution of money to the synagogue. But he was unlikely to do much actual reading from
the Torah scroll.

It would be nice to say that the chanting of Torah remained
the province of the few because Jews were so punctilious about
keeping Torah away from sinners, liars, and hypocrites. But
the main reason most Jews don't chant Torah, down to the
present day, is because it is very, very hard to do. Even if one
learns to sight-read the Hebrew letters, vowels, and trop accents, that does not make one a competent Torah chanter. For
a Torah scroll contains only consonants, no vowel markings.
Aharon's vowels and trop accents are to be found in a codex
Bible that one might put on a bookshelf, but they are not
written in the scrolls found in synagogue arks. The members
of a choir might have perfect pitch and be able to sight-read
music, but how well would they perform if they opened their

sheet music to find only "GLR N XCLSS D" (for *"Gloria in excelsis Deo"*) or, in a setting of the Catholic requiem by, say, Mozart or Verdi, "TB MRM SPRGNS SNM / PR SPLCR RGNM" (*"Tuba mirum spargens sonum / per sepulcra regionum"*), stripped of vowels and of all musical notation? To chant Torah, one must insert the vowels in the mind's eye, then marry that image to the memorized trop. To chant the entire Torah, as the best ba'alei k'riyah can, is akin to singing all the parts in Wagner's *Ring* cycle from a text that has neither vowels nor any musical notes.

At some synagogues, the only congregant who can read even one line of Torah competently is the rabbi, and sometimes not even she or he can competently chant what is being read. The majority of Reform and Conservative rabbis have an adequate but hardly easy way with trop. Only in some Orthodox communities is there a surfeit of men who can leyn Torah.

Which makes Kol Ami, Judi Gannon's shul, one of the remarkable exceptions to the rule of Torah illiteracy. Like BEKI in New Haven, Kol Ami employs no cantor to chant the prayers, nor a ba'al k'riyah to chant Torah. Rather, the congregation relies on the unusual number of its members who have learned, many in their adulthood, to chant. The folks of Kol Ami are not more naturally musical than anyone else. They are not always on key, and their voices do not always ring with the sacrosanct authority that cantors seem to perfect at cantor school. The doctors and lawyers of Kol Ami could surely afford to hire a cantor or a chanter, but they have decided that taking part matters more than singing well.

Not all of Judi's boys and girls will want to chant again; at every shul, the bar or bat mitzvah is for many children a valedictory, not a beginning. But those who continue to worship on Shabbos will help enact a profound shift in religious authority, and a peculiarly American one, by constituting part of a cadre of Jewish amateurs who know the trop, can read Hebrew from the Torah scroll, and choose to; the boys and girls who fall away from observance may forget their trop skills entirely, but they may harbor a residual pride in what they once did and a desire, one that will reflower in later years, to see their children do the same.

For most of Jewish history, leyning Torah, the highest form of public Jewish participation, was the preserve of the most gifted, learned, or honored. By contrast, certain other Jewish duties, like walking to shul and laying tefillin, were incumbent on the most humble Jewish layman. But now, at a participatory and egalitarian synagogue like Kol Ami, the situation is reversed: almost none of the members lay tefillin or keep Shabbos, but several dozen men and women, having learned as children to chant Torah, will continue to practice that art several times a year for the rest of their lives. If they move to a different part of the country, they will seek out participatory services, those that don't rely on professional leaders. They consider access to the Torah a basic right of Jewish adulthood, and seeing lay adults chanting is proof that a synagogue is modern and progressive. For them, Torah has superseded keeping mitzvot as the elementary grounding of Jewish citizenship. Rabbis would differ on whether this is a fair trade: more Jews who read the commandments, fewer who follow them.

The contemporary teaching of trop means that access to Torah has been democratized. It surely has helped that an increasing number of the Torah tutors are women; like Annie Bass, who studied with both her mother and a female rabbi, Judi Gannon's male and female students see religious leadership being transferred from a male clergy to a coed hierarchy whose members, from adolescent girls to old men, conceive of Jewish knowledge as accessible to anyone with the maturity and the training to comprehend it, and the desire to try.

. . .

One of Judi's relatives had heard about the research I was doing and gave me Judi's phone number, assuring me, somewhat
mysteriously, that I would not regret meeting Judi. When I
called to ask if I could visit, Judi said to me:

"Of course you'll come. You'll come for a whole week, I
hope. You'll meet me; you'll meet the girls I am working with.
I am working with two terrific girls right now, Amy and
Rachel. After them, I take a sabbatical. Our shul down here,
Kol Ami, is wonderful. Of course, to have a wonderful shul,
you need a wonderful rabbi, and we have a wonderful rabbi,
Joel Wasser. He's a Canadian. And a wife and three kids. He is
just great. They're all great, though we're afraid we could lose
them. Their kids are getting older, and there's no Hebrew high
school in Tampa for them, so they might go somewhere there's
a Hebrew high school. You should see my appointment book
for the past year. It has just been crazy. I need Judi time, that's
why I'm taking a sabbatical. Now, if someone offered me a
contract to come back, I would come back—maybe. And even
while I'm gone, I might give special lessons. But it's time for
me to spend time with my family. Do you know that I miss my
own family's weddings, bar mitzvahs, bat mitzvahs, because I
have to go—I want to go—to the simchas of the boys and girls
I teach? This job takes over your life. When are you coming?"

Two months later, I arrived in Tampa. I had several hours
before I was to meet Judi and watch her teach a lesson, so I left
the motel and drove back down 275 South, past the airport,
and onto 60 West, then out toward Clearwater, where I had
been told there was a nice public beach. I had a nagging sense
that I'd read about Clearwater, that it had popped up somewhere in my religion studies. Then, as I was driving through
the downtown on my way to the beach, I happened on a wide,

glassy, shimmering building: the international headquarters of the Church of Scientology. Much of their literature, so often stuck beneath my windshield wipers, refers to the "Church of Scientology, Clearwater, Florida." It is an appropriate city for the Scientologists, whose religion (sect? cult? system of belief?—scholars spend long hours debating exactly what Scientology is) promises that its adherents can become "clears," super-beings with new levels of consciousness and self-actualization attained in sessions with church "auditors."

At the beach, I dove into the water and discovered that it was far warmer than a New England boy expects from the ocean. When I came up, I saw a brown pelican gliding above. The pelican was my high school's mascot, taken from the crest of our school's founding family. The pelican is a Christ symbol, I had been told, because according to legend it vulns itself to feed its young. I saw a second pelican circling above; the two were flying side by side. One of them came lower and began making passes back and forth, its long, sleek body parallel with the ocean surface. After several trial runs, it plunged, dipped briefly underwater, and emerged, gulping something. Then its friend plunged, and then they took turns, as if daring each other, upping the ante, like fly fishermen in a fast brook, competing to see who can haul in the best catch.

The ocean and the pelicans matter, because they represent why the Jews moved to Florida. Jews did not come for the Targets and Wal-Marts that have arisen like Legos on the landscape, nor for the adult bookstores with names like XTC that line the highway just north of downtown Tampa. They came for the allure of paradise.

Jews settled in the Northeast because that is where their boats docked—at Ellis Island and at the ports of Boston and Philadelphia. Jews in the South and Midwest often came as peddlers, eventually settling down as dry goods vendors in growing towns that needed their commercial skills. But Jews settled in Florida, as in Southern California, because these regions offered a certain sunny version of the American Dream. In her book *To the Golden Cities*, the historian Deborah Dash Moore writes about the special hopes that Jews brought south with them after World War II:

> Miami and Los Angeles Jews drew upon childhood memories derived from an upbringing on the streets of a big American city like Chicago or New York . . . Recalling crowded, vertical, dark, and dirty cities, American Jews marveled at the clean, spacious, open, horizontal quality of Miami and L.A. In the daytime the cities were bathed in light, from the omnipresence of sunlight to the popularity of white and pastel-colored buildings. At night, streets were quiet and empty; in the morning, sounds of birds filled the air. Signs of prosperity abounded: almost everyone seemed to own an automobile—a luxury in the Northeast and Midwest—and most people lived in private, single-family houses with flowers and fruit-bearing trees in the gardens. Even the sweet smells signaled a reality sharply at variance with the acrid fumes of coal-burning heaters and incinerators. The pace was more leisurely, less harried. The long train journey to reach these two cities helped set them apart from mundane America.*

As distant from the Lower East Side as Miami was, its immigrants built up versions of the old cities up north. The populations of entire apartment buildings on the Grand

---

*Deborah Dash Moore, *To the Golden Cities: Pursuing the American Jewish Dream in Miami and L.A.* (New York: Free Press, 1994), 2–3.

Concourse in the Bronx moved, together, to condo developments in Miami Beach, where they could walk to new deli-
catessens, synagogues, bookstores, and senior citizens' centers
that could have been lifted straight from Coney Island or
Brighton Beach, right down to the last bridge table.

But Tampa really is a world apart. There have never been
enough Jews to achieve a New York or Philadelphia by proxy.
The strangeness of the city is its newness, its disconnect from
the embedded traditions of the northern cities. And Tampa's
growth spurt came late. A woman I met in Tampa told me
that while Kol Ami was a synagogue of new families, "the real
old families go to the Reform temple across town . . . They
have families there that have been in Tampa two, three generations." In Tampa, there never was a great influx of Jews.
There are no neighborhoods that feel distinctly Jewish, no one
shopping district for buying your Hanukkah menorah and
your kosher corned beef. The only reminder of New York is
the expansive green spring-training complex of the New York
Yankees on the western edge of town, to which the team repairs every winter. It is no accident that Scientology touched
down in nearby Clearwater (and has its other major center in
Los Angeles). New towns, with little history and no settled
ways, are welcoming to new religions, while old religions,
finding themselves somewhat at sea, have difficulty finding
solid land in which to replant.

The Christian churches, especially those of a conservative
bent, have done the best job of making themselves at home.
Driving up and down Dale Mabry Highway, the main drag in
Judi Gannon's part of town, I encountered Buchanan Baptist,
the Bible-Based Fellowship, Carrollwood Baptist, Idlewild
Baptist, St. Paul's Roman Catholic Church, and a dozen others, all with sizable parking lots that were full on Sunday
morning. The neighborhood could seem Christian, but only

in a rather cold and corporate sense, inflected by that other American creed, capitalism. Judi's house, like nearly all the housing I saw in Tampa, was hidden behind the shrubbery of a preplanned development, and the developments were connected to one another by six-lane arteries lined with chain stores like Applebee's restaurant, Publix supermarket, and Blockbuster video. Even the independent stores were named as if they had chain-store aspirations: Wing King, Tire King.

The megachurches and highways and malls create an anomic, irreligious feel. It is hard to picture a small, intimate church thriving there, and it is even more difficult to imagine an older Judaism, whether the small Old World shtiebl, or storefront synagogue; or the majestic, prewar, stone-cut temple with a thousand member families; or the families themselves, walking to shul on Shabbos morning with five children in tow; or the strips of groceries, butcher shops, and dry goods stores that mark a long-standing Jewish neighborhood. All the comforting stereotypes one can dream up are immolated by Tampa's history, landscape, and population of new arrivals. And there isn't even a beach, or anywhere for the old folks to play shuffleboard.

This alienation makes the job of Kol Ami, and Judi Gannon, especially important. In New York, it's easy to feel like a Jew, even if you're not Jewish. As Lenny Bruce said, "It doesn't matter even if you're Catholic; if you live in New York, you're Jewish." You are surrounded by hundreds of thousands of Jews; the public schools are closed on Rosh Hashanah and Yom Kippur; Mayor Koch was Jewish; Mayor Bloomberg is Jewish; Mayor La Guardia was half-Jewish. There are dozens of synagogues and a score of kosher restaurants on the island of Manhattan alone. Toronto has an extensive Jewish neighborhood, with all the same amenities. Boston has heavily Jewish suburbs. Miami, of course, has become something of a

Jewish town. But there is no fulcrum of Jewish life in Tampa, not even a centrally located temple: the synagogues are scattered on lots along boulevards, as if they were Gaps or Exxon stations. There are no visible reminders that Jews exist. For many kids, Judi's kitchen is the Jewish institution they see the most. As the big day nears, they glimpse as much of her husband, Tom, as they see of Rabbi Wasser.

Judi and Tom live in a one-story, two-bedroom house decorated in suburban pastel chic, with furniture various shades of blond wood. Tom is a computer systems analyst who converted to Judaism after meeting Judi and has become Commander of Albert Aronovitz Post 373 of the Jewish War Veterans of the USA; he also serves as membership chairman, program chairman, public affairs officer, and insurance officer. The dining area is given over to candleholders, menorahs, picture frames, donation boxes for tzedakah, or charity, and all kinds of household Judaica, gifts from grateful students. Her living area and bedroom both contain boxes of memorabilia. Judi sat me down in an overstuffed chair, pulled up an end table to display her wares, and crouched next to me, narrating the story of each invitation, program, and place card she had saved.

She showed me the seating chart from the 1998 bar mitzvah of Brad Wickson. The front of the folio was a mock magazine cover that read, in text surrounding a color photograph of Brad, "*Sports Illustrated*, February 28, 1998, Highlights, Brad Wickson." The back cover showed a montage of photographs of Brad at different ages, engaged in different sporting events, with jokey captions: Brad on a Big Wheel at age one ("I began practicing for the Daytona 500 very early in life," the caption read); Brad as a toddler holding a Wiffle-ball bat ("Watch out Phillies. I may be your next draft pick"); Brad at about age six, kneeling in a soccer goal ("Soccer is my favorite sport. I love to try and take the ball away"). The two inside

pages, the centerfold, divided the partyers into their tables at
the reception. Each table went by a different team name.
At one table were the Florida State Seminoles: Fred and Mar-
sha Villani, Garry and Candy Terrigno, Johnny and Carol
Riesinger, Don and Kathy Farmer, Mike Rowe, Vicki Kissick.
Other tables were named for the Philadelphia Phillies, the
Colorado Avalanche, the Chicago Bulls, the Florida Marlins,
the Houston Rockets, and the Tampa Bay Devil Rays.

Judi had saved the newspaper advertisement taken out by
Max Horwitz to promote his "mitzvah project." It has become
common for b'nai mitzvah to spend the year before their ceremonies working on an extended mitzvah, which, in addition
to "commandment," means "good deed." They might spend
one day a week visiting old people in a nursing home or reading to the blind; they might join with other b'nai mitzvah in a
group project, like cleaning up a blighted park. To help
achieve the goal of his mitzvah project, Max bought a quarter-
page ad in the Tampa *Jewish Press*. Next to a picture of Max, a
smiling boy with gelled hair wearing a black T-shirt and a gold
necklace, a letter read, "My name is Max Horwitz, and I am
twelve years old. Soon I will celebrate the most important day
of my life, which is my bar mitzvah. During the preparation
of this long-awaited day, I have chosen to do a mitzvah project
which is a community outreach for a charitable organization
. . . The organization I am raising money for is American Red
Magen David for Israel (ARMDI), which is the sole United
States support arm of Magen David Adom, Israel's Red Cross
Society. Magen David Adom is Israel's 'second line of defense,'
providing a medical / disaster / ambulance / blood / health care
network to the people of Israel . . . This particular project will
help save lives for children like me, in the shadow of death.
Very truly yours, Max Horwitz."

"You must call Max!" Judi said.

Judi had hundreds of these artifacts. She showed me Lindsay Lowe's bat mitzvah program, designed in the manner of
a Broadway *Playbill*, with comedy and tragedy masks on
the cover and an episodic description of the night's events
inside: "Act 1: Cocktail Hour. Act 2: Introduction of Star.
Act 3: Welcome, Speeches, and Candlelighting," and so forth.
On the facing page, one finds the dramatis personae: "Lead
actor: Lindsay Lowe. Directors: Rabbi Joel Wasser, Judith
Gannon, Renita Gomez," and other roles, including "culinary
preparation" by Banquetmasters 2. From one Hollywood-
themed bar mitzvah, Judi had saved her place card, a little
model of a cardboard director's board. One side of the board
read "Mr. and Mrs. Thomas Gannon," and the other side read
"Apollo 13," the name of the table at which they had been
seated. Judi found in her box another favorite place card,
which was not a card at all but a small paper box, stuffed with
crumpled paper to hold its shape, topped off with a miniature
yarmulke and tallis. I am not sure why, but my favorite pieces
from the Judi collection were two crumpled napkins, one red
and one blue, each printed with a simple legend: "Jacob
Joseph, Bar Mitzvah, July 27, 2002."

As she rummaged for more things to show me, Judi kept
up the narration. Everything prompted a story. She found a
golden plastic statuette sitting atop a marble base with an affixed plaque that read, "Sarah's Gala of Stars, March 16,
2002." "This is from Sarah's bat mitzvah," Judi said, dropping
the trophy onto my lap, already laden with invitations, clip-
pings, and small paper boxes wearing yarmulkes and tallisim.
"Her real mother died when she was two, and her father had
converted for her mother. He married a former girlfriend,
not Jewish, who never converted. Rinnie, her stepmom, did a
beautiful bat mitzvah. There was a slide show with slides and
slides and slides. They gave her a star like one of the stars on

the Walk of Fame in Hollywood. She was a star. The theme
was Broadway. They all want to be stars."

Sports stars, Broadway stars, Hollywood stars. One bat
mitzvah was decorated according to just that theme: stars.
"Kate's Cosmic Celebration," it was called. They all want to
be stars.

So a woman whose calling is to pass on an obscure tech-
nique of reciting a dead language seemed entirely comfortable
with the parties and tchotchkes with which her students celebrate their newfound knowledge—was this incongruous? If
anyone was to chafe against the bar mitzvah party industry,
wouldn't it be Judi, who labors so hard to get these children to
take their religious inheritance seriously?

But sitting there in her living room, admiring the pride
with which she played docent to her collection, I decided that
the mistake must be mine. It was one thing for Rabbi Posner
in New York to blithely assure me that all was well even as he
had to explain the diminishing requirements of his synagogue's Hebrew school. But here was Judi Gannon, queen of
rigor, the unbending, underpaid empress of the trop, who
does not rest until all the pitch changes tumble forth with the
precision of well-marked points on a graph, and she simply
delighted in the parties! Faced with the simple fact of Judi's
conviction, my assumptions had to give way. Perhaps a big
party can make sense when there is something big to celebrate. Sometimes, the more hard-driving the tutor, the more
seriously the student is forced to study and the more fitting a
grand bash at the end.

As Judi described them, the parties also seemed to sanctify
their occasions by guarding against sameness. There is a reason, after all, that Sweet Sixteen parties have themes or special
appointments: to remind us that it's not just another party.
Not only should one's Sweet Sixteen not resemble one's fif-

teenth birthday, but it should also be different from other girls' Sweet Sixteens. It must be unique. The simplicity of Annie Bass's luncheon did not diminish the significance of her big day, but she was a special girl with a special family, and her shul celebrates few b'nai mitzvah anyway; if she were one of eighty b'nai mitzvah her year at BEKI, I suspect that even she, no matter how modest her tastes, might have wanted a slightly different party. A fantasy novel theme? Not impossible.

Judi told the story of her life as if she were the emcee of a variety show, introducing one act after another. She graduated in 1967 from Montgomery Blair High School in Silver Spring, Maryland, which is, she said, "the alma mater of Goldie Hawn, class of '63, Connie Chung, class of '64, Ben Stein, Carl Bernstein, and Joan Jett." Her father, Aaron, a government statistician, was a part-time religious school principal, Hebrew teacher, and bar mitzvah tutor, and her mother taught piano in public and parochial schools. They kept a kosher household, never worked on Shabbos, and chose their neighborhood in Silver Spring so they could walk to shul. Her brother became a bar mitzvah, but Conservative girls were not yet allowed to celebrate the bat mitzvah.

She attended American University and planned to become an actress. She appeared on local stages and joined an experimental theater group in Washington. She still keeps a yellowed newspaper notice from 1970, a picture of a much younger Judi onstage next to a young man. It bears the caption, "ONSTAGE—Judi Sabghir and Norman Arnovic are among the cast of 'EH,' a comedy to be presented by the Silver Spring Stage . . . Admission is $2.50." Judi once performed a stand-up comedy routine, but "just once, and that was my secret life." She worked as a speech and debate coach and as an English teacher, and for fifteen years she taught classes on how to take the SAT. She once met with a publicist

in Washington who wanted to help her break into show business or television broadcasting, but she was in the midst of a
depression that plagued her in the late 1970s and early 1980s,
the depression that convinced her to allow her ex-husband to
raise their daughter, Aleeza, in Cheshire, Connecticut—
where, Judi tells me, Aleeza attended Cheshire High School
with James Van Der Beek, later the star of *Dawson's Creek*, the
teen television soap opera. "We saw James Van Der Beek grow
up," Judi told me. "His mother was a hoofer."

Judi never became Goldie Hawn or Connie Chung, but she
did emerge from her depression to become a happily married
woman, respected in her community, with a high reputation
for her unusual skill. What Torah trop has given her, she re-
turns tenfold in gratitude.

"Religion saved me," she said. "I say God sent me to my
rabbi to return me to what I love doing, singing and dancing.
I definitely have a true calling: teaching. My parents were both
teachers. The problem is that a different part of my calling is
performance. You must have a venue for depression, for your
depressed feelings. If not theater, then something else. For me,
that was the hazzanut," the music of prayer.

A tiny woman with short, curly black hair, a dark complexion,
and an improbable number of freckles, Dora Mattes met her
husband, Max, when he was in medical school. They left their
native Brazil for Ontario in 1983, for Max's cardiology residency, and they stayed ten years. Their three daughters were
all born in Canada: Esther, fifteen; Miriam, eleven; and Sofia,
almost ten. Shortly after Sofia's birth, the Matteses moved to
Tampa, where Max now has a cardiology practice. The Mattes
girls would be unusual Judi clients if only for their Brazilian-
Canadian-Jewish heritage, but Esther, the eldest, is a Judi

favorite for another reason. She was born with Turner's syndrome, a chromosomal disorder that causes mental retardation and some physical abnormalities, like unusual shortness, a webbed neck, and heart defects. Esther is in an EMH class—educable mentally handicapped—at the local high school. With Judi Gannon's help, she became a bat mitzvah in 2001.

"Going to synagogue, we had always seen Judi," Dora said, in her careful English, when we met at her house in Tampa. "When the time came and they started giving dates, I liked her. We started with Esther early, a year and a half before the bat mitzvah instead of nine months. Esther has learning disabilities and is in a special class at school. What we can do, it's ten times harder for her."

Judi put Esther's parashah on tape. It's a standard practice in many shuls, but Judi does it only in special cases. "Before going to school, she would study for half an hour every morning," Dora said. "She would listen to her tape again and again. If you pointed out a word to her, maybe she can't tell you what it is. She knows the main words. So she learned by listening. She learned it by heart. She took it very seriously. She knows things are harder for her.

"On the day of the bat mitzvah, Judi was beside her the whole time. Even when they say something like 'page 415,' Esther has problems finding the page, so Judi would turn the pages for her. So she could practice, I made a binder for her with bigger letters. Those Hebrew letters are so small.

"She reads at a second-grade level, math even lower. But culturally she knows everything. She knows everything on the radio—I always have to ask her who the singers are. She speaks better Portuguese than the other two. This year in school, she saw a girl trying to speak to a teacher using Portuguese words, because she didn't know the English words she was looking for, and Esther went over and translated for her."

Dora showed me a photo album filled with pictures of Esther's bat mitzvah party, a fairly simple affair at the Marriott Hotel. There were pictures of extended family doing the horah; pictures of her father, Max, raised high on a chair held by strong Brazilian men; and pictures of Esther smiling.

"We had family from Brazil, Canada, California. Friday night after service, we had a dinner here for family from out of town. Saturday there was a big luncheon at the synagogue, and then there was this big brunch on Sunday. It was very emotional. Esther was so proud that she was able to do it."

The bar or bat mitzvah is a celebration of the book, and for children who are not on good terms with books, it can be a point of entry, a new chapter in their relationship with the printed word. It can draw them into a tradition that sometimes seems to honor its smart people as more godly. Being a Christian brother or a Buddhist monk requires a certain level of devotion and discipline, but being a Talmudic sage requires devotion, discipline, and an extraordinary facility with words. It also helps to have an eidetic memory and a functional knowledge of several dead languages, including Aramaic and Old French. Few Jews have the brains or the devotion to ascend very high on the ladder of Jewish learning. Some quickly forgotten passages of Torah may be as high as they will ever go. B'nai mitzvah ceremonies are not just points of entry, however; they are also fixed, irrevocable points in a Jew's personal history. Faith and religious feeling are not constants, and all religious people know what it is to feel a desperate loss of belief, accompanied by the fear that the loss is permanent. Even in such times, when a Jewish future is hard to imagine, it helps to have a tangible, memorable Jewish past. In this respect, the party planners, photographers, and caterers, those who suffer the most derision and seem most disposable, perform a valuable service.

The memories they foster carry a special weight in a town like Tampa, where children are bereft of other identifiably "Jewish" memories. For children born to a young landscape like Tampa's, only recently built up by real estate developers, b'nai mitzvah are like initiations—even more so when one of the parents is a convert and so is herself new to Judaism. Judi introduced me to Deb Goldman, a toned, tanned, brightly blond woman in stretchy athletic clothes, who, like Judi's husband, Tom, is a "Jew by choice," a convert.

"I was raised Catholic, went to Catholic school, with the nuns ripping the hems out of our dresses," Deb said. I was, once again, sitting at Judi's kitchen table. "And then we would go in the bathroom and staple them back up. That's why little red staplers were invented, you know: for Catholic-school girls." Deb giggled at the memory.

"I married a guy, my ex, who didn't believe in anything. I had Mike, who is now sixteen, and Kate, who is now thirteen. When Mike and Kate were little, there were lots of problems in the marriage, but the clincher for me was when Mike was five, and Kate was maybe two, and we were having a discussion at bedtime about our prayers to God. And their father came in and said nastily, 'Do you see God? If you don't see him, there's no God.'

"I tried to explain to Mike that there were differences of opinion, but we were having other problems, already looking to go different ways. I had personally a little bit of drug use problems, pot and pills. I was going to AA and NA, and that spirituality got me away from Roman Catholicism. It was another way of being close to God, my own understanding of God."

Deb met her second husband, Todd Goldman, when she was going through her divorce and working as a sales representative for Colgate. Todd worked for a dentists' professional association, and he and Deb met at a dental show. By the time they met again, at another dental convention, Deb's divorce was final, and they began a courtship that lasted six months and was conducted mainly at dental shows. When they began to discuss marriage, they talked about religion. Todd said that Deb would not have to convert, but it was very important to him that his children be raised as Jews. "Todd is very strong for the six million who died," Deb told me.

When David, her first of two sons by Todd, was a newborn, Deb started to think about conversion. She began to study, and by the time David was a toddler, she was ready for her immersion in a mikveh. To most Jews, the mikveh is the indoor bath in which observant Jewish women immerse themselves after their monthly period. But immersion is also required of converts, and the mikveh need not be manufactured; where no proper mikveh can be found, natural bodies of water may suffice. If a mother brings her young children with her into the mikveh, they are converted too.*

"Later that winter, there was a mikveh going on, and we all got in the water and did our conversion in the ocean." The next order of business was a bar mitzvah for Mike, who had already begun his studying. "Mike was a little behind and started with Judi on trop and Hebrew. I did my class with him, when Mike was in the seventh grade. His bar mitzvah was February 12. The New Year's Eve right before, we went over to Clearwater. It had to be forty-five degrees out, just unbelievable. The beit din"—the rabbinic court that effects a conversion—"was over there, so we had to go over there. It was New Year's of '98–'99. I had Stephen"—her second son by

---

*According to Jewish law, a mikveh may contain no liquid other than water; the water may not be manually drawn; and, unless a spring, river, or ocean is used as the mikveh, the water may not be flowing.

Todd—"on my hip. We went in our bathing suits. Stephen was on my hip, Kate was in this hand, Mike was in this hand, and we dashed in. Stephen was climbing up my body trying to get out. We all dunked three times, got out, and got in robes and blankets. There were a man and two women, sisters. Then we got out and said prayers. The kids were like, 'That was cool.' That night at shul, the rabbi called us up as a family to open the ark.

"Mike had his bar mitzvah. Judi would put the service on tape, and I would practice so I could follow along with his service."

Deb and Todd got remarried under Jewish law, and Deb continued her studies. Three years later, she read trop at her daughter Kate's bat mitzvah.

"The rabbi and Judi are the two most beautiful-to-the-core Jewish people I have ever met in my life. People might say that sounds cliché-ish, but it's true."

"Both my parents were raised Orthodox, kept a kosher home, with separate dishes, the whole thing," Rita Schonwetter said. The mother of Rachel Schonwetter, who that week would celebrate her bat mitzvah, Rita was taking classes with Judi to brush up on her own Hebrew, so that she could stand on the bimah with her daughter and participate. "My grandmother died, and for some reason my grandfather moved into our home for a while, and then he moved back to Israel. My father wanted to keep the home kosher, but my mother said forget it, we're not going to keep the home kosher but still eat out. So I was raised Reform. My father died when I was just eleven, and my mother didn't believe in bat mitzvah. I studied with a cantor and became a bat mitzvah at sixteen, but I lost my Hebrew afterwards, because I had no reason to use it.

"My husband grew up Orthodox, Ron. When we got married, we looked at a Reform shul. To be honest, though, we're more comfortable as a couple at Kol Ami, which is Conservative but very egalitarian. The women can do everything here.

"When we were at Maxine's bat mitzvah, I distinctly remember Sarah saying to me, 'That's a cool thing,' that her parents read. For me, I had to relearn Hebrew again, and I also had to learn trop. I started with Judi late. I had picked out which portion would be trop-wise a little easier."

Rita told me about all the work that her daughter Rachel had been doing. Rachel would be leading Friday night services and Saturday morning services, and she would be reading Torah. The other readers on Saturday would include her mother and a host of friends. At some shuls, all the aliyot are given to visiting relatives, as a way of honoring them and also thanking them for making the trip. But Judi prefers that the oldsters stay in the pews.

"There's a big risk when you let out-of-towners read," she said. "I discover all the out-of-towners' backgrounds before I let them read. They say all the time, 'Oh, I know how to read.' But it's a big risk, and in front of strangers."

Rita nodded and said, "For both my daughters, we kept the readers to their inner circle of friends."

"We know they're equipped," Judi said. "We trained them."

Rita mentioned a practice that, I learned, is not unique to Kol Ami. "There is a minimum requirement of Fridays and Saturdays," she said. "My oldest is the first to attend ninety services. They get credit even if they're at a bar mitzvah at another synagogue—that's very important. You get a certificate if you go to thirty-six. It's all in multiples of eighteen." According to the ancient Hebrew practice of assigning numerical values to letters, eighteen is the value of the word "chai," meaning "life." Jews often donate money in multiples of eighteen dollars: $18 or $36 or $180. Getting a certificate for attending eighteen or thirty-six Shabbos services does not seem a very holy practice, but as I saw at Rachel's bat mitzvah, it does work. The rituals of synagogue and Torah reading, mysterious and daunting to the neophyte, were familiar to Rachel and her friends.

The Wednesday afternoon before her bat mitzvah, Rachel and her close friends and family assembled at Kol Ami for a rehearsal. I went early with Judi to take the scroll out of the ark. In the most traditional synagogues, the Torah would never be removed just for practice, only for obligatory reading on a Saturday, or for the traditional weekday readings on Monday and Thursday. But I had already seen a liberal, "modern Orthodox" Jew—the Joe Lieberman kind—remove a Torah on a Tuesday so that a bar mitzvah photographer could take pictures of his son pretending to read, so I was not surprised by this casual use of the Torah at Kol Ami.

Soon, the inner circle of girlfriends, the ones who would get aliyot on Shabbos, arrived and did brief run-throughs of the Hebrew they would chant. Rachel came a bit later, like a star at her own movie's premiere. She and her mother chanted their sections, Rachel with greater sureness. And then Rabbi Wasser arrived and, taking charge of the sanctuary, kicked out everyone except me, Rachel, her parents, and Judi.

Rabbi Wasser—trim, tucked-in, and efficient, with a well-knotted tie and close-cropped blond hair under his yarmulke—wanted to hear Rachel practice her speech. She began: "Shabbat Shalom. Every time you walk through Publix, do you go past the kosher meat section, Campbell's soup aisle, or bottled water and think about the Torah? This week's parashah, Toldot, really made me think about the grocery store. First, there is the selling of Esau's birthright for a bowl of lentil stew and bread, then Isaac's wealth in farming and building wells, and finally, Jacob stealing Esau's blessing by tricking Isaac and serving him the meat which Esau was supposed to be preparing—"

"DON'T MUSH YOUR WORDS TOGETHER!"

When he hollered, Rabbi Wasser stopped pacing up and down the sanctuary aisles, approached the bimah, hopped onstage, and leaned over Rachel's shoulder.

"Is this a new paragraph?" he asked. "How do I know? Right, I don't. Now, is that a new paragraph? How do I know? Right, because you paused. Good. Okay. You're going a little too fast. Slow down." He removed from his shirt pocket a blue ballpoint pen and a yellow highlighter. He began to trade off between the two, writing over Rachel's shoulder, highlighting some passages and writing "SLOW" at the top of each page. His annotations complete, he hopped off the stage and resumed pacing, clicking the ballpoint pen in and out nervously. I was reminded of the old *Saturday Night Live* skit "High School Chess Coach," in which a Bobby Knight type stands on the sidelines in a gymnasium, watching two students hunched intently over a chess board. He is tearing his hair out, yelling commands like "PAWN TO ROOK FOUR!" and when his player makes the wrong move, he throws a chair onto the court. Rabbi Wasser was something of a bar mitzvah coach, poised to yell, "It's a TEVIR, you IDIOT! A TEVIR!"

Rachel read the rest of the speech more slowly. When Rabbi Wasser did interrupt, she glanced up at him, skeptically, with the doubtful eyes of a born wiseass. She could handle him.

And that Saturday, she chanted Torah better than at the rehearsal, and better, I expect, than she ever had before. From the bimah, wearing a Moroccan satin tallis that she had bought on the Internet, her reddish brown hair crimped the way that girls in the 1980s worked hard to achieve, Rachel chanted one-third of Toldot, the story of Jacob and Esau.

"I had worked with Judi before," Rachel told me afterward. "Learning Torah for religious school. I was kind of a little excited, but it wasn't—it hadn't smacked me in the face that I was going to have a bat mitzvah in ten months, and then when the time came it would be here.

"The whole summer I was on vacation and at camp and stuff. Judi told me what to work on when I went on my cruise. I had two friends at camp who were having their bar and bat mitzvahs—Max was in August and Amy is in December—and we were doing the same thing. So it wasn't bad. I didn't mind reviewing it. When we had rest time, it would give me something to do, if I didn't feel like writing a letter.

"Judi's a lot of fun. I'm going to miss Judi's house. I never thought I would ever say that. I learned everything. She made it okay to mess up. She was real patient and fun to talk with. It was more personal than 'I'm your teacher and you have to learn this.' "

There is no such thing as the perfect bar or bat mitzvah, Judi tells her kids. "God wants us to make one mistake to keep us humble." And learning to chant Hebrew is, in a sense, a modest and humble act. It won't make a Jew rich or famous. Trop will not get you the hottest date for the prom, and it wins you no admission to Harvard. Learning it is an act of devotion to a book written in a language that nearly died of old age. But chanting it well can be religious, as surely as eating matzoh or saying Kaddish for the dead. "I know they're ready for their bar mitzvah," Judi said, "when I hear them do the blessing and I get goose bumps." What the experience means to the boys and girls themselves, Judi can't say for sure. Hazzanut saved Judi's life, to use her words, and she can hardly expect it to do that for others. Torah chanting might not save the children, but they, at the very least, will save it.

4

The Small Town

*O*n the morning of Jacob Newman's bar mitzvah, the members of Temple Shalom of Northwest Arkansas, who usually meet at a small white house on Storer Street in Fayetteville, met at the nearby Unitarian Universalist Society, which lends space on the rare occasion that it's needed. I arrived at 9:45 in the morning. The seats were arranged in several nestled semicircles, with the open end reserved for the bimah; sitting at the bimah were Jacob Newman; Jacob Adler, the student rabbi who would lead the service; and a young woman in a flowing dress who was holding a guitar. The room was square, and there were about seventy-five people in it. Of the men, three wore a tie, one fewer than had a ponytail. It was evident that many of the guests at Jacob Newman's bar mitzvah were disposed to enjoy what Jacob's mother, Darla, would call a "renewal" experience. Many, it seemed, had already been renewed: they were from the generation of 1960s immigrants to the Ozarks, and their children, many of whom were present, were second-generation Arkansas counterculturalists. On my seat I found a homemade siddur, stapled together with a yellow cover that read, "Bar Mitzvah Service for Jacob Chasin Newman—December 28, 2002—23 Tevet 5763."

On the inside cover of the siddur was a diagram showing

the various aspects of God according to Kabbalah, the mystical tradition followed mainly by ultra-Orthodox Hasidic Jews; more lately by those celebrities, like Madonna, who are attracted to its numerological, quasi-astrological properties; and, finally, by Jewish Renewal mavens like Darla Newman. Jacob Adler, the student rabbi, got up and began the service by explaining the diagram's four sections: the physical, the emotional, the intellectual, and the spiritual. The bar mitzvah, he said, would have four parts, following a roughly analogous scheme. The people seated around me nodded with approval.

Leslie, the guitarist, began to strum and sing. The words to the tunes were printed in our siddurim. The first song was "Eheyeh Esher Eheyeh," the words uttered by God in Exodus 3:14, which mean, roughly, "I am that I am," or "I will be who I will be." As the song began, Jacob Adler passed around the room a sack filled with musical instruments for our taking: mariachis, wooden eggs, tambourines, glockenspiels, at least one pan flute. As we picked instruments out of the bag, we joined in with the guitarist, shaking and rattling and tapping in time with the music. Old men closed their eyes and rocked from side to side, humming, stroking their beards. There were more songs over the next hour, and although there were few traditional prayers, there were versions of traditional prayers, including an English-language "Morning Prayer" that Darla Newman led responsively, with semaphore hand movements. As we sang "You lift us up when we are down," we all raised our hands up, and as we sang the words "beyond imagination," we swept our hands from one end of our wingspan across to the other, like the men with hand lights who direct airplanes on the runway, to represent the whole imaginable universe. On the line "We're rising," we all stood up, the toddlers hopping off their parents' laps and the elderly struggling to their feet.

During part two of the service, "The Emotional World,"

we sang a song of prayer for peace in Israel, and Darla asked us to put our arms up so that along with our heads they made the letter *w*, which resembles the Hebrew letter shin, the first letter of the word for peace, "shalom." With hands lifted upward, and people swaying, and words being sung in Hebrew by people who knew no Hebrew, the effect was positively Pentecostal. They were the exact signs of Christian charismatic worship: palms raised, eyes closed, speech in a mysterious language one does not understand. During an interlude in the song, Darla asked us to call out the names of other places that needed our prayers for peace.

"Iraq," someone immediately answered.

"Chechnya," someone else said.

"North Korea."

"Venezuela."

"Israel."

When the Torah was removed from the ark, instead of giving it to the bar mitzvah boy to parade around the sanctuary, Jacob Adler handed it to a man at the end of the innermost concentric half circle and asked that it be passed around so that everyone had a chance to hold it. At other synagogues, I had seen a variation: the Torah would be passed, on the bimah, from grandfather to father to bar mitzvah boy. I had never before seen the Torah passed around the whole room, to be held by every Jew, Gentile, Pagan, and other.

I am by nature suspicious of this sort of freestyle, folksy innovation, because I think that spiritual yearnings need tradition, the kind that comes from books, to stay meaningful. But as the Torah was passed around, cradled and kissed by old women and young bearded men and a middle-aged lesbian couple—one woman of the couple was the bar mitzvah boy's aunt—with their newborn daughter, and old Gentile men in denim shirts and their wives wearing an abundance of Native

American turquoise jewelry, I was unexpectedly moved to a poignant gratitude, one that persuaded me to quiet my cynical side, just for a moment, and sway in time to the guitar. An old woman wearing a tallis and a woven yarmulke held the Torah and rocked it like a baby. A man in a Guatemalan beret inspected the backside of the parchment with the reverence he might usually reserve for something whittled or carved. A little girl, maybe six years old, smiled with pride because she could hold up the Torah without help.

Jacob Newman chanted Exodus 3:1–10, the section of parashah Shemot that includes the story of God's speaking to Moses from the burning bush, and then read the haftarah, from the Book of Isaiah, in English. When he was done, he gave a short speech, a brave effort given that he was fighting a debilitating flu that made this small boy look even smaller; he would obviously have been happier vanished beneath a down comforter. His father, John, stood up and read the speech he had read on a snowy day thirteen years earlier, the day of Jacob's circumcision, a speech that referred to the current events of the time, including a bad cold snap and the fall of the Berlin Wall. Jacob Adler spoke, then Darla Newman, then John Newman's brother, Bob. Jacob's paternal grandmother rose to speak of her father, for whom her young grandson Jacob was named. "My father came here from Russia," she said, looking right at Jacob. "He worked at a variety of menial jobs while going to night school at the City College of New York, and eventually became a certified public accountant. You share some of his traits, Jacob."

When the mourners' prayer was read, the whole congregation stood together. Traditionally, only mourners stand to say Kaddish, but at some synagogues everybody stands, on the principle that we can all say Kaddish for those who have no one else to say Kaddish for them. Jacob Adler asked if any of us would like to say the name of a friend or relative who had recently died. Some names were called out, and then Jacob added one. "John Rawls," he said. The philosopher, whose class Jacob Adler had taken in graduate school, had died on November 24. "He wasn't a relative, but he was a teacher, and a teacher can be like a father."

When the service was over, I was immediately drafted to help bring long folding tables up from the basement, and to move the chairs from their semicircles and arrange them around the tables. A buffet luncheon was served: hummus, a green salad, fruit, tabbouleh, turkey sandwiches on whole wheat bread, wine, soda, and spring water. As I sat down to eat, the Po' Goys, a klezmer band, set up at the back of the hall and began to play Yiddish folk tunes.

To my left was a man with sandy hair and a droopy mustache. His name was Scott Sutton, and he was a psychotherapist, he said. He had lived in Fayetteville for twenty years. Of the twenty-five or so people I met at the bar mitzvah, none, except the children, was a native of Fayetteville. They had all come by way of somewhere, their paths often loopy and circuitous. Scott was part of the social work–and–therapy contingent at Jacob's party; his wife, sitting to his left, was also a therapist, as was another friend he pointed out across the room. "There's a bunch of us," he said.

I asked Scott to tell me more about himself.

"I went to Trinity College in Hartford, and I graduated in 1970," Scott said. "It went from being a place in 1966 where boys were walking around with frat initiation beanies on their heads and there were no women to being a place where men and women were living together in dorms. It was an exciting time to be there. So I have mixed feelings about Trinity. Hartford was a pretty boring place, and so was Trinity in a way, but it was an exciting time to be there. Afterwards I went to Episcopal Divinity School in Cambridge and took a master's but never got ordained. My dad had been a priest, and my great-uncle had been a bishop, so I had to get that out of my system. But I don't go to church anymore."

Like most of the Ozark-dwellers I met, Scott was an enthusiastic partisan of the region.

"I love it here," he said. "This bar mitzvah is pretty typical of cultural life here. You have to make stuff happen yourself. I wanted to start a fencing club, and I put an ad in the paper asking for fencers. First calls I got were 'Barbed wire?' 'Electric fence?' But then some people called who fenced, and we got it going. You make it happen yourself.

"I'm not Jewish, but I know half the people in this room."

In the most Jewish of Jewish towns, a bar or bat mitzvah can become, paradoxically, a rather private affair. In Scarsdale or Newton, Massachusetts, if everyone invited all the neighbors to their b'nai mitzvah, nobody would ever have a free Saturday. So the kids go, the parents only rarely. But in a small town in Arkansas, inviting only one's Jewish intimates would mean a dinner party, not a big celebration. So Gentiles are necessary. You need a decent Christian showing to fill the seats. The circle is widened, beyond family and close friends, even beyond all the Jews in town. At Temple Shalom, the very occasional bar mitzvah, perhaps one a year, is a gathering of the Jewish and the Jewish-*ish*—the fellow travelers, the onlookers, the bookish folks and literati, the liberals and hippies, the somehow different—and a sizable cluster of sympathetic but more clueless Gentiles, the classmates and co-workers who are happy to see what this Jewish stuff is all about. It is a natural opportunity for Jews to proclaim that they exist and to perform their existence in a way that the neighbors can see.

Even for a southern and rural state, Arkansas has a tiny Jewish population. According to the 2003 *American Jewish Yearbook*, 0.1 percent of Arkansans are Jews; there are 175 Jews in Fayetteville and 1,100 in Little Rock. Unlike Mississippi, Illinois, Louisiana, and other states along the Mississippi River, Arkansas never drew Jewish peddlers and dry goods salesmen in meaningful numbers. Jews arrived in staggered steps and settled in scattered pockets. The first Jewish congregation in Arkansas built a synagogue in Little Rock in 1870; by World War II, there were congregations in Pine Bluff, Fort Smith, and Hot Springs, with a total membership of almost five thousand.* The Jewish population began to grow in the late 1960s, when hippies, artists, New Age spiritualists, and back-to-the-land enthusiasts filtered into the Ozarks, buying patches of bucolic land on the cheap. It was cheap for a reason: it is rocky and difficult to farm, prone to harsh, high-altitude winters and humid, steam-boiler summers. Nobody looking to make a buck farming would choose the Ozarks, but these new arrivals, many of them Jews, were not seeking profit, not of the financial kind. They were fleeing suburbs, big cities, and college campuses, baffling their parents, who had worked hard to provide comforts their children now ostentatiously rejected.

John Newman, father of the bar mitzvah boy, was part of that wave of immigration. In 1968 he had dropped out of college in Albany, moved to Berkeley, and married. A friend of his in Berkeley, someone he looked up to, asked if John had ever thought about heading for the country. John had not thought about it, but he liked the idea. In 1970, after stopping back home in New York for a spell, he and his wife, Chanda, packed up their Volkswagen van and headed for

Arkansas: A Guide to the State (New York: Hastings House, 1941), 86.

points west—Colorado, California, British Columbia, they were not quite sure where—and took a detour into the Ozarks, fell in love with the land, and bought forty acres in the mountains. The land was seventy-five dollars an acre, three thousand dollars total. John got one thousand dollars from his brother; the other two thousand came from a savings account he had opened ten years earlier with his bar mitzvah money.

John and Chanda erected a teepee, planted a garden, and had a baby girl named Apple, in that order. They lived in the mountains for three years, with occasional forays into town to work odd jobs and make some money. Then Chanda said enough, no more, and left. At the time, John was working for the local food co-op. When he was promoted to manager, he discovered that he enjoyed the business aspect of his work. He enrolled at the University of Arkansas to study accounting, and finally he earned his college degree. He had been intermittently interested in Judaism, and in 1978, 1979, and 1980, he helped plan community seders with a friend. They were a success; the last one was attended by eighty people. John, who was already thinking of leaving Fayetteville to further his career, now decided that he might like to wander in search of a Jewish bride, too.

"The way I tell the story, which is an exaggeration, is I had already proposed to both the Jewish women in Fayetteville," John told me. "So in June of 1980 I went out to Los Angeles." His parents had moved there from New York, and he'd heard that the city had a vibrant dating scene. I asked John, whose first wife had not been Jewish, why finding a Jewish woman was important to him this time around.

"It was two things," he said. "I was reconnecting with my Judaism, starting with those seders. I certainly wasn't keeping kosher or going to services on any regular basis, but it was growing in importance to me in a hippie sort of way . . . The other thing was, in that period—I got divorced in '74, moved out to L.A. in '80—in that period, I had had a lot of relationships with women, but none of them seemed to last very long. So I had kind of taken a break from relationships and all, and I think that was part of just feeling maybe I would find something more lasting with a Jewish woman."

In Los Angeles, John was set up on a date by his mother, Leila. She was on the board of the local food co-op, and she was asking her friends there if anyone knew a nice Jewish girl for her son. A woman named Lottie Cohen suggested her friend Darla Long, the daughter of a Jewish mother from New York and a Gentile farmer from Dodge City, Kansas. Darla and John met, fell in love, and, in 1985, got married.

When John first mentioned moving from Los Angeles back to Arkansas, Darla thought he was crazy, and for two years John dropped the topic completely. Then, one night, lying in bed, Darla asked John what he was thinking about. To be honest, he told her, he was thinking about moving back to the Ozarks. And to his surprise, she said okay, they could start planning a move. They returned to Arkansas with Darla's son, Sean, then eight years old, and their daughter, Jenny, who was one. The Newmans joined Temple Shalom and soon became active members. Darla began teaching in the religious school. Sean and Jenny celebrated their b'nai mitzvah at Temple Shalom.

Now it was Jacob's turn. His simcha, like his sister Jenny's, was different from their older brother Sean's, because what their father, John, now a clean-cut man with an M.B.A., had lost in hippie vibe, their mother, Darla, had since absorbed. In 1995, after being given a brochure by a friend, Darla spent a week at Elat Chayyim, a Jewish spirituality retreat in the Catskill Mountains, north of New York City. In Jewish circles, Elat Chayyim has become an instantly recognizable marker of all things innovative or, some might say, fringe. One gets a good sense from the description on its Web site: "In an age when time is a rare commodity and our lives seem to center on rushing from one activity to the next, going on a Jewish spiritual retreat is a great gift to give oneself. A typical day on retreat at Elat Chayyim might include yoga, meditation, experiential prayer services, classes with incredible teachers and an evening program." Seminars offered include sacred dance, Jewish feminism, Jewish mysticism, and "Jewish healing practices."

"I felt we had established for the family and children that they had a Jewish identity, and now it was time to find our Jewish path," Darla told me after the bar mitzvah. "So I went to Elat Chayyim for a week and thought it was wonderful." One of her teachers there was David Zaslow, a rabbi from Oregon and a prominent avatar of Jewish Renewal, a form of emotive, spiritual, left-leaning Judaism, "a worldwide, transdenominational movement grounded in Judaism's prophetic and mystical traditions," as one of its Web sites puts it. Zaslow, who is by all accounts a terrific orator and song leader, made a deep impression on Darla. Jewish Renewal's combination of music and mysticism was, she decided, something that she might be able to take back home. At Elat Chayyim, Darla had met a woman from Tulsa, Oklahoma, two hours from Fayetteville, and together they brought Rabbi Zaslow to the area; but there were not enough Jews in either town to start a Jewish Renewal congregation.

Instead, Jewish Renewal became the province of a few enthusiasts like Darla. As a religious-school teacher at Temple Shalom, Darla ensured that the young Jews of northwest Arkansas would all get at least a little mystical flavor, but Jacob's bar mitzvah was her masterpiece, the culmination of her study; the day's rites, the music and prayers and their explications in her homemade photocopied siddurim, were her way of explaining Judaism to the Gentiles, and of explaining her particular brand of Judaism to other Jews.

The delight she took in showing off Judaism—a delight that had he not had the flu Jacob might have mirrored—was something common to the small-town b'nai mitzvah I saw. For Jews in heavily Jewish areas, the bar or bat mitzvah can be a ticket to be punched, a social expectation as much as a religious rite of passage. In other words, it can be like a wedding, which, no matter how joyous and sincerely emotional, is also satisfying an expectation and, in that regard, is a highly functional affair. One gets married (in part) to win certain legal protections, to get health insurance, to ensure that one's children are not stigmatized. And in Jewish neighborhoods, one becomes a bar or bat mitzvah in part because it is a Hebrew school expectation, a way to repay numerous party invitations, and an important form of social networking for parents. But while it would be noticeable for a young Jew in Miami Beach not to become a bat mitzvah, it is even more noticeable for anyone in Fayetteville to celebrate any Jewish ritual. Jacob Newman's bar mitzvah could not help but be a declaration of sorts, just as it was a declaration for Reform Judaism to bring back the bar mitzvah ceremony: it is an anti-assimilationist measure, a statement of religious pride.

So its success requires an audience, someone to listen. Jacob's bar mitzvah affirmed to local Jews the Renewal Judaism that Darla had injected into her Reform community, and it reminded local Gentiles that there were Jews in their midst. In a community like Fayetteville, more easily identified with people trying to convert Jews than with Jews themselves, the bar mitzvah is a performative gesture, a communion of Jew and the majority other; and Jacob's bar mitzvah, this oriental irruption in the countryside, was, even more than most, a demonstration of one family's unique search for religious meaning.

Temple Shalom had an ordained rabbi, Laura Lieber, but she lived in Chicago and flew down only one Saturday a month. Three weeks out of four, the head Jew in town was rabbi-in-training Jacob Adler, whom I met the night before the bar mitzvah. I had stopped by the Hillel house of the University of Arkansas, figuring that on a Friday night I could find someone who would know something about Jewish life in the sticks. I ended up eating a vegetarian Shabbos dinner with two old ladies, only one of whom was Jewish; a tall man with a ponytail who had given up wearing socks (and was also not Jewish); and a young woman who reported for the local newspaper (and was Catholic). The college students were home for Christmas vacation, so these were older folk, but not the older Jews one might expect at a Shabbos dinner. Rather, they were a motley group of questers and seekers, curious about Judaism, hoping to glean some wisdom from the rabbi, who of course was not the rabbi at all.

On Sunday, the day after the bar mitzvah, I met alone with Jacob at Arsaga's, a coffee shop in a strip mall on Gregg Street. At fifty, Jacob is an old student even for the rabbinate, a profession that many come to late. He is five foot three, with a very dense, well-trimmed salt-and-pepper beard. That morning, his balding head was topped by a square, fezlike yarmulke. I had just seen the second *Lord of the Rings* movie, and I decided that Jacob looked like a Semitic version of Samwise, the merry yet pugnacious hobbit. I spotted Jacob in the back left corner of the coffee shop, reading the *New York Times*, and I approached him rather gingerly, as if wishing not to disturb this homuncular, otherworldly specimen.

Jacob folded up his newspaper, invited me to sit down, and asked what he could do for me. I asked him to explain yesterday's unusual bar mitzvah.

"The division of the bar mitzvah into four sections is fairly common in Jewish Renewal circles," he said. "Emanation, creation, formation, making physical"—different words from those used in the siddur, but I got the idea. Jacob had listed them in descending order, from the highest principle to the lowest, the earthly aspect; but in the bar mitzvah, he said, we had started with the physical and worked our way up.

"The Jewish Renewal grandfather, or zayde, is Zalman Schachter-Shalomi. He used to be Zalman Schachter, but he didn't like the connotations of his last name—a schachter is a butcher—so he added 'Shalomi,' for peace." According to Jacob, Schachter-Shalomi originally conceived Jewish Renewal as a kind of "hippie Orthodoxy," traditional Judaism infused with a neo-Hasidic vim. Jacob compared Schachter-Shalomi to Shlomo Carlebach, the famous "Singing Rabbi" who in the 1960s founded the House of Love and Prayer, a countercultural synagogue in San Francisco; what Carlebach did for Jewish music is what Schachter-Shalomi wanted to do for daily Jewish practice, Jacob said. But over time, as he discovered that the hippies were unwilling to be bound by so many rules, Schachter-Shalomi spoke less of stringent observance and more of spiritualist passion. His hippie Orthodoxy became more hippie, less Orthodoxy. It fused with other strands, from the communes of the havurah movement to the theological insights of Jewish feminism. Today, the most popular emanations from Jewish Renewal are the kinds of kabbalistic prayers that Darla Newman led at her son's bar mitzvah, dressed up with hand movements and new melodies, often accompanied by drums or guitar.

"It's not how I most express my own Jewish practice," Jacob

said at the coffee shop. "For me, a lot of the traditional practices work as they are. A lot of the consumers—they wouldn't use that word—of Jewish Renewal were alienated from Judaism or didn't have a lot of Jewish education." When they return to Judaism, they often do not have the patience for traditional Jewish disciplines, the thrice-daily prayer and three-hour Saturday services. "To have intense religious experience can take commitment and practice," Jacob said. "If I say, 'Sit down and meditate,' you can't do it." Jewish Renewal, he was saying, offers a bridge to spiritualism with fewer demands. "As a whole, it's a movement open to people without experience or commitment. They need some gate into Jewish life. That's fine."

Jacob added that he is hardly a model of strict observance; his own Jewish commitment has been in flux over many years. Jacob was raised in Cranston, Rhode Island, in "a typical inconsistent Conservative Jewish family": his mother kept a kosher kitchen—she still does—but his father was not so religious that he could stay away from his army-navy surplus store on Saturday—customers know no Sabbath. For Jacob's parents, Judaism was a given, a comfort and a kind of habitual routine, but hardly a font of deep piety. For Jacob, religion had always had greater weight. "I always experienced a connection with Judaism," he said. "It seemed like something real to me. We used the old Silverman prayer book, and the English seemed kind of boring, but the Hebrew part seemed amazing. The Hebrew letters seemed alive. I went to Hebrew school and Hebrew high school, through the eleventh grade, evening classes.

"I went to Harvard College starting in 1971, finally graduated in 1976. At school, I started questioning what I believed in, and I did not have any good answers. It was a difficult time, filled with a lot of distress. At the same time, I was more observant than I had been. I had my first real experience of Shabbat with Aryeh Frimer, who was one of the Hillel rabbis. I think he was a Bostoner Hasid," from a sect of Hasidim who follow a rabbinic dynasty with headquarters on Beacon Street in Brookline, just outside Boston. "And he was also a graduate student in chemistry, which tells you what kind of guy he was—that's an unusual combination. He would sing the shirim on Shabbat with an intensity that was really amazing. I was blown away. It was ironic, because I was questioning my own beliefs at the time, but I was experiencing this on Shabbat."

The tension between his intellectual doubts and his fervent observance began to overwhelm Jacob—too much cognitive dissonance, too much self-recrimination, fears of hypocrisy— leading him into a crisis, a breakdown, whatever you want to call it.

"It got to be too much. I had to stop everything: stop being observant, stop questioning. I couldn't eat; my stomach was tied in knots. After I stopped, I gradually started to feel better.

"And none of that changed until I came here."

In 1984, almost done with his Harvard philosophy dissertation, "The Urgings of Conscience: A Theory of Punishment," Jacob moved to Fayetteville to become an assistant professor at the University of Arkansas. "This is not where I wanted to come," he told me. "But then as now, in philosophy, if you were offered a job, first you accepted, then you asked where it was. So here I was." Having once chosen his mental health over his Judaism, Jacob now decided it was safe to venture back. "I would go to shul just to be with other Jewish people, not because I believed."

And so it was for three years, Jacob occasionally venturing to Friday night services, not feeling commanded but wanting to go anyhow. Then, one night, the rabbi couldn't come: "And I was the only one there who could read from the Torah on short notice. It was a challenge. How could I be a public reader of a book that I didn't believe was what it claimed to be? On the other hand, it bothered me that a group of Jews should miss a Torah reading. So I read it, and it was a transformative moment."

Jacob began leading services more often. He returned to Scripture, brushed up his Hebrew. He taught himself Aramaic, the late antique language of some Jewish prayers, the language that Jesus spoke; and he offered the first class in Aramaic at the University of Arkansas. With no permanent Hillel rabbi at the university, and with only occasional visits from part-time Temple Shalom rabbis, Jacob became the town rabbi. He decided to be ordained, and in 1998 he enrolled at the liberal Reconstructionist Rabbinical College; on sabbatical from his teaching, he spent a year at the RRC campus in Philadelphia, then another year in its Jerusalem program. With some advanced credits for the language work he has done on his own, Jacob will be ordained a rabbi in 2006. With Rabbi Lieber gone three weeks out of four, student rabbi Jacob runs weekly services and Friday night dinners and teaches Saturday Torah classes.

The academic study of philosophy is not known to be healthy for one's Jewish devotion, and moving to the Ozarks even less so. Jacob has puzzled at length over this irony, that the Judaism he lost in Boston he recovered while teaching Kant in the mountains. Some would say that it was precisely the absence of Judaism in the air that called him back: we only notice oxygen when it's gone. Jacob has tried that theory and found it wanting.

"My left brain would say that this was a natural process, based on what the academic market is. I would come out here, there would be few Jews, and sooner or later this was bound to happen. My right brain says this was divine intervention. If I had landed in Boston, which is full of Torah readers, this wouldn't have happened. It felt like the divine finger was pointing at me, saying, 'Now I guess you'll read my book.' "

Like theism and evolution, the two theories are not incompatible, of course. Just as God could have created Darwinian natural selection as his instrument of divine change, God could have created the natural conditions of a bad academic job market precisely to send people like Jacob Adler to places where they might learn unexpected things. And it could be God's intention that some very gifted but dormant Jewish souls find themselves alone in the wilderness, much like the earliest Jews, consciously having to huddle together for security. "If I had landed in Boston," indeed: Adler would never have been called to read Torah, and he would not be a rabbinic student today. Jacob did land in Boston once, at the feet of Jews far more observant and passionate, and the conflict aroused by his religious doubt nearly destroyed his mental health. Far away, surrounded by a far more relaxed group of Jews, he could become the leader I saw, teaching Jacob Newman about Jewish manhood.

John Knoderer, another guest at the bar mitzvah, was the eccentric, sockless man I had met Friday night at dinner. He had twice the hair, twice the height, and ten times the religions of Jacob Adler. He was well over six feet tall, with blue eyes, a long, untrimmed beard, and a long, whitening ponytail. I asked him why he was not wearing socks with his sandals, even after the fresh snowfall, with the temperature below freezing five nights in a row. "I am not outside enough for it to be worth it," he said. "And I'm trying to simplify my life."

John told me he was a "multidenominational cafeterealist": "cafeteria," he said, because in a cafeteria, just because you don't take the spinach, that doesn't make the spinach bad; and "realist," because all paths to God are equally real. Although he was raised a Lutheran and is not a Jew, John knew dozens of people at the bar mitzvah, and his was the kind of eccentric presence that everybody else notices. "Oh, *I* know who he is!" people must say, with a knowing smile, perhaps a roll of the eyes. John Knoderer is the kind of sincere, gregarious guy who after his second visit somewhere seems perfectly at home.

"I don't go to any particular church on a regular basis," he told me. " 'Attendance' implies regularity. Probably I'm visiting Temple Shalom more than the average right now because of Talmud class. I've visited a variety of others. For example, one year on my birthday I managed to visit a Lakota Sioux sweat lodge ceremony. That's their purification ceremony, and I got some illumination from that. My father was a Lutheran minister. My second major membership was Quaker, throughout my college years."

John attended Indiana University in Bloomington for six years, taking first a degree in management and then two years of education classes. Afterward, while living with his parents and volunteering with VISTA (Volunteers in Service to America, President Johnson's domestic counterpart to the Peace Corps) he began to worship at the nearby Presbyterian church—which his father, the Lutheran preacher, had begun attending—and the Quaker meeting. The Presbyterian church adult education class was reading *The Chronicles of Narnia*, by the Anglican apologist C. S. Lewis, and John, devoted since childhood to science fiction and fantasy literature, was powerfully moved.

"In the seventh book," John said, "a soldier from the evil army approaches on Judgment Day and is surprised to find himself passed to the good side. He's wandering about to figure out why he was not destroyed with the rest of the people. Aslan's answer was that when you said Tash's name, you had good thoughts in your heart, so you weren't worshiping the false god—you were worshiping me. That's where I come

from: it doesn't matter what you say you believe, what matters
is what's in your heart."

I wasn't sure what John was talking about. I once tried to
read the *Narnia* books, when I was ten, but I got scared by the
scenes in the first book, *The Lion, the Witch, and the Wardrobe*,
in which a little boy disappears into a closet and becomes ad-
dicted to Turkish delight; so I never even finished the first volume, and I have been unable to return to the series, despite its
reputation as a literate Christian parable suitable for adults as
well as children.* Nor had I read any of the other seminal texts
of John Knoderer's multidenominational cafeterealist theology, including Robert Heinlein's *Stranger in a Strange Land*
and, more important, Piers Anthony's seven-book series *Incar-
nations of Immortality*. "The first book is from the point of
view of Thanatos, or Death," John said. "The second book is
from the point of view of Time. Et cetera, et cetera." Those
books gave John the belief that Satan, should he exist, is not
exactly evil, for he is doing what God wants him to do. "So
he's not going to end up cast into the fires and destroyed, because he is doing what he is meant to do."

Some years ago, John began collecting different versions of
the Golden Rule—"Love thy neighbor as thyself," "Do unto
others as you would have them do unto you"—and he believes
that some version of the rule is found in all the world's religions.

I asked John if his long hair had any religious significance,
and he said yes, indeed.

"Around six years ago, probably February or March of

---

*To some, C. S. Lewis is best known as the author of *Mere Christianity*, the
1952 collection of three lectures, originally delivered on BBC radio, in which
he attempted to discern the essential principles that unite Christians of different
denominations. That book has probably made more Christian converts in the
last hundred years than any book except the Bible.

1997, I woke up out of a dream. And all I could remember was a feeling: *Don't cut your hair.* I thought, I don't understand it but I think I'll pay attention for a while because I can always go ahead and get it cut later. I didn't say anything to my mom about it. (I lived behind her and still do.) There were occasional hints made—'Time to get a haircut'—and I would give a mild 'yes' without really meaning it. Then at one point I come over and in the chair which is considered *my* chair there's an advertisement about a barbershop soon to open. I'm not happy about it, but I figure maybe the whole purpose of the dream was to make sure he had a customer on the first day." John borrowed a twenty from his mother, went to the barbershop, and was greeted by a sign on the door: "Newspaper wrong—Open next Monday." He took the sign on the door as a sign that he was not supposed to cut his hair, and he has not cut his hair since.

John works part-time as the director of a literacy counseling center in Gravette, Arkansas, helping students with their homework, helping adults prepare for GED examinations, and teaching English as a second language. He has lunch every day at Shiloh Farms, a Christian farming community that offered him meals in perpetuity in exchange for his help fixing bugs in their computer systems. His vocation is not, however, his avocation. What he loves to do is make mazes. As a child, John loved solving mazes, so when in 1977 he got his first personal computer, a Radio Shack TRS-80 Model One with sixteen kilobytes of memory, the first thing he did was write a program that created mazes. He began encoding written messages inside his mazes, and at science fiction conventions he would give away his mazes, to what one may safely assume was an audience inclined to mazelike mind games. One year, at a convention in St. Louis, somebody looked up at him and said, "Hey, it's the maze man." That has been his nickname ever since, and mazes have become an increasingly important part of his life.

Sometimes, he brings his computer to crafts fairs and makes mazes for show. Several years in a row, he made mazes for children attending the Labor Day Youth Gathering of the Lutheran Youth Organization for Oklahoma and Arkansas; he stopped going to the Lutheran event the year that it conflicted with a theosophical camp at which participants would attempt to construct a walkable labyrinth. "Had to do that, of course, since a labyrinth is a maze with no dead ends," John said. He has created a Web site where he has uploaded mazes containing, encoded in their walls and paths, hundreds of popular first names.* They are personalized puzzles, perfect gifts for young children. If you find a maze with your name in it, you may download it free of charge; otherwise, John asks that you make a voluntary payment. "I spend most of my time as a volunteer," he writes on his Web site, "and do have substantial bills, so every amount will be fully appreciated. I feel that creating these puzzles is part of my ministry, so you will be supporting a personal ministry that includes messages that have been received in dreams. If you'd like to know more about my heaven-sent dreams, feel free to ask."

I did ask, and John told me that on a May night in 1997, shortly after he hadn't cut his hair, he was in Conway, Arkansas, for Third Wave, a three-day technology conference. After a day of seminars, he retired to his hotel room with a large root beer float to watch the season finale of *Star Trek Voyager*. At 7:30, with the television tuned to the right station, he began reading a favorite *Star Trek* book, getting his mind primed for an hour of far-out, spacey TV. And for some rea-

---

*When I asked John how to refer to parts of a maze, he told me that he called the black lines "walls" and the white spaces "paths," but he cautioned me that these may not be the correct terms, technically speaking.

son John, a night owl about to watch a favorite television
show, was overcome by fatigue. He couldn't keep his eyes
open. After fighting off sleep for several minutes, he resigned
himself to going to bed. He turned off the television set,
placed a bookmark in his book, turned out the light, and fell
asleep. And that night he had three dreams, which he recorded
on hotel stationery after waking.

In the first dream, John felt himself floating off the earth.
He cried out, "Yes, yes, yes!" because he knew he was going to
heaven. Later he decided the dream was "somewhat Rapture-
like." In the second dream, he found himself on a plane from
California to New York, two places he has never lived. Somehow, he knew the plane was going to crash, but he was not
afraid: "I find myself talking in my mind," John described it
to me, "not praying, but saying, 'I'm coming home, I'm coming home.' And I know I'm saying it to God.

"In the third dream, I find myself in a group of people,
standing in front of a long table around which are seated
many, many men. They are there to challenge me in my beliefs, and my reply is, 'I believe in God, Jesus, Buddha, the
Great White Spirit'—in my dream, I name every name God
has ever used to walk the earth. It's obvious they don't like my
answer, but it's obvious there's nothing they can do to change
my mind so they let me go. I find myself in a huge room filled
with people, a cross section of every ability, every disability,
every orientation, every disorientation, every belief system,
every disbelief system. And I feel the presence of God, Jesus,
Buddha, the Great White Spirit, saying, 'Support those who
are in doubt, those who are wavering.' So I go up to each person wavering because of the pressure of the committee, and I
say these five words: 'Do not deny your God.' With the emphasis on 'your.' With those five words, I knew they were getting my meaning, which is 'Just because what you believe is

different from what I believe, or what the committee believes, we shouldn't deny what we all believe.'

"And that to me has cemented my firm belief that every religion has part of the truth, and no religion has all of the truth."

Although John had no plans to become a Jew, was not studying Hebrew, and had a spotty record of synagogue attendance, he knew more about Judaism than many Jewish members of Temple Shalom. In his way, he was a typical member, almost. As Jacob Adler told me, Temple Shalom gets a "good number" of non-Jews. "They tend to be of three kinds," he said. "First there are the 'universal religion' people, like John, whom you met. The second are the people who are exploring Judaism in some way. And the third are the strangest: Christians who think they should go to synagogue. At some point, they come to the realization that Jesus was Jewish, and they figure if their savior was, maybe they should be too."

In Greater Fayetteville, where the nonexistent Introduction to Judaism classes meet at the nonexistent Jewish Community Center, these curious souls learn a little something about Judaism by showing up at Temple Shalom, where, if they come around often enough that people know their names, they get invited to events like the Newman bar mitzvah. There, they get a further introduction to Jewish religion and, not incidentally, Jewish culture, courtesy of other non-Jews like Carol Widder, the accordionist for the Po' Goys, the four-piece band that provided the music at Jacob Newman's bar mitzvah luncheon. The Po' Goys play klezmer, a Jewish musical style with roots in Israeli, Russian, and other Eastern European folk music traditions; it became a genre of its own on the Lower East Side of Manhattan, where in the early twentieth century all those musical idioms got stewed together. The language of klezmer lyrics, when there are lyrics, is Yiddish, a language spoken by none of the Po' Goys.

Carol had white skin, reddish cheeks, and blond, red, and brown hair; she looked a lot like the actress Sissy Spacek. Born in Boston to an Irish Catholic surgeon and his wife, a registered nurse, Carol moved as a young girl to Springfield, Missouri. The family always knew some Jews; her father's partner, a Jewish doctor, went to Israel in 1967 to help the war effort. When Carol was sixteen, she spent a summer at symphony music camp at the university in Fayetteville, where she met Mark Widder, who instantly became her first and, it turned out, only love. When it came time for college, she turned down scholarship offers at big-city conservatories and enrolled at the University of Arkansas, where Mark was already a student. She started college in 1974, and she was married the next year at a wedding not attended by her parents, who disapproved of her groom. They told her it would have been far better if she had decided to marry a Jew. "It was okay to play with a Protestant," Carol told me, "but you sure didn't marry a Protestant bicycle mechanic."

Mark Widder dropped out of the University of Arkansas and became, in addition to the area's leading bicycle mechanic, a curator of Fayetteville's thriving bicycle culture, marking bike trails and becoming a spokesman for the nonpetroleum movement. Carol worked as a special-education teacher, and the couple had two daughters. Later, when Carol enrolled at the University of Wisconsin to study communicative disorders, they moved to Madison, which at the time had more bicycles per capita than any other city in the United States. Mark quickly found work in a bike shop, and Carol became an expert in suprasegmentals, the features of speech, like volume, rate, and stress, that are not letter sounds; knowledge

of suprasegmentals is necessary to research in speech impedi-
ments. Carol now does freelance transcription work: she is
sent tapes of families having conversations, and she transcribes
their dialogue so that it can be analyzed for abnormalities.

"I'm trained to hear all kinds of *s*'s," she said, when we
spoke at her house. "There's the dental *s*, the normal *s*, the lat-
eral *s*, and a few more. Musicians are often the best phonetic
transcribers, because we're not listening to content, but listening to sounds as they are." Her mentor in Madison, in fact,
was a musician, a Jewish musician, "a bass player named Larry
Schreiber."

Back in Fayetteville, Carol was invited to join the Po' Goys,
a project of Keefe Jackson, the local music prodigy, twenty-
four years old when I saw him play. "He is an incredible jazz
saxophone and clarinet player," Carol said. "He formed the
band four years ago. I originally played piano and contrabass.
I worked my way through school playing in orchestras. But I
picked up the accordion six years ago, and Keefe needed an
accordion player." Carol loved all the music that klezmer
sounded like—folk music from Old Europe, Celtic fiddle music, accordion music—but she knew nothing about klezmer.
Keefe, on the other hand, knew close to everything about it.
"Keefe studied in Portland, Maine, for two years with a guy
who just lived klezmer. He told him, 'Klezmer *is* D minor.' So
yesterday, when I wanted to know what key to play 'Hava' in,
Keefe just said, 'How about D?' "

At first, the four members of the Po' Goys played together
just for fun and to satisfy Keefe's obsessive connoisseurship.
They would get together to play classical klezmer, one might
call it, stuff from the thirties and forties, with jazz and ragtime
inflections—not the standard simcha fare, "Hava Negila" and
the melodies from *Fiddler on the Roof*. But then "the jobs just
happened." Someone asked if they could play a bar mitzvah,

then a bat mitzvah. "I never realized how many Jewish friends I had until this happened," Carol said. "I'm drawn to Jewish people."

There were even some Jews at Jacob Newman's bar mitzvah. Daniel Levine, professor of classics at the university, past president of Temple Shalom, and a man almost too refined to live so close to Wal-Mart's world headquarters, greeted me at the church on Saturday morning. He shook my hand, smiled brightly, and said that he had heard I would be coming. Yes, he said, he would be happy to talk.

I visited Daniel later that week at his house, which had a cultivated appeal, a studied indifference akin to its owner's perfectly disheveled silver hair. The garden outside was well tended—even in winter, with nothing in bloom, you could tell. In the kitchen, Greek script was stenciled around the top of the walls where they met the ceiling. Daniel led me downstairs to his renovated basement, home of the master bedroom and some very large closets; the adjoining bathroom had a walk-in shower stall, its concave ceiling tiled in a style Daniel called "Santorini/Jerusalem/Morocco/Greece/Temple of Poseidon at Cape Sounion." It was an intentionally worldly house, even eccentric, befitting the one man in Fayetteville who regularly leads tours to Greece.

Like Jacob Adler, Daniel had come for the academic job and stayed. He is well known in the community, in part because the *Northwest Arkansas Times* calls him when it needs a quotation from a local Jew. The son of a rabbi and the grandson of a Hebrew Union College professor who wrote books on the prophets Isaiah and Jeremiah, Daniel avoided the rabbinate but could not escape Jewish leadership. He gives good comment, and his family gives good photographs: for years, whenever the *Times* wanted to run a story explaining this strange festival of Hanukkah, it called on the Levines. Daniel showed me an album containing three newspaper photographs, from three different years, of his wife and daughters lighting the candles on a menorah.

Daniel plays the role of town Jew with considerable aplomb. Invited to represent the Jewish community at the mayor's annual prayer breakfast, Daniel read aloud the Ten Commandments, and the obvious simplicity of that choice impressed people; afterward, several men and women approached to thank him and say things like "You know, I never read the Ten Commandments." His daughter Amy, ten years old, has twice visited the kindergarten class at her school to tell the story of Hanukkah. "Christians are real curious about Jews," Daniel said, "and ignorant, and not very sensitive, but that doesn't make them antagonistic."

Daniel told me something that I had also heard from John Newman, and that Jacob Adler had seemed to suggest: being in a town with few Jews, no Jewish money, and no synagogue enhances Jews' sense of Judaism, and it can prompt them to higher levels of observance. Though raised by a rabbi, Daniel goes to Shabbos services more now than he did as a child. He and his wife, Judith, have imposed a rule that he did not have growing up: the children may play with their friends on Friday night, but only after the family has lit the candles and made kiddush with the wine. Some weeks, they light Havdalah candles to mark the end of Shabbos.

The Levines go to services more often in Fayetteville than they would on Long Island, for sure. Amy and Sarah Levine probably think more about their Judaism, and have more sophisticated thoughts on the matter, than their young peers from towns with large Jewish populations. Those peers have more rigorous Hebrew school classes, and a better sense of kosher dietary laws, but they lack what used to be the normative experience of world Jewry: diaspora. The twentieth century was the first in history when Jews began to move closer to each other; before that, Jews were always being dispersed, and that dispersal reminded them of their outsider status. Two hundred years ago, cities like Amsterdam and Vilnius, with large Jewish populations, were the exception, while towns with a smattering of Jews, like Fayetteville today, were the rule. When there were fewer Jews in any one place, more of them had to represent their people to curious, or hostile, Gentiles. The "town Jew" used to be a recognizable figure, one that Daniel Levine rather embodies today.

The Levines, like the Newmans and Jacob Adler, strayed away from the big city and, accidentally, toward their Judaism. That was not the case for Hank Kaminsky, another Jew I met at the bar mitzvah. Hank's only religion is art. He's the town sculptor, and he looks it. Everybody in Fayetteville looks the part, actually—a feature of small towns, where people are assigned roles by their neighbors: Jacob Adler, the yeshiva bocher in his yarmulke; Daniel Levine, the hip young classics prof; Darla Newman, the earth-mother Jewess; and Hank Kaminsky, the artist, six foot five with a ponytail and blue eyes, not unlike the multireligionist maze-maker John Knoderer, but with a self-abused Jackson Pollock swagger that was all his own, a face addled with gin blossoms, and a John Wayne body packed into jeans, a red shirt, and shit-kicking boots.

He took me to his studio, an old warehouse on Government Street, and showed me his metal-casting implements, rubber molds, wood frames, and clay models. But to see his masterpiece I had to meet him downtown, at the Town Center Plaza. "The World Peace Prayer" is a bronze globe, ten feet in diameter, which Hank built on a commission from the Bradburys, local patrons of the arts. Raised in the bronze are the words "May Peace Reign on Earth," rendered in English, French, German, Japanese, Turkish, Hopi, and about a hundred other languages (Kaminsky had lost count at one hundred). The phrase, in an array of alphabets, is written again and again, arranged in meaningful ways. For example, the Cyrillic script of Serbian is across the globe from the Roman script of the Croatian. The Tibetan and the Chinese intersect. It was a brilliant concept, marred by small flaws in the execution, more of which came to Hank's attention every week. Jacob Adler found an error in the Hebrew, the dalet, or *d*, of *Adamah*, "earth," looking like a resh, which makes the *r* sound. The Seneca contains an error. It fell to Daniel Levine to tell Hank about an error in the Greek: what is supposed to be a nu is actually an upsilon, turning *eirene*, "peace," into the meaningless *eireue*.

When Hank showed me the peace sculpture, it was not quite operational. The fountain at the top, which was to bubble water over the north pole to cascade down the globe and collect in a small reflecting pool at the bottom, was undergoing some last-minute plumbing repairs. The sculpture was already $50,000 over the $250,000 budget, and Hank did not stand to make much money on this piece. He earns his living, he told me, doing busts of people. He has done both Sam and Alice Walton, the First Couple of Wal-Mart, who, if not quite the Victoria and Albert of Arkansas, are the Rainier and Grace. He did Congressman Wilbur Mills and a teenage Chelsea Clinton.

"I went through my period where I wore the Domino's cap and delivered pizzas so I didn't have to take these bust commissions," Hank said. "I wanted to stay true to my art. The original urge to be an artist is the urge to create. But I eventually made my decision that my role was as a village artist. Every village needs its sculptor, and I do a service to the community."

Like the Levines and the Newmans—like all the Jews I met in Fayetteville—Hank came from elsewhere but had no plans to go back. He loves the Ozarks, although he regrets that you can never feel alone there the way you can in New York City. There is no anonymity in the small town. "I get alone by getting stoned," Hank said. And leaving New York, he left the art world. You can't get famous doing busts of Arkansans. But that is an acceptable price, especially since he did not leave New York on good terms: in 1969, he told me, he was fired from a job teaching sculpture at the Cooper Union after he wrote an article about the pro-Vietnam activities of some of the school's trustees. When a friend invited him to join a crafts cooperative in Eureka Springs, Arkansas, Hank left everything behind, including one and a half marriages. "One of the marriages, I was married to her, but she wasn't married to me," he said.

When I asked Hank about his Judaism—I had, after all, met him at a bar mitzvah—he quoted the spiritual guru Ram Dass, né Richard Alpert: "I'm Jewish on my parents' side." Hank's mother was an observant Jew, his father was not. "He was raised in an Italian neighborhood, and he changed his name from Samuel Avram, or something like that, to Frank." The Kaminsky family attended a shul in Valley Stream, Long Island. "My bar mitzvah was very organized and short compared to Jacob's," he told me. "I was amazed at how long his was, but meaningful, and people paid attention through the whole thing." He clearly was impressed by Jacob's experience, but of his own he retained just one image: "The thing I still remember was holding the pointer. It was a very powerful image, and it stayed with me my whole life."*

And yet: "That was the day I quit Judaism. I made a decision. If I had had the language at the time, I would have said I didn't feel comfortable being held to traditions that limited my thought patterns. I thought I needed to travel in different realms." To reach those realms, Hank did copious amounts of drugs, and he spent a short while practicing yoga with a swami who came up to him one day and suggested that he leave. "Kaminsky, you don't need this," the swami said. Now, sculpting is his religious practice. "When I start a sculpture, whether stoned or not—and marijuana is one of my favorite activities—I get to a point where I am being led by the sculpture. And if I need to know where to go next, I ask the sculpture."

Before I left, Hank sold me a small plaster sculpture, Greek letters used in the making of the large bronze globe. He wanted fifty dollars, I countered twenty-five, and he said, "Deal—if you promise to write about me."

Nobody had less to say about Jacob Newman's bar mitzvah, after the fact, than Jacob Newman. I asked him if he enjoyed it, and he said, "I think I enjoyed it up to the bar mitzvah, because, mostly because, I had gotten sick that week. I had the flu, I think." I asked him if he knew many other Jewish chil-

---

*The "pointer" is the yad (*yad* is Hebrew for "hand"). It is typically a metal implement, sculpted into a hand at the end, used to follow the Hebrew letters as one chants. One uses the yad to ensure that Torah letters are not scraped or blurred through years of touching by human hands. Also, Jewish tradition requires that the Torah be read, not recited from memory, and using the yad is a reminder to look at the scroll.

dren at his junior high school. "I can think of one, and I know of one Jewish kid whose mother isn't Jewish, and another who was born Jewish and now considers himself an atheist." I asked him if he would keep going to synagogue as he got older. "Sometimes," he said, "but probably not as often as I do now." At the time, I could think of nothing more to ask, and he had nothing more to say.

But Jacob was more loquacious in an e-mail exchange a couple of months later, when his health had returned and he had had some time to think.

"I actually enjoyed the bar mitzvah," Jacob wrote, "and will look back at it fondly. The training and preparation was tedious (I had to remember and receive training on how to read Hebrew again), but I think it paid off in the end. One thing that I was not satisfied with was my speech. I was planning on a much-better-thought-out one, but I procrastinated too long and I got sick, and I eventually ended up having my dad write most of the speech for me the morning of the bar mitzvah. He would ask my thoughts about my Torah portion and everything else. I really disliked it.

"Despite my being sick, my speech, and the training, I thought it was a great experience where it all paid off in the end."

It sounded as if his bar mitzvah experience was rewarding and memorable, but not quite profound. I suspect that he was tolerant of his mother's New Age, Jewish Renewal enthusiasms, but I doubt that Jacob would have chosen her folk songs with accompanying hand gestures. I am skeptical that, given his druthers, he would have hired a klezmer band. He might, in fact, have envied the flashy bar mitzvah parties in L.A. and Miami, if he had known about them. They definitely seem to be reflections of the boys and girls themselves—the music is by Beyoncé, 50 Cent, and Coldplay, not the Po' Goys.

The test might not be, however, whether Jacob would prefer a big-city, big-money affair. Humans have wide eyes, and
there are things that all of us, children and adults, mistakenly
think we want. Some bar mitzvah parties in New York might
be genuine expressions of the child and his family; others
might be designed by parents, or by hired professionals whose
wholly unique parties somehow fail to celebrate the unique
children. It is impossible to say how the deepest feelings, or
the most affecting memories, are produced: if a boy sincerely
wants the Jets' quarterback to sign cards at his bar mitzvah,
and if his parents make that happen, does it matter that his
goal was to outdo the bar mitzvah at Yankee Stadium? If he remembers his bar mitzvah clearly, but only as a triumphant
party, how do we measure that against Jacob Newman's fainter
but more religious memories?

The argument for a bar mitzvah like Jacob's is not that he
would have planned it that way, but that in being an expression of his family it is an expression of him; perhaps it was the
day his mother gave him Jewish Renewal as his own, to keep
or to reject. When you hear Jews talk about other Jews' b'nai
mitzvah, they often say, "It was really his mother's chance to
shine," or, "His father invited all the partners from his firm,"
and you can be sure that those comments are meant unchari-
tably. To the yentas—the gossips, the critics—the bar or bat
mitzvah must center on the boy or girl, and any twisting of
the event into a party for the adults is a perversion of its true
spirit. But that is not the right criterion at all.

That Jacob's bar mitzvah was his mother's big day—and, at
the last minute, his father's, when he had to assemble Jacob's
speech for him—is supposed to be a problem, and to the extent that a bar mitzvah can be written off as business entertainment for the boy's father, the critique is valid. But a family
enterprise is normally seen as a good thing—Americans need

more family time, not less; more cooperative projects, not fewer. They need more community. There is nothing heretical about a bar or bat mitzvah that ends up meaning more to a circle of older folks than it does to the child. Even if—and it's an if—Darla Newman, overjoyed to put her Jewish Renewal into public practice, was more thrilled by Jacob's bar mitzvah than Jacob was, or if John Knoderer the Amazing Maze Man was helped further along his spiritual path by being a guest than Jacob was by being the host, that is not necessarily a problem.

We assume that it is a problem because we insist that the child becoming an adult appreciate how profound a passage he is making, and if he doesn't feel it in his gut, then we worry that something has gone awry. Maybe the boy has not studied hard enough; maybe his day has been ruined by crass materialism. We also worry about the adults' having a better time than the child because our culture makes a fetish of childhood. We have a tendency—perhaps owing to romancers of childhood like Rousseau and Montessori, perhaps owing to capitalism's commodification of all things young—to make of children something precious. Like their football victories and spelling-bee triumphs, children's religious rituals become opportunities to honor the beauty of unspoiled youth. We like turning them into stars, as Judi Gannon said. Their star power both compels us and makes us ashamed of how compelled we are. Nobody likes the sports dad or the stage mom, but we're all in danger of becoming them.

If we understood the bar and bat mitzvah as important mainly because they signal a child's entrance into the far richer, deeper world of adulthood, then we would expect that the boy or girl would not fully understand the day's import, not until some years later. It would be the adults nearby who would be most affected—relieved, delighted, overwhelmed. That would not be a sign of anything disordered, but rather an acknowledgment that religion is a process of constant growth, one that yields its sweetest fruits only with time. The earliest religious rituals—the circumcision, the First Communion—are obviously occasions for parents' joy more than children's. The older child, of bar mitzvah age, is more capable of appreciating religion than the infant or six-year-old is, but it would be sad if his parents were not more appreciative still.

In a small Jewish community like Fayetteville's, there is even greater reason to think that bar mitzvah memories age well. Even if Jacob forgets his bar mitzvah, watches it fade into the gray evanescence of time, and decides in the end that it was just an excuse for people to dance about and eat health food, he could still take pride in having perpetuated Fayetteville Judaism. He hosted a community simcha, bringing together, for one day, Fayetteville Jews and their Gentile friends. That is a good thing, and whether or not Jacob knows it now, he will. A bris, after all, is not much fun for the baby, but someday he will be at his own son's bris.

It would be nice if, even without religion, families and neighbors regularly got together for picnics or for large, joyous dances; maybe we should bring back the barn raising. But usually it's religion that provides the occasions. It commands us, by virtue of tradition, to take the good suit out of mothballs. The bar mitzvah does not serve that function everywhere. In cities with a bar and bat mitzvah season, with party after party, at least some of the parties feel like rote obligations. These b'nai mitzvah are none of the things that Jacob Newman's was: a gathering of the whole Jewish community, a party for their Gentile friends, and something old-fashioned, from the era before Jews were concentrated in big cities, from a time when small villages—not unlike Fayetteville—would have their own traditions, rites, and melodies: a chance for a few families, far from the centers of learning and wealth, to make their own Jewish culture.

5

The Boy

In a neighborhood filled with pickup trucks tucked in for the night, resting in their driveways, attached to the heating blocks that help Alaska's engines wake up every morning, sat the small chalet-style house of Rabbi Yossi Greenberg. Out front, the snowbanks along the road were about three feet high, low for an Anchorage January. The winter had been mild, the temperature dropping only a little below zero at night and creeping into the teens during the day. But it was still always well below freezing, and the two-foot ice sculpture of the Star of David that sat beside the Greenbergs' front door would not melt for at least another two months. Right above the ice sculpture, next to the door, a wooden plaque was affixed to the house. It read, in Hebrew letters, "Beis Chabad," Chabad House. I knocked on the door, and it was soon answered by a string bean of a boy wearing black pants, a white dress shirt, and, over his bowl of brown hair, a black yarmulke. I had not expected one so young at ten-thirty at night, when it had already been dark for nearly eight hours. I looked back at my rental car, sitting in the road like a child abandoned to the elements. Then I turned to the boy in the doorway, and I asked him if his father was home. He disappeared within, leaving me there, the cold night at my back. Thirty seconds later, he returned.

"Come in," he said.

I stepped onto a landing at the meeting of two stairwells: the stairs ahead descended to a dark basement, the stairs to the right led to a lighted living room. From above I could hear men laughing, and I could smell chicken. The skinny boy nodded toward a mat on the floor, and as he watched patiently I took off my shoes and left them there. In my stocking feet, I followed him upstairs toward the noise and the men and the food.

Three men in full beards were sitting around a circular kitchen table in the back right corner of a big contiguous living room, dining room, and kitchen, eating chicken with slices of bread and pouring Coke and Sprite from two-liter bottles into plastic cups. They looked over and motioned for me to join them. They introduced themselves in turn.

"I am Rabbi Yossi."

"I am Rabbi Zushe."

"I am Rabbi Israel."

At the table there was a woman in a housecoat, with white hair cut close to her scalp. Rabbi Yossi nodded toward her and said that this was his mother, also mother to Rabbi Zushe, Rabbi Israel, and fourteen other brothers and sisters. I nodded to her, but I did not offer my hand, knowing that an ultra-Orthodox Jewish woman would not take it. Another brother walked in, younger, college-aged, bearded like the rest, in the same black pants and white shirt and yarmulke. His pregnant wife, also in her early twenties, was with him, and they both smiled at me, said good night to everyone, and left. Newlywed sex, I thought. I sat down at the kitchen table with the old woman, her three rabbi sons, and her grandson—the little boy, I now realized, was Mendy Greenberg, the bar mitzvah boy.

Excited about his party the next day, Mendy had trouble sitting still. He kept hopping up from his seat, eager for a chore to do, like getting more Coke from the refrigerator. "Go get Mark a yarmulke," Rabbi Yossi told his son, who ran off, returning immediately with a white satin skullcap.

"You eat yet?" Rabbi Yossi said.

I had, but it seemed that Rabbi Yossi wanted to feed me.

"I'm a little hungry."

Rabbi Yossi smiled, and his smile made him broader, pudgier, livelier than before. He fixed a paper plate of dark meat chicken, filled a plastic cup with Sprite and no ice, and slid them both to me.

Rabbi Israel, the eldest of the three rabbi brothers, reached between the Coke and the Sprite to pull out a half-empty bottle of Crown Royal. He poured a shot into a small plastic cup and passed it to me.

"And now," he announced, "we say a l'chaim. Because some people would call all over the world doing interviews by telephone, but you came here, to Alaska, to be with us. That is the spirit of bigness that is in Judaism. You ever hear the expression 'There's a minyan in him,' there are the souls of ten Jews in that one man? That's what I mean. You're here with us. So now, *Baruch atah Adonai*"—he waited for me to repeat after him—"*eloheinu melech ha-olam, she-hakhol nihyeh bi-d'varo*"—the prayer over foods which are not the product of the soil, like meat, fish, milk, eggs, and cheese, and all liquids except wine and grape juice. And then he raised his cup of whiskey and said, "L'chaim! To life!" And he and I did a shot together; then he did another shot, and, to be polite, so did I. And his younger brother Rabbi Yossi said, "This is probably the first Orthodox bar mitzvah in Alaska history!"

I had been invited to a rare family reunion. These brothers do not see each other often. Rabbi Israel, forty years old, of El Paso, Texas, had a red beard and amused blue eyes and an impish smirk; he had the swagger but also the chummy approachability of George W. Bush, and I wondered if it was a Texas thing. Rabbi Zushe, thirty-six, lives in Cleveland, where he runs a Chabad house in the suburbs. "We get four hundred people for High Holidays," he told me. And Rabbi Yossi, thirty-eight, lives in this split-level chalet in Anchorage, with his wife, Esty, and his four children: Menachem Mendel, the bar mitzvah boy, known as Mendy; Chaya Mushka, eleven, known as Mushky; Levi, seven, known as Levi; and Rivkah, two and a half, known as Rivky—two boys, two girls, so far. Mendy does not really live in Anchorage, though. He goes to school in Queens, and before Queens, he went to school in Chicago. Before that, he was home-schooled by his parents, and now, when he is home, he studies with his father, in preparation for when he will become a rabbi like his father and uncles: Greenberg brothers also serve as rabbis of the Chabad sect in Shanghai, China; Oceanside, California; and six other cities around the world.

"Where there is Chabad, there is a Greenberg!" Rabbi Israel said.

As the uncles talked, I asked Mendy about going to school so far away. Did his plane rides to New York and back bother him?

"I change in Minneapolis," he said. "But it's six hours to there. I read, or I talk to people."

Rabbi Yossi had been talking to his mother, but apparently he had been listening in with one ear, for now he looked at us, his smile returning, fattening his merry face.

"He gets in arguments about religion!" the proud father said. "One time, he gets in a discussion with someone, an older man, who wants to argue which is true, Jewish or Christian. And at the end, he says to Mendy, 'I wish my son knew as much about his religion as you know about yours!' "

It is queer to be an Orthodox Jew in Alaska, but then it is

queer to be anyone in Alaska. Everyone who moves there has
to explain why. Even Alaskans who think they are normal
think all other Alaskans are strange: "People here in Anchorage are more or less sane, but out in the wild, you find sur-
vivalist types, men with guns, men who moved there so their
wives would have nowhere to escape to." "Well, Juneau is just
another state capital, but out in the islands, you find those
fishermen types, alone with just their boats all year round.
Odd birds."

Alaska has more than its share of alcoholics, and less than
its share of women, which means more than its share of strip
clubs.* One that I drove by in Anchorage was called the Great
Alaskan Bush Company. The local bookstore, one of the best
I've seen, also has a great name, Title Wave. Much about the
city is typical: the Wendy's, the Barnes & Noble, the business
district of skyscrapers nestled into a valley, surrounded by hills
of houses, stores, and nightlife.

In the winter, by day it is white, but it is rarely day. In summer, by day it is green and inviting, and it is rarely night. The
constant daylight can feel assaulting, and it is a problem for
Shabbos, which is supposed to begin at sundown on Friday
and end at sundown on Saturday.

"In the winter, it's not so bad," Rabbi Yossi said, when I
commented on the dark. "Shabbos begins at three-thirty; you
light the candles, you pray, you eat." The odd thing is that the
three daily prayer services, which in, say, New Hampshire or
North Carolina would be spaced out from about 7 a.m. to
2 p.m. to 6 p.m., tracking sunrise to sunset, are crowded together here. "It's a little weird doing Shacharis at 10 a.m., then

---

*According to the 2000 census, the Alaska population is 48.3 percent female,
less than the 50.9 percent for the United States as a whole. The American government estimates that 5.7 percent of Americans over age twelve are alcoholics,
while 7 percent of Alaskans are.

Mincha two hours later, and Ma'ariv a couple hours after that. But it's okay.

"The problem is the summer. If the sun doesn't go down until 11:30 at night, that's difficult for the children, to wait to eat until then."

Rabbi Yossi turned to his brothers and said something in Yiddish. Their mother, a Russian immigrant to Israel, speaks Russian, Yiddish, and Hebrew, but very little English, and she was sitting quietly through all this talk. It suddenly occurred to me that these three rabbis had had a long day of reunion, catching up on the news of each other's lives, and, of course, planning the last details of the bar mitzvah party the next day. They were tired.

"I'll see you tomorrow night," I said.

"Yes," Rabbi Yossi said. "And Thursday, I will take you around and show you our new state-of-the-art mikveh, and the site of our new synagogue we're going to build, and our school. And we'll find other people for you to talk to." He looked at the top of my head. "You keep the yarmulke. And Friday night, you'll have Shabbos with us, yes? And Saturday, of course, you'll be with us, yes?"

He handed me an invitation to Mendy's party the next night, at the downtown Marriott; the invitation was in both Hebrew and English. He asked me if I needed directions, and I said no, I thought I could find it. Esty, his wife, came in to remind him that they still had more place cards to finish. And, its being midnight, I left.

One very adult lesson that the bar mitzvah teaches children is that there is usually a gap between the ideal and the real. There are expectations: parents expect one thing, friends expect another, the rabbi another—and the ancestors, too, they expect you to be a credit to their good name and to the good names of those murdered by Hitler and in the czar's pogroms and by the communists, the flame of whose memory you must keep lit! But beside those great expectations sits a human-sized boy or girl who must balance responsibility to the Jewish people with all of life's other responsibilities, like tending goal in the soccer game on Friday, taking out the trash, and doing math homework, leaving little time to be a perfect Jew.

The liberal branches of Judaism try to make sense of this gap. They say that it is possible to be a good Jew and still be a member of this society of sports and summer camps. Reform, Reconstructionist, and Conservative Judaism negotiate a road between strict observance and total secularism. There is, they say, a third way, and although each branch describes its third way a little differently, somewhere nearer to or further from the traditional ideal, they all agree that to be a good Jewish man or woman does not have to be a full-time job. Being a good Jew can be sort of like being a good person, but with special holidays.

Most of us say *Thank God for that.* Traditional Judaism is awfully demanding. I, for one, believe that there is beauty inherent in rigor, and I suspect that most of us need more, not less, discipline in our lives; but I also know that Orthodoxy is a high tree to climb. Most people lack the commitment—not to mention the time in the day—to get to the top, and it's good that there are resting points along the way, levels of observance that we can more reasonably expect to reach. Most of the children I talked with used the occasion of a bar or bat mitzvah to begin finding that appropriate level for themselves. Sizing up that gap between the ideal and the real, locating the possible, was one of the first struggles they would undertake as Jewish adults, and it raised big questions, adult-sized questions: Would I play in a big football game on Yom Kippur?

Will I date only Jews? Answering those questions is a very grown-up job.

For some Jews, however, the whole business of finding the right level of observance is nonsense. For the very, very religious, like Mendy Greenberg, manhood has prescribed meanings. It is a job, with responsibilities like laying tefillin, fasting on Yom Kippur, giving charity, and joining a minyan when nine men at prayer need a tenth. It also means beginning to think about taking a wife and maybe studying for the rabbinate—not tomorrow, but not so far away as ten years, either. In ultra-Orthodox communities, especially among the Hasidic sects, it is not uncommon to marry around age twenty-one, or even younger; and, because they shun secular education, many ultra-Orthodox boys are ready to enter business, or take rabbinic exams, very soon afterward. For these b'nai mitzvah, real manhood—supporting a family, holding a job—is approaching fast. The challenge is not to discern the important obligations—they are all important. The job is to be worthy of them. For an ultra-Orthodox boy, becoming a bar mitzvah means entering a new relationship with God, the covenant of Abraham and Jacob.

To understand the particular kind of manhood that is expected of Mendy, it helps to understand what it means that the Greenbergs are Hasidim (from the Hebrew *hasid*, "pious"), members of a tradition founded by the Polish rabbi Israel ben Eliezer, who lived from 1700 to 1760 and was known to his followers as the Baal Shem Tov, the Master of the Good Name. The Baal Shem Tov taught a mystical theology of creation based on the Jewish oral tradition known as Kabbalah. In the last few years, it has become chic for celebrities, like Madonna, Britney Spears, Courtney Love, and Mick Jagger, to study Kabbalah as a kind of self-improvement regimen. But the study of Kabbalah was never the main attraction of the

Hasidus movement. The Baal Shem Tov taught that the sim-
plest peasant, so long as he was devoted to God and prayer,
could be as good a Jew as the most erudite melamed, or
teacher. That emphasis on the common man attracted many
people on the fringes, poor and marginal souls who were of-
tentimes a little crazy. The first Hasidim were known to turn
somersaults during worship, to dance outside under the stars,
to laugh and sob in turn. Ecstasy mattered more than book
learning.

By the late 1700s, the movement had become more routine.
The distinctive dress of the Hasidim—beards, black coats, fe-
doras or fur hats—remained, but the trances and physical exer-
tions became infrequent. Its earliest leaders gone, Hasidus split
into factions, each following a different rabbinic dynasty. The
dynasties were named for the towns where they were founded:
the Satmar Hasidim were from Satmar, in Hungary; the Ger-
rer, from Ger, Poland; and so forth. Rabbi Schneur Zalman,
from the Russian town of Lubavitch, founded the Lubavitcher
Hasidim, the sect of the Greenberg family.

Except to a connoisseur, these black-hatted men all look
alike, but after the war they brought with them to Brooklyn worlds of distinctions—variations in dress, liturgy, and
theology—that they guard jealously. They also brought their
unique snobberies. Lubavitchers will tell you that they are the
brains of the Hasidim, dedicated to *chochmah* (wisdom), *binah*
(comprehension), and *da'at* (knowledge)—from which they get
their movement's other name, the acronym "Chabad."

The Lubavitchers have school curricula different from those
of the other Hasidic movements, and their rites of worship
differ slightly too. But what mainly sets Lubavitchers apart is
their attitude toward less observant Jews. While other Orthodox movements can be indifferent to secular folk, Lubavitchers reach out to all Jews—fervently, persistently, some would

say annoyingly. They are known for their "mitzvah tanks," modified U-Hauls that young Lubavitcher men park in areas with heavy Jewish traffic, like financial districts or college campuses; the driver and his friend look for passersby who might be Jewish, inquire about their religion, and invite any Jews they find to come inside the vehicle to lay tefillin. On the holiday of Sukkos, the mitzvah tank is outfitted with lulavs, the palm branches that Jewish men are commanded to wave about in celebration. During Hanukkah, they pass out boxes that contain menorahs and instruction booklets detailing how to light the menorah and what prayers to say. Young Lubavitcher girls have a role too, passing out Shabbos candles to Jewish women on the street or in office buildings and suggesting that they light candles on Friday night.

After these teenage endeavors, a Lubavitcher man takes a wife and, if he is fortunate, is sent on shlichus, which translates roughly as "mission." The emissary and his wife, shliach and shlichah, who probably grew up in Brooklyn, Detroit, Seattle, or Sydney, decamp for an area that, in the judgment of the Lubavitcher elders, needs a stronger Orthodox rabbinic presence. In their adopted towns the couple teach classes and host Shabbos dinners. They offer private lessons in Torah, run summer camps, and open religious schools. Lubavitchers go to Belarus, Siberia, Thailand, Alaska, anywhere there are Jews. Unlike most Christian missionaries, the Lubavitcher couples go to their destination and stay for life. In 1991 Yossi and Esty Greenberg arrived in Anchorage, a city of fifteen hundred Jews, a city where Esty must go to the airport to meet her weekly shipment of kosher food from Los Angeles, and—like the Israel Greenbergs of El Paso, like the Shalom Greenbergs of Shanghai—they will not leave. Chabad watchers guess that there are about two hundred thousand Lubavitchers in the world, of which perhaps 10 percent are in families on shlichus. Nearly one million children attend Chabad schools, camps, and other events every year, and at least as many adults are touched, in some way, by Chabad outreach. That's out of a world Jewish population of twelve million.

Lubavitchers are moved to their evangelism by their devotion to "the Rebbe," Menachem Mendel Schneerson, who died in 1994 at age ninety-two, after leading his sect for forty-two years. He took the Jewish notion of "shelichut" (in Yiddish, the Lubavitchers' language, "shlichus"), according to which one may deputize another to act in his stead, and began sending young rabbis and their wives on missions. As his shlichim, they would be like instantiations of the Rebbe himself. When they taught a class or hosted a Passover seder, it would be as if the Rebbe were teaching the class or hosting the seder. To be a shliach of the Rebbe became the greatest honor, and the best career, for a Lubavitcher man—and to be a shlichah, the greatest path for a woman. What this all means is that a Lubavitcher boy like Mendy, from a family of shlichim, sees manhood as the onset of his responsibility to save the souls of world Jewry.

The farther he travels and the more hardship he endures to bring Jews back to the fold, the nobler his efforts. Mendy is heir to a Chabad machismo, one that does not manifest itself in fistfights or leather jackets but is not really so different from other American machismos—it's a Jack Kerouac or Hunter S. Thompson kind of manhood, on the road, a gonzo Judaism, doing whatever it takes.

The next night, Wednesday, I went to Mendy's bar mitzvah party in the Marriott ballroom. By Lubavitcher custom, the party is midweek, to reduce the risk that any of the work associated with throwing the party will affect the leisure of Shabbos. At the entrance to the room were two small tables, one filled with place cards and the other laden with black felt yarmulkes, embossed on the inside with Mendy's name and the date. Inside, twenty set tables were arrayed around a parquet dance floor. Banquet tables were piled high with fruit. At the front of the room was a lectern with a microphone, a bar mitzvah cake iced with the words "Mazel Tov Mendy," and an electric keyboard. Behind the keyboard, playing background music as the guests mingled, stood Israel, a young rabbi who goes by the American name Raleigh (from the last two syllables of "Israel"). He teaches at the Rabbinical College of America in Morristown, New Jersey, and for extra cash he travels the world providing low-cost music for Lubavitcher simchas. About 150 guests, half of them Jews, no more than 20 of them Hasidim, were mingling. A few, I saw, were black. Someone pointed out the mayor, a white-haired man with a practiced high-beam smile.

In many ways, it was a typical American celebratory meal: place cards, round tables with white tablecloths, middle-aged men dressed by their wives, chicken. One man looked as if he would have liked producing coins from the ears of delighted children. Another man wore a toupee. As waiters served the main course, Raleigh played "Sunrise, Sunset," which I found funny, because it is not a traditional Jewish song but one Broadway composer's idea of a traditional Jewish song. Just as "Edelweiss," written by Rodgers and Hammerstein, is now considered an Austrian folk melody.

After dinner had been served, Mushky, Mendy's eleven-year-old sister, rose to the lectern as emcee. In ultra-Orthodox Judaism, there are things women may not do, like sing by themselves in front of men, which is considered immodest (although they may sing in a mixed choir), or read from the Torah in front of men; but there is no prohibition against working outside the home, dealing with finances, or learning or teaching anything. Women may speak publicly, too, and it was no doubt an intentional gesture by Rabbi Yossi to have his daughter be the main voice of the night. Lubavitchers are sensitive to criticism that their tradition is antifeminist; yes, women may have different roles, they say, but a Lubavitcher woman is no barefoot housewife. A rebbitzin—a rabbi's wife—is likely to be a prominent woman in her community, offering religious counseling, women's discussion groups, and Torah classes for women.

Mushky introduced the mayor, who greeted everybody and assured them that in Anchorage the "community holds out its arms to all religions, creeds, and colors." Mushky next introduced Mendy, who gave a speech on his parashah, Bo, the portion of Exodus that describes the last three plagues in Egypt, the locusts and darkness and killing of the firstborn; the commandment to celebrate the Exodus every year at Passover; and the commandment that men wear tefillin. He concluded his speech by saying a little something about his family's calling, to which, even before becoming a bar mitzvah, he had considered himself an heir.

"Many people ask me how it feels to be a shliach," Mendy said. "It's not always easy. When I was eight years old, I was at my father's office on International Airport Road, and a man came in looking for my father, but my father was not there. The man was looking for answers to questions. And all I knew to do was help the man put on tefillin. Because I knew that a synagogue was holy because it had a Torah in it, and a house was holy because it had a mezuzah on the door, and a Jewish man was holy because he put on tefillin. And when the man put them on, he began to cry. He said it was the first time he had put on tefillin . . .

"I want to thank my mother and father for raising me to be

a shliach of the Rebbe. And I know that when I grow older, I will be a shliach myself."

Mendy's last act was to recite the traditional bar mitzvah Maamer, or discourse. It's a speech in Yiddish, several pages long, that Lubavitcher boys are supposed to recite from memory on the day that they become b'nai mitzvah. Hasidim are the only large Jewish community in the world that still uses Yiddish regularly; without them, Yiddish would pass into an afterlife as a classical literary language, studied and admired by people with doctorates. As his watchful father unconsciously mouthed along, Mendy tore through the speech. He stumbled at one or two places, but otherwise he nailed it.

Mushky next introduced Rabbi Yossi, who had his own speech to give: "If Judaism means to be in a gulag for seven and a half years, as my father was, then so be it. If the survival of Judaism in this generation means to be twenty hours away from your parents in Israel, so be it. If the survival of Judaism means flying in kosher food, so be it." Someday, he said, Chabad may be called to spread Judaism beyond the earth's seven continents. "Mendy," he said, turning to his son, "I hope that your Chabad house will be the first one on the moon!"

Everyone laughed, and then Rabbi Yossi yielded the microphone to his wife, Esty, who gave a proud speech about her son the bar mitzvah boy, then offered a special thank-you to her friend Ron Hightower for flying to Los Angeles to get the food for dinner, thus averting a crisis. Since the World Trade Center was destroyed, not just anyone can ship large amounts of food via cargo shipping; only certain superauthorized shippers can. And the kosher butcher providing the food for this feast ships in boxes covered with Hebrew letters that are not, it turns out, on the list of authorized cargo shippers. So Ron, a pilot for Alaska Airlines, flew to Los Angeles to pick up the food himself, without which we would have had no chicken.

We all applauded Ron, and then Mushky introduced her little brother, Levi, who sang an a cappella rendition of "The Little Bird," a popular Hasidic parable about the Messiah. Then the room went dark, and Mushky introduced a video to be shown on the screen in the back left corner. As the movie began, white letters on a purple background said, "Bar Mitzvah Celebration of Mendy Greenberg, January 8, 2003— 5 Shevat 5763." The letters dissolved to scenes from Mendy's childhood, including a story on the local news about his first haircut, which by Jewish tradition comes for a boy when he is three years old. In another scene, Mendy was shown receiving the blessing of the late Rebbe, Menachem Mendel Schneerson, shortly before his death. And then the movie became about the Rebbe, with testimonials to the Rebbe's greatness from Yitzhak Rabin, Elie Wiesel, and Benjamin Netanyahu.

The dinner over, the speeches made, and the movie shown, it was time to dance. As Raleigh played klezmer, a circle gathered on the parquet, all male except for little Rivky—still young enough to dance in mixed company—in her father's arms. The men held each other's hands and danced in a circle, singing about Yerushalayim and shalom. It was mostly not Hasidim, but the Hasidim, the father and uncles, set the tone, giving the other men permission to dance in ways not normal for American men. Mendy was passed from one to the next, sitting on the shoulders of bigger men as they danced and sweated, shouted and whooped. For a minute, the mayor, overcome by the contagion of joy, lost his anchorman polish, threw his head back, and smiled broadly at the ceiling as he danced a horah. Next to the men, there was another, much larger circle, all female, holding hands and dancing. Outside that circle, three teenage girls did the Electric Slide, the old dance step from my high school years, as Raleigh the Hasid played on and on.

. . .

Thursday, Rabbi Yossi took me across Anchorage to show me
the land that had been bought for the new Chabad synagogue
and community center. The rabbi's operation had outgrown
his basement and dining room, and he was raising money for
the new building. Months later, reading Sue Fishkoff's book
about Chabad, I discovered that Rabbi Yossi had taken her on
the same tour and told her the same stories. I recognized in
her book the same mikveh, or ritual bath, where women immerse themselves after their periods (and where men too may
immerse themselves before Shabbos or their weddings or as
part of a conversion ceremony). Rabbi Yossi obviously has a
standard tour, but it is a good one, narrated with enthusiasm.
The mikveh was necessary because many Orthodox women
will not move to an area without one, so raising the money for
its construction had been a signal accomplishment.*

Later that day, Raleigh, the keyboard player, and Baruch,
the young Greenberg brother with the pregnant wife, invited
me to go snowmobiling with them, and so I found myself rid-
ing in the rabbi's minivan out to Big Lake, forty miles north
of Anchorage by Route 1, where in a little hut two very non-
Hasidic, non-Jewish men with a NASCAR swagger rented us
three snowmobiles. We cruised around the frozen lake for an
hour, all of it well past the 2:45 Alaskan sunset, wind blowing
through our helmets and through their beards. I was snowmobiling with Hasidim. ("*Snowmobiling with Hasidim*, A New

---

*I found the Fishkoff book, *The Rebbe's Army: Inside the World of Chabad-
Lubavitch* (New York: Schocken, 2003), to be an entertaining, smart, and even-
handed discussion of the Chabad movement. For a dissenting view, consider
the work of David Berger, who argues that the messianic strains in Chabad
place it outside the bounds of proper Judaism; see *The Rebbe, the Messiah, and
the Scandal of Orthodox Indifference* (Oxford, England: Littman, 2001).

Play by Neil Simon," I thought.) At one point, I noticed that
Raleigh, who was perhaps half a mile across the lake the short
way (it was six miles across the long way), had stopped and
turned off his snowmobile completely, no headlights and no
motor. He seemed to be standing next to the vehicle, and I
wondered if he needed help, if he was hurt or freezing, or if
anything on him or on the snowmobile was broken. I zoomed
over, braked to a stop, turned off my motor, and asked him
what was wrong.

"Nothing," he said. "I realized I had forgotten to daven
Mincha, so I just did it right here on the lake."

The next day, Friday, I arrived at about one o'clock, hoping
finally to chat with Mendy while it was still possible, before
sunset. In this house, once the sun was down I could not take
notes, as one does not write on Shabbos. Sensing I had a little
extra time and might be of some use before the interview, I
asked the rabbi if there was anything I could do for him.

"Read to Rivky," he said.

Rivky, of the little blond ringlets and permanent smile,
took me to her room, where she picked out a book about a
classroom of Jewish children following their teacher on a mag-
ical trip inspired by the mezuzah on their classroom door.
("That's the only book she ever wants to read," groaned
Mushky, her older sister.) I took Rivky back to the living
room, where Karen Greenberg, a friend (no relation) of the
Greenbergs, was studying a bit of Torah with Mendy. As
I began reading to Rivky, she nestled into me with the comfort of a child used to having strangers about.

When I finished the book, Rivky showed me her doll,
which made a noise when squeezed. But it was an electronic
noise, one dependent on some battery inside, and it was Friday evening around dusk in an Orthodox Jewish home. So
Mendy, distracted from his learning with Karen and possessed

of a new, adult sense of responsibility, leaned over to our sofa and told Rivky she had to find another doll. She began to tear up, then seemed to choose anger instead of hurt, and gripped the doll powerfully.

"No, it's Shabbos," said Mendy, trying to be patient.

A short tug of war ensued, and then I said, "Rivky, why don't you leave the doll here and go to your room to find another book for me to read to you?" She smiled, dropped the doll, and ran away.

But just as Rivky got back with another book, the rabbi found me again.

"I need to send you on a mission," he said, handing me a yarmulke from Wednesday's party. "Take this yarmulke and this challah and this bencher"—a small book containing the prayers and songs for before and after meals—"to Providence Hospital. Sid Klevens, room 416. He just had an operation and couldn't come the other night. Tell him the rabbi says Good Shabbos. And then hurry back, before sundown."

I got directions and drove to Providence Hospital, fifteen minutes away. Inside, with the help of a nurse, I found room 416, Sid Klevens. Sid, who looked about seventy years old, was sitting up in bed in a blue bathrobe monogrammed "SKK" across the left breast pocket. He looked fit and comfortable, ready to go home. He was bald and had a happy, hale face. I handed him the challah, the bencher, and the yarmulke, and I told him that the rabbi wished that he not be alone on Shabbos evening.

"Are *you* a rabbi?" he asked.

"No, but I study religion. I'm studying religion."

I could tell that he immediately interpreted my studies as rabbinic school and me as a student rabbi, because that made sense to him and because he wanted me to be a rabbi who had come to visit.

"Are you a Lubavitcher?" he asked.

"No."

"The Lubavitcher students, they used to come up to see me when I worked at the Air Force base. I'm an airplane mechanic, still am, work part-time. It's my hobby and my career. For forty years I've been tinkering with planes and getting paid for it. The Lubavitcher students, they used to come visit the Air Force base, where I was the Jewish lay leader. And before they'd come, I didn't keep kosher, you see, so I would throw out all the ham and things.

"I used to have a Hanukkah party on the base every year. And I'd take a little money out of the fund we had for Jewish activities and then invite all the Jews. And at the end of the party, we'd have more money than we started with. They felt guilty, you know. This was like putting money in the collection plate. So the priest said to me, 'We should let you run our Easter Mass!'

"Well, I wasn't going to do that, but I said I would hold a seder for them. They didn't know that the Last Supper was a seder, so I taught them. And that year, we had a seder, right before Easter, and read the story of the Exodus. With all the Christian chaplains.

"When I was in Germany on a base, I took a history class offered on the base. The teacher, he didn't know anything about Jewish history, and he got some things wrong. I corrected him, and he said, 'Klevens, from now on you get twenty minutes at the end of every class to teach the history of your people.' Of course, I didn't know that much! So I asked the rabbi at the base to borrow some books, and I just spent the rest of the course staying one week ahead of everyone else. Learned a lot that way, you know.

"I'm a member of the Reform temple here. I went in December to say the yorzeit for my wife." On the anniversary of a Jew's death, relatives say the prayer for the dead and light yahrzeit (anniversary) candles—"yorzeit," some Yiddish speakers say. "She died two years ago. They want me to say the yorzeit on the date she died, but I follow the Jewish calendar. They don't understand that."

I told Sid I was in town for Mendy's bar mitzvah, and I thought to ask about his.

"My bar mitzvah? I was in Boston. I was raised Orthodox, but don't ask me to read any Hebrew. I got kicked out of Hebrew school. I was a bit of a rebel. But they let me finish, and I did my bar mitzvah, and that was it. Didn't go back after that for a long time."

But he married a Jewish girl, the one who had just died. They had four children and eight grandchildren, and now there were some great-grandchildren.

I wished Sid Klevens a Good Shabbos and said I had to get back for dinner before sundown. I asked when he would be leaving the hospital, and he said a granddaughter was coming for him in a couple of days. As I left, he thanked me for coming.

When I got back, a little after sundown, I found the house filled with people and the dinner table set for twenty-five. Yossi asked me how it had gone, and I said that Sid and I had had a really nice conversation. Yossi and Esty looked at each other, and Esty said, "He comes here and is already a shliach!" —which I could tell she found a wondrous thing.

They were seating men at one end of the table, women at the other. Esty was a little embarrassed by this, but it was the rule of her father-in-law, who kept motioning for me to move to the men's section. Finally, I got what he was saying. "This isn't law, it's tradition," Esty told me. "Not our tradition. But my father-in-law likes it that way."

After the prayers over the wine and the bread, we began to

eat, and Shabbos dinner quickly became more and more celebratory, drunken, and loud, with Mendy and Levi and Chavi
and Chaya and Mushky and Rivky and Karen and Gavriel and
David Ben Ezra, who had moved with his bride, Sigrid, back
to Alaska to take over his parents' insurance company, and the
grandfather Moshe and his wife and Yossi and Esty and the
whole mishpochah. We did shots of Crown Royal and gave
numerous l'chaims, which Rabbi Yossi would punctuate
with "L'chaim l'chaim, Mendy!" or "L'chaim l'chaim, Dovid!"
Then, during a calm moment, Yossi asked his father, Grandpa
Moshe, who had a long, white beard and looked as old as the
Bible itself, to tell the story of his time in the gulag after the
war. Moshe finally agreed, shushed everyone with little waves
of his hand, and started speaking in Hebrew. Mendy, his
grandson, translated.

"We had Polish passports," Moshe said, "because after the
war Stalin said that the Polish people who had fled from the
Nazis into Russia could go back to Poland; he had no use for
them in Russia. And so a group of Lubavitchers, we got Polish
passports, paid a lot of money for fake documents, and were
trying to escape to the West. But the man who was supposed
to smuggle us across the border turned out to be a double
agent, and he led us right to the police station, where he
handed them all our fake passports. I was sentenced to
twenty-five years in a gulag in Siberia.

"But I would not work on Shabbos. I would work from
4 a.m. until sunset every day, but not on Shabbos. And for
every Shabbos I refused to work, I was sentenced to five days
of solitary confinement. So I would not work on Shabbos,
then on Sunday until Thursday I would be in solitary confinement, and then on Thursday I would get released, and I
would work on Friday, and then not on Saturday, and I would
go back into solitary confinement. This went on for two and a

half years, until I reached an agreement with the head of the camp. I would be allowed to pretend that I worked on Shabbos. I would go out in the camp with the others, and I would not be doing anything, but if they asked me what I was doing, I would say, 'Oh, I was sent over there to get something for him,' and I would always have to have something I was supposed to be doing, but would not really do anything. It was hard, remembering not to work when surrounded by two thousand people working.

"I would not eat treyf"—nonkosher food—"in the camp. And on Pesach, I would not even eat their bread. During Pesach, I lived on sugar alone.

"I discovered one guard was a Jew. I said to him one day, 'I don't understand Russian, tell me in Yiddish.' And he did, so I knew he was a Jew. I asked him right before Yom Kippur if he could get us a machzor for the holidays. We all had the daily service memorized, but not for the holidays. This was very dangerous, but he brought us one, and I copied it over. When the guards asked what I was doing, I said, 'Learning English.' They didn't know the Hebrew script from the English script. And we used that to daven on the holidays. A little later, a man who worked at the camp, not a guard but a man who worked there, brought us another machzor from his girlfriend, who had taken it from her father, who was religious. Nobody was supposed to have these, of course. And if this one had been lost, if she hadn't gotten it back to him, he would have had a heart attack. He couldn't get another. But I copied that one too. So we had two. And she got it back to him."

Moshe was paroled after seven years, and the guards were probably glad to be rid of him. So was Russia.

"I was in one of the first groups given permission to make aliyah to Israel. With six children, I went. I got to Israel, and

then to the United States. I gave one of our secret machzors to
the Rebbe as a gift."

Someone called out a question: "But doesn't Jewish law allow you to eat treyf in a situation like that, where your life
depends on it?"

Mendy translated the question, then translated his grandfather's answer: "You don't make calculations like that in the
gulag. You are going to die anyway. You're there for twenty-five
years. You have to hope for a miracle. You keep your religion."

The next morning, the day of Mendy's bar mitzvah service, I
arrived in the Greenbergs' basement about 10:45. They appeared to have started, even though the rabbi had promised
me that the 10:30 start time was only on "Chabad time."

So they were praying already, and there was a minyan and
more, maybe twelve men, with about as many women on the
other side of the mehitzah, the barrier that separates men and
women at prayer. Unlike the mehitzah at many liberal Orthodox shuls, this was a real mehitzah, with wood going up about
four feet and a curtain affixed above the wood on spokes, so
that you really couldn't look over and see the women, and they
really couldn't look over and see you. As the two hours passed,
people kept arriving, so that by the time the Torah was passed
around, first to the men's section and then, in a nod to gender
equity, to the women's section, there were maybe twenty men
and fifteen women there, plus more women and children running around upstairs preparing lunch.

The basement was just a big central room, behind which
were a bedroom and a bathroom. There were two lonely bookshelves pushed against the wall, which was painted a harsh institutional white, and there were long folding tables pushed to

the side. Otherwise, it was empty. It was a basement synagogue, like the storefront shtiebls of Brooklyn, and except for the unnatural bright light it didn't for a minute feel like anything else.

Mendy was leading the service. He had on his broadbrimmed hat and his special Shabbos jacket, longer than his normal coat and belted with a silk sash. He shuckled—rocked his torso back and forth from the waist—enthusiastically, not nervously. Nervous shucklers tend to be a little embarrassed by a display of religious abandon, but Mendy was an enthusiastic shuckler, pivoting energetically from the hip fulcrum, like a miniature model woodpecker. This style seemed original to Mendy rather than learned from his father, who spelled him from time to time. Mendy led about four-fifths of the prayer service, read about four-fifths of the weekly parashah, and read the entire haftarah.

He had not yet mastered all the tricks. Any good Chabad rabbi knows, for instance, that because it is all about outreach, about making the neophytes feel that their participation counts, one must periodically call out page numbers to let the newly Jewish Jews know where in the siddur they ought to be. Following a siddur is not easy, even for someone with excellent Hebrew. There are parts that are read aloud, signaling the beginning of a new section, and then there will begin a quiet part, which is done either silently, to oneself, or in a whisper, loud enough that people can hear you praying but not so loud that they can hear what you are praying. And then, when the leader thinks everyone should be ready, he'll bring it back to the head, as they say in jazz music, gathering all the players together again, away from their private riffs and solos and back into a tight prayer band, ready to begin a fresh part of the service. It's easy to get lost in all of this, and the people most likely to get lost are the very ignorant, whose Hebrew is either weak or nonexistent, and the very devout, who spiral inward with their praying and lose all sense of where everyone else is and when it's time to join together again.

Mendy forgot to call out his page numbers, but you forgave him that, because otherwise his hand was so sure: chanting with confident rhythm, sliding into the notes at times, other times hitting them perfectly—and sometimes holding off to prompt a sense of anticipation, as with the word "baruch," or "blessed," giving us a long *"baaaahh-"* and rounding the corner with an impassioned *"ruch!"*

When it was all over, the children threw hard candy at the bar mitzvah boy, the custom in all American synagogues, Reform to Orthodox. And Mendy smiled and collapsed into a chair, exhausted.*

Immediately afterward, everybody swung into action, transforming the synagogue into a banquet hall. We moved the mehitzah, put away the chumashes and the siddurim, and opened long folding tables for the fifty people who would eat the kiddush luncheon. One table became a buffet and was soon loaded with cholent, whitefish, lox, bread, hummus, salad, and soda.

After three hours of praying, all I wanted to do was eat, and only reluctantly did I greet the woman seated next to me. Deborah Ferrell, a massively barrel-chested black woman, told me that she had come to Alaska with her parents in the 1970s and had vowed to stay as long as they did. She was just back from Luxembourg, where in December she had set the world women's bench-press record by lifting 396.8 pounds. I asked her how she knew the Greenbergs.

---

*People wonder where the custom of throwing candy comes from. My friend Rachel Goodman makes an observation that I am sure is right: it comes from the aufruf, the tradition of honoring an engaged couple by calling them to the Torah in synagogue shortly before the wedding. At the aufruf, candy may be thrown at the couple. Now, as to where *that* tradition comes from . . .

"I'm converting to Judaism," she said, then went back to her bagel with egg salad.

When people were almost finished eating, Esty Greenberg stood up, holding aloft her little daughter, Rivky. We went quiet with anticipation. At first, Rivky needed a little prompting, but as her mother whispered something in her ear, she overcame an initial shyness, pumped her little fist in the air, and began.

"Sh'ma!" she yelled with a fist pump. Everyone repeated after her, "Sh'ma!"

"Yisrael!" And everyone cried, "Yisrael!"

"Adonai!" And we all cried, "Adonai!"

"Eloheinu!" "Eloheinu!"

"Adonai!" "Adonai!"

"Echad!" "Echad!"

(Which means: "Hear, O Israel! The Lord is our God, the Lord alone.")

Rivky smiled and giggled. Rabbi Yossi, his face red, fat, and merry, raised a glass of wine, looked down at his daughter, and said, "L'chaim l'chaim, Rivky!"

I did not have a chance to ask Mendy about his bar mitzvah, or about doing the Rebbe's work, until the following month, when I visited his boarding school in Queens. It was a frostbitten day in February, the snow from the great blizzard of 2003 not yet melted and still gathered by the roadsides of the Cambria Heights neighborhood. I drove slowly through the streets, watching black men lean exhaustedly on their shovels, resting from the labors of patiently moving snow from one place to another, trying to make room in their driveways for their Fords and Buicks. They stopped to look over at each other and smile hapless smiles. Past all the small, kempt front

yards, at the far east side of Cambria Heights, I found the Old
Montefiore Cemetery, a Jewish burial ground.

The visitors' pavilion at the cemetery entrance was not
large, the size of two school classrooms at most. Inside there
was a coffee machine, some card tables, and, against one wall,
a glass case holding books by and about the Rebbe. An old
man and his wife stood inside the entrance, speaking in
French. Out the back door of the pavilion was the graveyard,
and in the graveyard, one minute's walk from the entrance, set
back from roads with names like Benjamin Avenue and Abraham Avenue that separated districts of tombstones, was a
small building. It was the Rebbe's mausoleum, called the Ohel,
from the Hebrew for "tent" or "tabernacle."

I had planned to visit the Rebbe's grave after meeting with
Mendy, but I had arrived before the appointed hour of 1:30,
so I thought I might pay my respects first. Before exiting the
visitors' pavilion, I sat at one of the card tables and, with the
pencil and lined paper laid out for this purpose, wrote a letter
to the Rebbe. I asked for his advice about some religious questions I had been unable to resolve. I folded the letter up, left
through the back door, and walked thirty seconds down a
slight slope, dodging the headstones in my path, until I came
upon the two entrances to the Ohel, one for men and one for
women. Inside the men's entrance was an antechamber whose
only contents were a small bookshelf, the siddurim it held,
and, on the floor, canvas slippers. It is customary not to wear
leather shoes inside the Ohel, so I changed into slippers, removed a siddur from the shelf, took a suede yarmulke from
my pocket, and opened the door to the small courtyard in
the Ohel's center. The yard was modest, just big enough for
the Rebbe's grave, his wife's grave, and the ten or so mourners
standing around. I walked to the foot of his grave and said
a psalm in Hebrew; by tradition, one says the psalm that cor-

responds to one's age plus one, so mine was the 29th psalm. Then I said the Rebbe's psalm—his age plus one, so the 93rd psalm. I tore up the letter I had written, as is tradition, and scattered it over his grave. There were three-foot snow-drifts atop the two graves, his and his wife's, and torn letters on Mead composition paper sat placidly on the snow, neither scattering to the wind nor spreading outward in a blanket of prayer, just clumped together.

I left the Ohel walking backward, according to the tradition that one never turns one's back to the Rebbe. I walked slowly up to the visitors' pavilion. Inside, it was drafty, not much warmer than outside. I sat down and rubbed my hands to-gether, wondering whether it had been respectful or shameful to petition a dead rabbi who I didn't believe had any real pow-ers. I assured myself that it was an important scholarly en-deavor, because this was the kind of thing that Lubavitchers do every day, these acts of strident irrationalism, asserting their faith through constant prayers—over fruit, over wine, after one goes to the bathroom, when one wakes up in the morning. Hopeful trips to gravesides. Mendy's school had been built here because it was a good thing to learn close to the Rebbe.

Sitting in a cold metal folding chair, I heard Mendy before I saw him.

"Have you put on tefillin yet today?"

I turned in my chair to see the small boy, awaiting my reply.

"*Yet?*" I wanted to say. Such confidence the boy has in me. But instead I said, "No, I haven't."

Mendy motioned for me to follow. We went out a door, then right into another one, and we were inside his school: no more than a few cheaply built classrooms, stitched together and leaned, almost flush, alongside the pavilion, just well enough to keep the wind from blowing in, but not nearly well enough to look elegant or clean. I had seen the school from the outside and adjudged it nothing but trailers, ghetto class-rooms. On the inside were tables and books and a dozen small boys, some with the beginnings of peach fuzz on their upper lips, yarmulkes capping their heads. They were reading Bible and Talmud in Aramaic and Hebrew. Teamed in twos, each boy facing his chevrusah, or study partner, they talked excit-edly in Yiddish. They could have been memorizing, arguing meaning, or struggling with possible interpretations. The air held a quiet polyglot thrum. Two young men in their twenties were supervising, hopping from table to table and offering suggestions, perhaps etymological wisdom, keys to unlock the mysteries of Talmud; and the two young men were supervised by two older men with whitening beards. The boys were on lunch break, and there were some empty spaces at a table. Mendy produced a small velvet bag, removed his tefillin, and told me to roll up my left sleeve.

It had been one month since Mendy's bar mitzvah, one month that he had been a man. By being there at his school, and by not yet having davened with tefillin that day, I was giving Mendy the opportunity to fulfill the central mitzvah of his Jewish adulthood, which was to help me be a better Jewish man. For as it says in *Yalkut Bar Mitzvah*, the Chabad move-ment's 169-page guide for bar mitzvah boys, these are some of the things a boy must keep in mind on the day he becomes a bar mitzvah:

> On the day of Bar Mitzvah the boy joins the ranks of *Klal Yisrael*. Especially in light of the ruling of the *Ram-bam*, that each additional thought, speech, and action can sway the scales of merit and bring salvation and de-liverance, it follows that each additional Bar Mitzvah,

with its accompanying *mitzvos*, sways the scales of merit
for the Bar Mitzvah boy and indeed for *Klal Yisrael* and
the whole world.

It should be noted that the number 13 is numerically
equivalent to the word *"echad"* (aleph-chet-dalet), one.
This demonstrates that at the age of Bar Mitzvah, the
boy becomes one with his people, united in their
shlichus of making the world a *Dirah b'tachtonim*, an
abode for the Divine.

A Bar Mitzvah boy must always have in mind that:
(*a*) G-d created the heavens and earth and is therefore
the one and only *baal habayis* over the world. (*b*) The
portion of the world granted to each person rests in a
state of darkness and it is the responsibility of the individual to illuminate it and change it for the good.
(*c*) The first stage in *avodah* is the recognition that
through learning Torah (which is the word of G-d, as re-
peatedly emphasized in the Torah by the phrase, "And
G-d said . . ."), and keeping *mitzvos* (which are the will
of G-d), one may illuminate the world, as the verse
states, "a *mitzvah* is the candle and the Torah light."

Since the entire Torah is compared to the *mitzvah* of
tefillin, and in the light of the aforementioned, that the
boy should try to persuade others to keep *mitzvos*, it follows that every Bar Mitzvah boy should actively involve
himself in the Tefillin Campaign, using his new tefillin
not just for himself but to follow the Rebbe's directive
and put on tefillin with another Jew.

The Bar Mitzvah boy should accept upon himself to
keep *mitzvos*, not only in strict accordance with the rules
of the Torah, but he should also accept to do them in a
beautiful way, above and beyond the letter of the law—

middas chasidus—all being permeated with the light and warmth of *chasidus*.

It should be noted that in the last *Yechidus* (prior to the revelation of *Mashiach*) which the Rebbe gave to Bar Mitzvah boys—on the 17th of Shvat 5752—the Rebbe demanded that the boys use all their energy "to bring the days of *Mashiach*."*

To sum up: a bar mitzvah, having officially joined the community of Jews, is now responsible to help bring light to a dark world by studying Torah and keeping commandments, especially the commandment of tefillin, praying with small wooden boxes filled with scraps of prayer affixed to the arm and head. Furthermore, it is the bar mitzvah's obligation to become involved in the Tefillin Campaign, initiated shortly before the Six Day War in June 1967 by the late Rebbe Menachem Mendel Schneerson, to get as many Jewish men as possible to lay tefillin. The boy should undertake all these obligations not with bland dutifulness, but in a beautiful way, permeated by the warmth of Hasidus, pious religious fervor. Thus shall the boy fulfill the Rebbe's injunction to use all possible energy to hasten the arrival of the Messiah.

In more secular families, laying tefillin is hardly ever done; when it is, it's an exercise of passion or perhaps connoisseurship, a way to act like a really excited Jew, eager to go beyond the call or to venture into the more mystical aspects of the religion. But for Hasidic Jews like the Lubavitchers, as for most Orthodox Jews, tefillin is the most important obligation, exceeding even Torah study.

*Nissan Dovid Dubov, *Yalkut Bar Mitzvah: An Anthology of Laws and Customs of a Bar Mitzvah in the Chabad Tradition* (Brooklyn: Sichos in English, 1999), ch. 1.

The laws of tefillin are many and pertain to all aspects of this curious ritual, recalled every day in the Jewish prayer known as the Sh'ma—the beginning of which Rivky declaimed to much applause in her basement—which quotes Moses' proclamation in Deuteronomy 6:4–9: "Hear, O Israel! The Lord is our God, the Lord alone. You shall love the Lord your God with all your heart and with all your soul and with all your might. Take to heart these instructions with which I charge you this day. Impress them upon your children. Recite them when you stay at home and when you are away, when you lie down and when you get up. Bind them as a sign on your hand and let them serve as a symbol on your forehead; inscribe them on the doorposts of your house and on your gates."* The commandment to inscribe the Lord's words on the doorposts is fulfilled by mezuzot, the small, rectangular, decorative boxes containing passages from the Torah that Jews affix to the front doorframe, and sometimes all the doorframes, of their houses. The other command, to "bind them as a sign on your hand and let them serve as a symbol on your forehead," is fulfilled by the laying of tefillin, two small boxes, also containing bits of Torah, that are fastened to one hand and to the forehead by long leather straps that coil around the arm and once around the head.† If you have never seen one before, then at first glance a Jewish man wearing tefillin can

*From the Tanakh, or Hebrew Bible, as translated by the Jewish Publication Society (Philadelphia, 1985).

†The mezuzah is a rectangular box, often made of wood, glass, or ceramic, containing a piece of parchment on which is written the text of Deuteronomy 6:4–9 and 11:13–21. The two tefillin boxes, the tefillin shel yad (tefillin of the hand) and tefillin shel rosh (tefillin of the head), each contain the same four passages from the Bible: Exodus 13:1–10, Exodus 13:11–16, Deuteronomy 6:4–9, and Deuteronomy 11:13–21. In the tefillin shel yad, the prayers are written on one piece of parchment, while in the tefillin shel rosh they are written on four different pieces of parchment, each of which is placed in its own subcompartment.

look as if he is being attacked by two long, black vipers slithering up his bare arm and neck and resting their square heads on his hand and the top of his head.

As the Jew shuckles in tefillin, he might seem to be praying for release from these beasts holding him captive. The intertwining of a man and his tefillin appears atavistic and scary, especially because it seems to answer no purpose except fealty. The Jew is engaged in an act of deliberate, daily obedience, prescribed by God. *Yalkut Bar Mitzvah* devotes a detailed chapter to tefillin, describing their application in intricate detail:

> Just as in the physical sense tefillin are put on two months before the Bar Mitzvah to allow the boy to learn to perform the *mitzvah* properly, so too in the spiritual sense there must be a period of preparation. It is therefore correct that the Bar Mitzvah boys should learn the laws of tefillin . . .
>
> Among the positive commandments there is no *mitzvah* greater than the *mitzvah* of tefillin, and every Jewish male should be very careful to keep this *mitzvah* properly. One who is meticulous in the *mitzvah* of tefillin will merit long life, and is promised a share in the World to Come. The fire of *Gehinom* [hell] will not touch him and all his sins will be forgiven.

But what does it mean to keep this mitzvah "properly"?

One may not lay tefillin until the break of dawn, when it is possible to recognize one's friend at a distance of four cubits. Tefillin may not be laid after sunset. The tefillin must be removed from their bag in a respectful way, never shaken out. The tefillin for the head must rest above the hairline, or the hairline that existed when one had a full head of hair; if it rests on the forehead, one has not properly fulfilled the commandment.* The tefillin shel yad, of the hand, is to be worn on the left biceps, facing the heart. A left-handed person may wear tefillin on his right arm, but an ambidextrous person must wear them on his left. No wristwatch may be worn. The strap is to be wound seven times around the forearm, and it is Lubavitcher custom to divide the seven coils thus, according to *Yalkut Bar Mitvah*: "After winding the first coil on the forearm, a small space is left, then one winds two coils close to each other, then another space is left, and then we wind the final four coils. Then a final half-coil is made diagonally so as to wind the *retzuah* around the palm, resulting in the shape of an inverted letter '*Daled.*' The winding is always made in an out-ward motion away from the body." It is prohibited to speak be-tween donning the tefillin of the hand and the tefillin of the head. The tefillin should be kissed after they are removed. One may borrow another's tefillin without asking, but only in an emergency; and if one must adjust the straps, one is obligated to readjust them to the original size before replacing the tefillin where one found them. These things one may not do while wearing tefillin: eat a meal, enter a bathroom, pass wind. "The Baal Shem Tov said that a soul may descend to this world for no other reason than to do a favor for another Jew; it could be that putting on tefillin once with another Jew was the reason for descent of one's own soul—who can tell!"

As I laid tefillin in the chilly classroom trailer, Mendy pa-tiently talked me through the steps, offering help when

*In response to an inquiry from a Mr. D. Lent of Manchester, the Rebbe wrote, "The location of the tefillin on the head is, of course, explicitly given in the Shulchan Aruch. If you have noticed that a certain person seems to have placed the tefillin lower than the original hairline, it is undoubtedly because the hair of that person had receded, and from the distance it would have been difficult for you to determine actually where the original hairline was."

needed. (This was my second time, and the first had also been with a Lubavitcher.) He adjusted the straps on my left arm, deftly positioning them over my biceps into a Hebrew letter shin. He coached me all the way down to my middle finger, which gets its own wrap. He then placed the second box on my head and fastened it with the straps. Handing me a siddur, Mendy suggested that I recite the extended version of the Sh'ma. Reading slowly in Hebrew, I stumbled, and Mendy supplied the difficult word with an eagerness appropriate to his life's work, laying tefillin with Jews who may be saying the prayers for the first time. These Jews, Mendy hopes, will be inched just a bit closer to saying the prayers every week or every day, and maybe to donning Jewish garb, shunning impure foods, and ceasing work on Shabbos. Adjusting my tefillin straps and correcting my Hebrew, Mendy worked with the pride of a medical student giving his first shots.

After I had prayed, I unwrapped and kissed the tefillin and handed them back to Mendy, who zipped them into their velvet pouch. We walked back to the visitors' pavilion, away from his schoolmates. It had gotten colder, and an old disheveled man drew coffee from a large thermos on the card table.

Mendy sat down at the table with me, and I asked if boarding school made him lonely. He told me that he had gotten used to it.

"Before this year, I spent two years in Chicago," he said. "I was taught at home before that, by my father and girls who would come to Anchorage."

At Mendy's party in Anchorage I had met two such women, eighteen-year-olds, one from Los Angeles and the other from Baltimore. Young Lubavitcher women who are not yet married sometimes go where an elementary school or Lubavitcher family needs their help, then move on after a year or two.

I asked about the Maamer, the bar mitzvah discourse in Yiddish that Mendy had recited by heart at his party. He told me that the previous rebbe, the Rebbe's father-in-law, had recited the speech at his bar mitzvah, and that his father, the fifth rebbe, had recited it too—it had been written by *his* father, the fourth rebbe. But it was the seventh rebbe—the Rebbe—who had insisted that it be the custom for every Lubavitcher boy to memorize the Maamer, which takes for its theme the ultimate importance of tefillin, a favorite theme of the Rebbe's too.

"I studied about an hour a day for a month to learn the Maamer." It was not so difficult, Mendy said. He has known Hebrew script, in which Yiddish is written, since his mother taught it to him when he was three or four. He has been able to lead daily and Shabbos services, a small book's worth of Hebrew, since he was ten.

He told me that he had first said the Maamer here in Queens, where his first bar mitzvah service had been held, a week before the one in Anchorage. I asked why there were two. Because, he said, it was good that a bar mitzvah should be near the Rebbe's grave. I had heard that weddings were held at the Ohel, but I hadn't known about b'nai mitzvah. I was sorry I had missed it, I said. I flew all the way to Anchorage, not having known I could have seen Part I much closer to home. Mendy said that was okay—even his mother couldn't make the one in Queens.

I asked who had come to the simcha in Queens.

"A lot of my friends and relatives came to say mazel tov," Mendy said. "It was a little Hasidische farbrengen," a Hasidic gathering. "Mainly Lubavitchers, but also some other guys."

I had many more questions. For instance, had anyone in his family fallen away from the faith?

"Not by us."

I loved the way he spoke, the Yiddish and German inflections—"a Hasidische farbrengen," and "not by us," diction
imported from the German and Yiddish *nicht bei uns.*

I asked Mendy about the preparations for his bar mitzvah,
and he told me that he had learned more than what was required.

"I wanted to learn the halakah"—Jewish law—"about tefillin.
I wanted to learn a lot of it by heart. At thirteen, I am responsible for the whole Torah and mitzvos. I started preparing for
my bar mitzvah a half year before it. I first laid tefillin two
months before—that's what the Rebbe says a boy should do."

Mendy was one of fifteen boys at his school, but his time
with them was drawing to a close. The school year would end
in June, although that was not the way he put it: "I am not so
good with the English months. It goes . . . till about two
months after Pesach."

Saturdays were days off, and half of Friday, sort of.

"Every Friday, school ends early and we go to ten offices
in Manhattan and put on tefillin with them, give them a
paper about that week's parashah, give candles to the ladies.
School ends in the morning, and we go until Shabbos. I
can't go to other people's places"—offices claimed by other
young Lubavitchers. "I got my route from a friend."

What psalm, I wondered, will I say for the Rebbe when it
has been, say, 160 years since his death, and we have run out
of psalms?

"We're not going to have such problems, because the Rebbe
will be back to tell us."

At that, I must have had a surprised look on my face. The
question of messianism is fraught for the Lubavitchers: some
believe that the Rebbe was the Messiah and will return soon,
while others find such a belief laughable and embarrassing.
The issue could eventually lead to schism, and most shlichim,

who tend to be in the antimessianist camp, try to avoid the question. Seeing my surprise, Mendy quickly explained himself: "It's a mitzvah to think that the Rebbe *could* be back any second, even right now."

Good save, I thought. "Have you considered any careers besides shlichus?" I asked.

"Shlichim are what you really want. Nowadays, most newly married men are planning to go on shlichus."

"Who studies here?"

"Here, they have a first through eighth grade, then also here a special yeshiva for people over twenty, to become rabbis. Between that, they don't have yet. For high school, I could go to Chicago, Monsey, Detroit, France, Israel. There's a special school for kids of shlichim in Sfat.*

"You start Torah when you are five years old, then Mishnah when you are eight or nine. Talmud at the end of fourth grade or beginning of fifth grade, then higher levels of Talmud, more commentaries. You learn the Shulchan Aruch in different ways too."

At this point, it pays to remember that the languages needed for the study of Talmud are Hebrew, Aramaic, and a smattering of Old French, and at Mendy's yeshiva conversations are held in Yiddish and English.

"At 6:45 you wake up. At 7:30 some Hasidic philosophy before you daven, so when you daven you have a better mind, think about God with love . . . so the first thing you think about is God—not cows, not Pesach."

At 8:15, Mendy said, you daven Shacharis, the morning service. From 10:30 to 1:45 you have Talmud class. Lunch is at 1:45; then the fifteen boys and their teachers daven Mincha, the afternoon service, at 3:15; then go back to studying

*That is, Monsey, New York, and Sfat, Israel.

Talmud until 4:30. After a half-hour break, they relearn the Talmud portion by themselves or with their partners. From 5:45 to 6:30, they study the Shulchan Aruch, the important sixteenth-century legal code compiled by Joseph Karo. At 6:30, they daven Ma'ariv, the evening service. At 6:45 they eat dinner, and at 7:45 they study Hasidic philosophy.

There are thirty-six tractates of Talmud, Mendy explained, and you learn them all in detail between eighth grade and marriage. This year, Mendy and his friends were studying Tractate Pesachim, about the rules for Passover, "when you're allowed to eat the lamb and when to slaughter it," that sort of thing. There is no television, no field trips to the movies. During breaks in class, Mendy and his friends study the week's Torah portion along with the commentary by Rashi. They also squeeze in three chapters a day of Maimonides, another medieval rabbi, "because," Mendy said, "the Rebbe has a campaign to unite the Jewish world by learning Rambam," as Maimonides is known. For students too young to learn Rashi or Rambam, free time may be spent learning a mitzvah of the day. At that rate, they can learn all 613 biblical commandments in less than two years.

I asked Mendy if he was worried about not being part of the greater American culture, not seeing movies or reading comic books.

"No," he said. "Because I have friends who are like me."

These little pishers of thirteen, these future emissaries of the Rebbe, look forward to lives of shlichus, accompanied by their wives, whom they will find through prescribed channels.* As one of the cadre raised to do the Rebbe's work—"I

---

*Lubavitchers are not forced into marriages, but it is the custom to marry young, and there is a strong, worldwide network of yentas and eager mothers who arrange meetings. If a meeting goes well, a courtship begins, and engagement and marriage can follow in a matter of months.

have friends who are like me"—Mendy is not typical of anything except himself and those friends; most Orthodox Jews
are not black-hatted Hasidim, and most Hasidim are not
Lubavitchers, and there is a lot of skepticism and enmity di-
rected toward Mendy's kind.

Mendy had two b'nai mitzvah, one in Queens and one in
Anchorage; relatives flew from as far as Israel to celebrate; the
mayor came, local businessmen came, and, although I haven't
asked, I bet that Mendy cleared enough in gelt to cover a year
of tuition at a private university, the kind that he would never
attend. There was a big movie on a big screen, and the hotel
had to kasher an oven just to make the food edible for its religious guests. The invitations were engraved, not printed, and
on good stock. It was a party that they should not be ashamed
of in Scarsdale or Skokie. For Mendy, though, the really important thing is that he now knows the Maamer in fluent
Yiddish, lays tefillin daily, and is ready for a new boarding
school, where he will learn no algebra, science will be taught
from the Book of Genesis, and his knowledge of Talmud will
increase so that he can go to a more advanced yeshiva, where
it will increase some more. So that he can be a shliach, and go
with his wife to live for a lifetime in New Delhi or Des
Moines, asking Jewish men to lay tefillin and keep mitzvot,
asking Jewish women to separate meat from milk and light
candles on Shabbos, raising thirteen children to do the same.

6

The Grown-ups

In 1885, nineteen rabbis met outside Pittsburgh to write a short document stating the essential principles of Reform Judaism. The Pittsburgh Platform declared Judaism to be "a progressive religion, ever striving to be in accord with the postulates of reason," no longer having any need for the "entirely foreign" laws regulating diet or dress, nor any need for a return to Palestine. It was the document that said, in effect, We Jews are a modern American people, with no need for the Holy Land or its outdated customs. The platform's third plank reads, "We recognize in the Mosaic legislation a system of training the Jewish people for its mission during its national life in Palestine, and today we accept as binding only its moral laws, and maintain only such ceremonies as elevate and sanctify our lives, but reject all such as are not adapted to the views and habits of modern civilization." One of the ceremonies "not adapted to the views and habits of modern civilization" was the bar mitzvah, which in Reform Judaism was already being replaced by confirmation.

Several miles from where the Pittsburgh Platform was written, my ancestors were among the earliest members of Rodef Shalom, the Reform temple in which my father was raised. Neither my father's mother, Eleanor Jacobs Oppenheimer

Freund, nor her second husband, Jacob de Sortis Freund, was particularly interested in religion, so it fell to Oscar Oppenheimer, my father's grandfather, to drive my father every week to Rodef Shalom, where he was a member of the confirmation class of 1958. Oscar, though guardian of my father's Jewish education, was known to attend the Jewish temple and a variety of Christian churches, in particular a Presbyterian church, as if to have a foot in all possible doors to heaven.

My father's confirmation must have been palatable, but just barely, to my grandmother, who most of her life was suspicious of all things Jewish. Her father had come from Arkansas, her mother from Columbus, Georgia, and her accent had traces of the southern belle's lilt, with no sign of either western Pennsylvania or anything "Jewish." She spoke no Yiddish. She was petite, with narrow bright blue eyes, defiantly good posture, and thick white hair. Had she not been gifted with that appearance, she would have willed it. Eleanor Jacobs, then Eleanor Oppenheimer, then, at her death in 2000, Eleanor Freund—at every moment of her life, she might have been mistaken for a society matron of German extraction, and I think she would have been pleased by the confusion.

In trying to explain her mother-in-law, with whom she did not always have an easy relationship, my mother occasionally referred to "Mother Ellie's childhood in Lake Charles," Louisiana, which was supposed to be shorthand for the difficulties of being the rare Jew in a swamp town and of being raised by a woman, my great-grandmother Bessie Straus Jacobs, with an inflated sense of class (and thus a deep pride in her distant cousins the Strauses, who owned Macy's and were prominent in New York civic affairs). As I was given to understand it, my grandmother's discomfort with Jews, and with whatever Judaism she thought remained inside her, was the ineluctable by-product of her own mother's shame and frustrated ambitions.

My grandmother returned to Judaism only for her funeral, held in a Jewish chapel in Pittsburgh. She was buried afterward in West View Cemetery, in the Freund family plot, several yards from the Oppenheimer family plot. Her coffin had a wooden Star of David carved on the outside, and the rabbi distributed cards printed with the words of the Kaddish, so that Ellie's secular descendants could chant her to sleep in Aramaic.

In a circular way, it made sense that I would finish a year of b'nai mitzvah in Lake Charles, the town that had nurtured my grandmother's indifference to Judaism, and thus indirectly my parents' indifference, and thus the secular childhood that had made me so curious about b'nai mitzvah in the first place. I found that the kind of person I was raised to be, one who knew he was Jewish but had no firm sense of what that meant, so was inclined to wander the country looking for meaning in other people's Jewish rituals, made more sense once I had seen Lake Charles. It proved to be the kind of town where Judaism lives but where Jewish rituals die.

But then they rise from the dead. In April 2003 I attended the b'nai mitzvah of Jacob Ecker and Rena LeJeune, sixty-five and sixty-one years old, respectively, both adult converts to Judaism. Whereas my grandmother was a Jew who would have preferred to be a German or a Cajun, here were a German and a Cajun who had decided to be Jews. (Rena, it turned out, had only married a Cajun.) For them, a bar and bat mitzvah were affirmations of their membership. Like immigrants to Israel who join its army, they wanted to have the full experience, proving beyond question that they belonged. I doubt that they knew that Lake Charles Judaism had until recently re-

jected the bar and bat mitzvah, and that when my grandmother was a child, any parents in town who wanted a bar
mitzvah for their son might be seen as not the right kind of
Jews. But if you want Judaism to persist in a small, poor back-
water, you're grateful for all the ritual you can get. The bar
mitzvah returned to Lake Charles—with the bat mitzvah
now—and it is not considered antiquated or embarrassing,
but desirable and joyous, a simcha, a bracing stimulant to remind everyone that Judaism endures.

Once I decided to go to Lake Charles, I found it mentioned
everywhere. The playwright Tony Kushner grew up in Lake
Charles, I read, and his widowed father, an orchestra conduc-
tor, still lives there and belongs to Temple Sinai—although he
was out of town the week I visited, in New York for Tony and
his partner Mark's commitment ceremony. In the play *The
Last Night of Ballyhoo*, by Alfred Uhry, better known for *Driving Miss Daisy*, the character Peachy Weil is described in the
dramatis personae as "a visitor from Lake Charles." The singer
Lucinda Williams was born in Lake Charles and wrote a song,
"Lake Charles," about a wandering man, born in Texas but
trying to make his way east: "He had a reason to get back to
Lake Charles / He used to talk about it / He'd just go
on and on / He always said Louisiana / Was where he felt
at home." An even greater song, The Band's "Up on Cripple Creek," mentions Lake Charles in the first verse: "When I
get off of this mountain, you know where I want to go? /
Straight down the Mississippi River, to the Gulf of Mexico
/ To Lake Charles, Louisiana, little Bessie, girl that I once
knew / She told me just to come on by, if there's anything she
can do."

Lake Charles is better known than any town of its medium size and middling prestige ought to be. Its seventy thousand residents work in riverboat casinos and pollutive chemical plants. Fine old houses line the lake, but the downtown is decayed and vacant. On the outskirts, strip malls slice up the mudbanks, and black people live in small houses on stilts. The mosquitoes are loud and hungry.

I first visited Temple Sinai on an April Monday, four days before the b'nai mitzvah I'd come to see, and my immediate impression was that the temple, like the town, had an admirably swollen opinion of itself. From the outside, Temple Sinai looked like a grand brick Romanesque cathedral that had been shrunk to miniature proportions, as if in punishment for uppity notions. A photograph I took of the building with my car in front makes the car look grotesquely large, because it seems impossible that a building of such architecture could be so small. As I stood with my back to the sparse traffic on Hodges Street, there was a silk-screener's shop to the left of the temple and a Masonic temple to the right. It was a quiet block, and I could not tell if this part of downtown was still downtown at all.

Above the doorframe were the Ten Commandments carved in stone, and above them was a stained-glass window under the temple's eaves, covered in Plexiglas, a precaution against vandals. To the right of the front door was a lantern, and beneath that a whitewashed wooden plaque with black lettering that read "C. 1904 TEMPLE SINAI." Beneath that was a metal plaque attesting to the building's placement on the National Register of Historic Places. A wheelchair ramp hugged the left side of the temple's facade, rising right to the front door. Near the bottom of the ramp, in the left half of the front lawn, was a sign that spelled out, in changeable white plastic letters,

TEMPLE SINAI

RABBI LEO R. WOLKOW

SHABBATH SERVICES
FRIDAY 6:00 PM

GOD BLESS AMERICA
SHALOM*

At the foot of the sign, I leaned down to pick up a discarded drinking cup from Popeye's Chicken and Biscuits. "We Do Good Ba-You," it said. The air was about sixty degrees at dusk, with no humidity, unusual for April. Far off, thunder rumbled. The temple was dark inside. I picked up the spent paper drinking cup and crumpled it into my pocket, restoring the lawn's dignity, I hoped.

On the far right quoin, past the lantern and the plaque, was an inlaid cornerstone of gray marble, set into the red brick. It said:

TEMPLE SINAI

ERECTED 1903.

L. KAUFMAN, PRES.

A. LEVY, VICE PRES.

M. MULLER, SEC.

D. REIMS, TREAS.

The social hall, offices, and rabbi's study were all in a newer wing that sat at a right angle to the sanctuary, jutting out to

*The "Shabbath" may seem erroneous, but it reflects an old Hebrew pronunciation, with the dental, lisped *th* at the end; in Ashkenazic pronunciation, this sound became the *s* of Shabbos, and in Sephardic pronunciation it became the *t* of Shabbat.

the left. Two walls of shrubbery formed the third and fourth sides of the temple's garden, a grassy courtyard nestled into the elbow of the sanctuary and the addition. A small gate set into a gap in the shrubs was open at a careless angle, and through the gate was a garden with three benches, arrayed in a semicircle around a birdbath and a small, struggling purple-leaf plum tree. Ceramic tiles decorated the seats of the three benches, each tile a painted Star of David with the name of a congregant written across it. At first, I assumed these were the names of big donors; then I realized these were the names of all the temple's members.

In the corner of the garden, diagonally across from this grotto of benches, tree, and birdbath, a small abstract bronze sculpture was hidden in the shadows of some bushes. I walked over to see that it was perched on a mossy boulder, and there was a plaque that said, "IN MEMORIAM, DAVID BARNHART, MAY 15, 1970." In front of the sculpture, there was a circular disk, perhaps eighteen inches in diameter. It was painted with a heart, and across the heart were the words, "A day that will live in our hearts forever. Always remember. September 11, 2001."

There wasn't much more to see at Temple Sinai. My meeting with the rabbi and his b'nai mitzvah students was not until the next day. So I took a stroll around town. I found the Calcasieu Parish Courthouse, about a quarter mile away. It was built in 1911 and was also on the National Register. It was wartime—we had just invaded Iraq—and a yellow ribbon was tied around each of the two Doric columns that anchored the courthouse. On the expansive front lawn, facing Ryan Street, there was a large statue, probably forty feet high, and at its pinnacle a green, rusted copper man held a flag and leaned into the wind. I searched the base in front of me, looking for an explanation, and I found these words:

THE SOUTH'S DEFENDERS

1861–1865

OUR HEROES

and in front of that, on the grass, a marble vase held fresh, dyed-red carnations, a sign that someone who cared had just stopped by.

The next afternoon, I went to the temple to meet Jacob and Rena, who were cramming Hebrew in the last days before their simcha. When I arrived, Jacob was not yet there, and the rabbi was in his office (I later learned) tutoring Sam, age twelve, son of recent Jewish arrivals in town and due to become a bar mitzvah the following year. In the social hall, sitting patiently, as if for a doctor's appointment, was a slender woman with brown hair, highlighted in places. She wore big glasses, and her ocher T-shirt was decorated with pictures of wild horses. With her unusual eyewear and the fauna shirt, she had something of the free spirit about her.

"Rena?" I said.

"Mark!" she replied.

The rabbi had told her I was coming, she said. What would I like to know?

So that I could better take notes, we moved from the seating area to a long cafeteria table. I wasn't sure where to begin. What makes a Christian-born Louisiana grandmother in her sixties become a bat mitzvah?

"My father was Presbyterian, from Massachusetts," she said. "He left home at about sixteen to go out on his own, and then he went to Florida, then Texas—he was a carpenter—then ended up here, where I was born. I got married, and my first husband was a Baptist. We went to an interdenominational church. He died after we were divorced."

I asked for that story and soon regretted asking—it involved a car falling on her ex-husband as her young son watched:

"My son, who was thirteen, couldn't get the jack to lift it off him. So he ran to the neighbor's house, but it was the middle of the day, nobody was home. So he ran to another neighbor's house, but nobody was home there. He went inside and called the operator, who called the fire department. And they finally got there. This whole thing took *hours*. And so my son was in shock.

"He couldn't be angry at me. He tried that for a while, but it just didn't work. So he got angry at God. A couple years later, a friend of his—well, someone he thought was his friend—took him down to shoot up Lake Charles with a rifle"—she meant Lake Charles the lake, not Lake Charles the city. "Thank God no one was hurt, and I went to court with him. It was a first offense, and the judge offered to let him go if he went to three years of counseling, plus restitution. We gladly took that. And now he is raising two children and doing great!

"I have a son with two sons and a daughter with two daughters. I met my present husband at my thirty-year high school reunion. He had sat behind me in class in high school, but he was the extrovert and I kept quiet."

It was the divorce from her first husband that led her to Judaism: "I had left my first husband and I went to live in a women's shelter, and that's where I met the rabbi"—Sherman Stein, then the Lake Charles rabbi. "The synagogue was quite involved in the women's shelter, and it still is. He tried to find me a place to live, and that's where Misty Green entered the picture." Misty Green, a member of Temple Sinai, invited Rena to move in with her while Rena attended nursing school.

"Misty lived in Hackberry, Louisiana, south of Lake Charles," Rena said. "It grew from the shrimping industry. Misty was a shrimper. She owned a shrimping boat, until it sank." The two women would drive to Lake Charles to see Rabbi Stein and attend services at Temple Sinai. "I started going to temple with her, and for the first time I didn't have to question everything I was hearing. It was the first time I was allowed to question, but also the first time I didn't have to. It all made sense. I fell away from it for a while, while I was working three jobs, but I came back after September 11."

By this time, Rabbi Leo Wolkow had joined us at the table. He listened with a proud smile. When Rena was done with her story, she turned to the rabbi and said that she wanted to show him the tallis that Jacob, the bar mitzvah "boy," had bought for her as a bat mitzvah gift. It was made of red and white silk and had scenes of Jerusalem embroidered on the back, with the prayer for the tzitzit stitched on the atarah. The rabbi held the tallis up in front of her, pulling it taut so that she could see the prayer, which she read aloud, haltingly. Then she draped the prayer shawl about her shoulders and sat down again at the cafeteria table, ready to practice.

As I took notes, I sneaked peeks at the rabbi, and I decided that he looked like a cross between Tevye the Milkman and Mr. Potato Head: short-waisted, bald, white-bearded, blue-eyed, stout (though less stout than before, thanks to the Zone diet, he told me). He looked like a fuller, puffed-up version of Jacob Adler, the student rabbi from Fayetteville. They all looked like rabbis. Perhaps rabbis grow to look like rabbis, the way people grow to resemble their dogs. They put on some pounds, grow beards, go bald, are indifferent to fashion. Rabbi Leo was wearing a navy blue T-shirt tucked into long blue shorts. From ten feet away, his outfit looked like a one-piece navy jumper. I half expected to look down and see attached pajama feet.

Rabbi Leo listened to Rena read her share of the week's haftarah, then the portion of Ma'ariv that she would lead on Friday. When the rabbi corrected her—which he did, ruthlessly and often—his voice came out of one side of his mouth. There was something pleasing about the palpability of his gnarled, thick words. They seemed substantial. I decided that Rabbi Leo's rumpled uniform and vocal tics served a good purpose: they said that the only things he bothered being careful with were his ideas.

"By Wednesday, you gotta have a speech," he said to Rena, "so I can see what you're doing. You got something there?"

Rena produced from her purse two pieces of paper. She seemed a little afraid to show the rabbi their contents. Before handing the pages over, she had to say something about them, in the manner of a student turning in a mediocre exam: "You had given us a list of things to consider as converts, and I started with them, and tagged some of my own stuff on. Anyways, it starts with 9/11."

Rena placed the pages side by side on the table. Rabbi Leo leaned over her and read the speech silently to himself. She sat with her hands clasped anxiously in her lap. I thought that this must be the first essay she had written since that high school class, seated in front of her future second husband decades ago.

"Okay," the rabbi said, a bit glumly.

"I thought I'd add some more on."

"Yeah, that's just the beginning," the rabbi assured her.

"I don't do your speech thing," Rena said. "Jacob walks in with five pages! I don't do that."

The rabbi nodded in sympathy, then asked me if I knew

that southwest Louisiana is the rice capital of the United
States and that the United States is the second-largest rice pro-
ducer in the world.

I hadn't known that, I said.

Lake Charles is about an hour and a half west of Lafayette,
which is the heart of Acadiana, the rabbi said. The next day,
he and his wife, Helen, were going to visit friends in Kaplan,
Louisiana, named after its Jewish founder, a Russian immigrant named Abrom Kaplan. Did I know that this was the bi-
centennial of the Louisiana Purchase *and* the centennial of
Temple Sinai? I hadn't known that either. The rabbi looked at
me as if I had a lot to learn.

A retired Reform rabbi from Chicago, Rabbi Leo was persuaded in 1999 to fly to Lake Charles to lead Rosh Hashanah
services. Retired rabbis often lead High Holiday services in
towns too small, or too far from the centers of the Jewish
world, to have a regular rabbi; Rabbi Leo was supposed to go
to Bombay that year, but the trip fell through, and at the last
minute he agreed to go to Lake Charles. The holidays were on
a Friday, and he arrived in Lake Charles on Wednesday.

"I had a poor night's sleep, and the next morning, I called
Helen. She says, What's the matter? I don't feel good. I call
Paul, my cardiologist, who as a kid I bar mitzvahed, and just
a month ago I was at his kid's bar mitzvah. And he says get
to the hospital. I call Bruce"—Bruce Katz, a member of
Temple Sinai—"who had just had dinner with the whole
mishpochah—you know, the Davidsons—and I said what's a
hospital that has a good heart division? Bruce says he's a young
guy, what does he know about hearts?

"It turns out St. Patrick's is good at hearts; DeBakey did
some training there. So I go there, Bruce goes with me. I'm

talking to Bruce, as he tells it, and then one minute I stopped talking. And it goes code blue, red, bells go off! I come to, I look up, and I say, 'Doc, what happened?' He says I had a heart attack. 'So what do you propose I do?' 'Angioplasty . . .'

"They stick in a stent or two, and I feel good. When are they going to let me out? I want to know. They wouldn't let me out until Sunday. I say, 'Can't you let me out for a couple hours on Saturday, I'll do yontuv, then come back?' No. So Bruce conducted Friday and Saturday, and I did Yom Kippur next week.

"So that's how I got here. So Bruce said, 'Why don't you move here?' I said, 'I just retired! But I tell you what. I know this guy in Alabama who's retired, but he does one day a month at some synagogue in Alabama. If you want me to do once a month, I'll do it.' So I started off Friday to Sunday. But the planes from Houston are unreliable, so if they delay the plane, it means I miss services Friday night. So maybe I should come on Thursday. Well then, I say, I'm here on Thursday, midweek, I might as well do something Thursday nights. So we start what we call Schmooze on Thursday nights. The first one I did was about Uhry's play *Last Night of Ballyhoo*, which mentions Lake Charles, and which has negative connotations for some. I call the talk 'The Ballyhoo about *Ballyhoo*.' I got twenty people. Now, I do Schmooze, sometimes it's three or four people. But I started teaching Hebrew Thursday night too. Now I teach it on Saturday. I figured if I do Sunday school, I don't get home until eleven o'clock Sunday night, so I stay until Monday. So now Tuesday and Wednesday is my weekend!"

Jacob Ecker arrived for his practice session. He had silver hair parted on the left and wore gold-rimmed glasses, neatly pressed trousers, and a short-sleeved Oxford shirt. He looked like a kind high school physics teacher, a bit square but entirely decent. I wanted to interview him right away, but he had only a few minutes to spare and wanted to practice his bimah skills, the removal of the Torah scroll from the ark and reading aloud. We could talk tomorrow, he said.

I followed him into the sanctuary, which, like the temple's exterior, suggested a grand cathedral shrunk down to proper small-town size. The miniature scale felt kitschy. There were two rows of eleven short pews each, enough to hold about two hundred crowded people—but up above, in the balcony, sat a pipe organ befitting a much larger congregation.

I sat in the front pew, and Rabbi Leo sat four rows behind me, so he could make sure his pupils' voices carried. Jacob and Rena went onstage. They faced each other at a distance of three feet and held each other's tallisim at eye level, so the prayer could be read from the atarah, the tallis's embroidered collar; each in turn read the prayer, then bowed his or her head so the other could drape the tallis over the shoulders. They had divided the Friday night prayer service into sections: each read aloud the Hatzi Kaddish, then each took half the extended, full-length Sh'ma. Rena read the shortened English version of the Amidah, or "standing" prayer, read while standing, which begins, "We praise you, Lord our God and God of all generations: God of Abraham, God of Isaac, God of Jacob; God of Sarah, God of Rebekah, God of Rachel, God of Leah; great, mighty, and awesome God, God supreme."

Jacob and Rena had each decided to read (not chant) portions of their birth parashahs, rather than the week's parashah. Thus, instead of hearing Acherei-Mot, the section of Leviticus that most congregations would hear that week, we would hear Jacob read a portion of Ki-Tavo, the passage from Deuteron-

omy in which God lists all the horrors that will befall the Is-
raelites if they do not keep God's commandments, and Rena,
a portion of Sh'lach, from the Book of Numbers, in which
God decrees that Israel's entry into the land will not happen
for forty years, during which time the entire living generation
will die out. To tie the service to the week of the Jewish calendar, they would each recite in Hebrew a portion of that week's
haftarah, from the Book of Ezekiel.

They removed two Torah scrolls from the ark, one for each
of them, and stood at the bimah, each taking a turn with the
Hebrew words, then politely stepping back, careful to share
the spotlight, like teachers team-teaching a class—with their
master teacher, Rabbi Leo, giving them tips from the back of
the lecture hall.

"The vowels weren't sharp in that at all," he said, interrupt-
ing Rena.

"*D'var law-more*—"

"LAY! *LAY*-more!" Rabbi Leo yelled. "L-A-Y M-O-R-E. If
you're going to write it in English, write it in English you can
understand. You'd do better just learning the Hebrew trop."

As Rena read her haftarah portion, the rabbi stopped her at
every line, correcting every mispronounced vowel. Rena
looked as if she was about to cry or scream, with some mix of
frustration and anger.

Thursday afternoon, sitting on the sofa in his hotel room,
Rabbi Leo told me that for years he had avoided doing adult
b'nai mitzvah, which have become rather trendy in recent
years. They were shallow, feel-good, not real Judaism. "I didn't
like shtick," he said. But he mellowed as the years went on. If
it gives them meaning, he figured, who was he to say no? He
decided that if the oldsters would agree to do some real studying for the event, then he would officiate.

But only if they really studied. "I made an eighty-three-year-old read Torah, chant haftarah, and come to classes with the kids," the rabbi said, proudly. "And tomorrow night, they're reading Torah, haftarah, giving speeches."

In traditional Judaism, an official called the gabbai stands next to the Torah reader, the ba'al k'riyah, and corrects every mispronunciation. Jews go to synagogue, the teaching goes, to hear the word of God as given at Sinai, not as improvised by a lazy reader. Jacob Ecker's Hebrew was respectable enough that he was spared the rod, but Rena LeJeune was getting a taste of Rabbi Leo's wrath, and it surely provoked humiliation more than reverence for Torah.

It was, of course, unfair of Rabbi Leo—who knew Rena had been converted rather painlessly, by a less rigorous rabbi, one who required a minimum knowledge of Judaism and only the slightest facility with shortened Hebrew prayers—to be a martinet about Torah. Having been exposed only to a lax kind of Reform Judaism, Rena was now studying under Rabbi Leo, who was by comparison a traditionalist, uncomfortable with the compromises that most Reform rabbis—certainly every other rabbi to pass through Lake Charles—accept as necessary to Reform. It was like having your regular teacher retire mid-year, only to get a substitute who graded twice as hard.

This variation among rabbis, from the pushovers to the firm hands to the taskmasters, is typical of the bewildering diversity of Jewish congregational life. Not only does every branch of Judaism have its own prayer books and liturgy, but every synagogue is free to add or subtract from the prayer book at whim. There are at least a dozen tunes for traditional Jewish prayers like Yigdal or Adon Olam, and the choice of tune can vary by region or even synagogue. Cantors and rabbis learn the hazzanut of their teachers, so turnover in seminary faculty has consequences across the country and even the world. Students trained in a new song style fan out to congregations and teach bar and bat mitzvah students tunes that parents hardly recognize and that grandparents find completely foreign.

The liturgical freedom is liberating, and it is not incidental to the intellectual freedom that drew Rena to Judaism. But as she stood on the bimah taking Rabbi Leo's stern corrections, Rena may have wished for a quick escape to Catholicism or to the Episcopal Church, where the language is English and where the prayers change at most once or twice a century, not with every incoming priest.

The diverse rabbinic styles allow for the shopping that brings some families to Emanu-El in New York City, others to Orthodox minyans in basements. You can bargain-shop bar mitzvah classes the way you can a health club or a mobile phone plan: lowest cost, shortest commitment, best customer service. The free market means high-end, cut-rate, and everything in between, and it also means some people will opt for do-it-yourself: children being tutored by parents, adults by their friends. But in Lake Charles, there was only one man selling what Rena and Jacob were buying; to have a bar mitzvah was to have a Rabbi Leo bar mitzvah.

The next day, I met Rena and Jacob at the temple again, and this time I had a chance to talk with Jacob a little more. It felt strange to me that I had already seen him rehearse his bar mitzvah parashah, yet I had no idea how old he was, what he did for a living, whether he had children.

Jacob was born, I learned, on August 23, 1937, and grew up in Harrah, Oklahoma, not far from Oklahoma City. His family were regular but not particularly devout members of Harrah Methodist Church, but his mother's sister Clara was one of the town's leading church ladies, "one of the people who did everything," as Jacob put it. While at the University of Oklahoma, in Norman, Jacob attended a Methodist church and was a member of the student Wesleyan society.* In 1959, after graduating with a degree in chemical engineering, Jacob moved to Brandenburg, Kentucky, to work for Olin Chemical Corporation. The man who hired him was also a Sooner, an OU grad, which is why he had been sent to Oklahoma to do the recruiting. He took a shine to Jacob, enough so that once back in Kentucky he introduced the new employee to his daughter, Carolyn Bess McReynolds, known as Betsy. Betsy suited Jacob, and Jacob suited her. In December 1969, five months after first meeting, Betsy and Jacob married in Brandenburg Methodist Church. Jacob jokes that his father-in-law "recruited me for two jobs."

In 1972, the Eckers moved to Lake Charles, where Jacob had found a job in the chemical plants. In their new town, they joined the Episcopal Church. Jacob had always admired Episcopalians as the progenitors of the Methodists, as if somehow the Episcopalians were the real deal. Jacob and Betsy attended St. Michael's Episcopal Church for fifteen years, and for three years Jacob was a member of the vestry.

I asked Jacob how he had come to Judaism.

"When I was at the University of Oklahoma, I never knew anything about it except where the building was. But I had a buddy who was the first person I knew ever to be Jewish. A lot of little old ladies in that town would rent rooms to students or prepare meals for students. So we became buddies because we went to the same old lady for lunch. He was at least Conservative, maybe Orthodox, because I remember him telling

---

*John and Charles Wesley were the founders of the Methodist movement in the Church of England; institutions that bear their name, like Wesleyan University in Connecticut, have historic ties to the Methodist church.

me the things he couldn't eat. I thought why couldn't he eat cheeseburgers! And then when he told me he couldn't eat shrimp, I thought, *You've got it all wrong!* And I've often thought, if I could get ahold of him, *Look what you led me to!*"

By the mid-1990s, Jacob had pretty well fallen away from the Episcopal Church, and he found his way to Temple Sinai. It was August 1994 when he "first wandered in the door. There was a public concert—maybe there's a better word? There was an Orthodox rabbi from New York who is known as the Singing Rabbi—a good friend of Barbara and Tony De-Bartolo's—so he came to visit them, and they put a notice in the paper: 'Everybody is invited to come see the Singing Rabbi.' So my wife and I came."

I never learned who the DeBartolos were, but after some digging I decided that the "Singing Rabbi" was Shlomo Carlebach, the great writer of Jewish folk melodies who in the sixties and seventies had presided over the House of Love and Prayer, the famous hippie shul in San Francisco.

Jacob enjoyed the concert, and afterward he said to his wife that he might enjoy returning on a normal Friday night to learn more about the temple. Jacob and Betsy went to services the next Friday, only to find that the part-time rabbi was out of town, in Houston. Jacob went again the next week and heard the rabbi, and he liked what he heard enough to go again: "And probably the third or fourth time, he led one of the services that had a particularly interesting meditation in it. He did it as a silent meditation that night."

Jacob reached across the table for a stray copy of *Sha'arei Tefila*, or *Gates of Prayer*, the Reform prayer book used at Temple Sinai. He opened the siddur, flipped through it until he found the right page, and read the meditation aloud: "Prayer invites God to let His presence suffuse our spirits, to let His will prevail in our lives. Prayer cannot bring water to parched fields, nor mend a broken bridge, nor rebuild a ruined city; but prayer can water an arid soul, mend a broken heart, and rebuild a weakened will."

Jacob was moved by this passage: "I said hey, I want to hear more of this." He went the next week, and the next. He became a regular, a lapsed Methodist and Episcopalian at the Jewish temple. But he was still going to the Episcopal church, because he had a good friend, a blind man thirty-five years his senior, whom he had begun driving to church. So he was going to Temple Sinai on Friday nights and St. Michael's on Sunday mornings, and soon he found that he was going to the Episcopal church "primarily to be with my friend." His friend died in 1998, and two years later Jacob began studying for conversion.

In the spring of 1999, Jennifer Weiner, Lake Charles's last full-time rabbi, left. The future of the Lake Charles pulpit was uncertain, and so was Jacob's conversion. That fall, with a little luck, a retired rabbi from Chicago was persuaded to come lead High Holiday services—but when he got to town, he had a heart attack, and so it did not seem a good time to talk to him about converting. But the rabbi made a full recovery. Soon he was back for a weekend, and Jacob found him. "It's going to be a lot of work," Rabbi Leo said. "Okay," Jacob said.

These are the converts, or, as they now say, "Jews by choice," whom I have known: David Brion Davis, the historian of slavery; Robert Forbes, another historian of slavery; Laura Leonhardt, a lawyer in New York who was two years ahead of me in college; Susan Shepard, a friend of my parents; and Robert Johnston, a labor historian. And these are some converts I know of, but do not personally know: Nell Carter, the late

Broadway actress whose performance in the revival of *Ain't Misbehavin'* made me want to be an actor when I was fourteen; Jamaica Kincaid, the Antigua-born novelist; Elizabeth Taylor; Sammy Davis Jr.; Kate Capshaw, the actress who married Steven Spielberg; and Nikki Schieler, the *Playboy* model who married Ian Ziering, the actor who played the louche Steve Sanders on *Beverly Hills, 90210*. In every case, the conversion was prompted, shepherded, or hastened by Jewish friends or immersion in a Jewish community. Rob Forbes and Laura Leonhardt each had dozens of Jewish friends. David Brion Davis married a Jewish woman, as did Robert Johnston (though Johnston's wife was herself a convert). Susan Shepard married a Jewish man. As for the famous converts, except for Sammy Davis they all married Jews (and Nikki Schieler Ziering told the host of the radio show *Loveline* that she continues to practice Judaism, even after her divorce from Ian); I would guess that they had also known many Jews well, so that even before falling in love and being moved to conversion they could have imagined being Jewish. They had attended a Passover seder, a bris, a Hanukkah party, or a Jewish wedding. They knew their way around the neighborhood.

Other converts talk of having lived in a Jewish neighborhood, being welcomed at numerous Shabbos dinners, or meeting the parents of their children's Jewish friends. Judaism had rubbed off on some part of their lives, and they had begun to wonder if spending more time with these people would make them feel more whole, better, happier. Some converts had an infatuation less with Judaism than with Jewishness: they liked Yiddish words, or bagels, or what they perceived to be Jewish intellectualism, and those bits of Jewish culture brought them to Judaism. Some converts wanted a religion that requires a day of rest.

Jacob and Rena did not remind me of the other converts I

had known. They had not come to Judaism through a bevy of Jewish friends (though Rena had had one, the roommate who was so good to her after her divorce), and they had not been enfolded in the arms of the community since converting. When I met him, Jacob was teaching Hebrew at the temple and was the designer and keeper of its Web page, but he was not part of the temple social scene.

"I'm not sure what my relationship is with the people here," Jacob said. "There's no one here I dislike. There is nobody here other than Rena who has become a personal friend. But somewhere in between are an awful lot of nice people . . . When you talk about the people here, what happens now is it seems like people are so busy. We come in, we do the thing we came to do. And we thoroughly enjoy it while we're here, and then we go back out to the other world."

Jacob paused for a moment, trying to decide if that's what he had meant to say: "I can't help but think that if I were you, writing that, it would sound negative."

I told him no, I knew exactly what he meant.

Rena, too, felt warmth, but not ardor, for her fellow Jews.

"No one knocked on my door and said, 'Come join the Hebrews,' " she said. "No one called me on the phone. There are, in other religions—there is that revival street-pounding type of search for new members. And it's good and it's bad. Because it's an emotional thing, and you can get emotional in any kind of religion, but I didn't want to be emotionally led into anything anymore. I had been there and had that."

Jacob, too, felt that sense of relief about what Judaism is not: not the holy rolling, not the altar call, not the preachers telling you what is and isn't sinful: "In churches, there are people who know the right way. They know what you ought to do, what they ought to do, what everybody wants to do. You can have discussions, but don't go off into weird ideas. And that's why this Jewish prayer"—the one he had discovered his third week in temple—"made sense to me. Because I was the guy who would go off into weird ideas, say, 'How do we know that?' "

A simple way of understanding what Rena and Jacob saw in Judaism would be to compare it to what some Jews or Catholics see in Unitarianism: a respite from judgment, proof that there can be religion without dogma.

I suspect that Jacob and Rena would be nonplussed to walk into a Conservative synagogue, the kind that hundreds of thousands of American Jews belong to, where nearly the whole service is in Hebrew; penitent Jews bow down to the floor, prostrate before God, on Yom Kippur; and rabbis urge the congregants, however gently, toward greater observance of the dietary laws, or toward forgoing automobile travel on Shabbos. There's the downside to Jewish diversity: converts to, say, Episcopalianism learn the Lord's Prayer and have something instantly in common with other Episcopalians, just as new Muslims learn the Fatiha, the first chapter of the Koran, and have that in common with all other Muslims—but converts to Judaism can't be sure what they'll have in common with other Jews. While becoming a bar or bat mitzvah helps draw one further into the family, it does not close a gap that, after all, often exists between two Jews who were born Jewish.

Stricter observance would be just one of the differences Jacob and Rena would find if they traveled the Jewish world. Most synagogues today vehemently discuss the tumult in Israel, intermarriage with Gentiles, and the malleability of tradition. May the names of the matriarchs—Sarah, Rebekah, Rachel, and Leah—be said after the patriarchs Abraham, Isaac, and Jacob in the Amidah prayer? May women chant Torah? Should children of Jewish fathers but non-Jewish mothers be considered Jews? For urban and suburban Jews,

these questions are old, common, and tiresome, but they are
not about to go away. Lake Charles Jews have an entirely different set of questions, far more parochial in nature: Will we
have a rabbi in town on Yom Kippur? Are there enough children to keep the religious school going?

This difference is in many ways a happy one. Temple Sinai
is not likely to suffer a schism over the question of the matriarchs or paternal descent. No power struggle over the synagogue presidency will tear friendships apart—the real question
is whether anyone will volunteer to be the next president. Jacob and Rena are thus spared some hard initiations that other
converts must pass through, the introductions to the rough,
competitive, nasty, and childish fights that can permeate congregational life. And they are lucky to have no conception of
the fashion wars that can erupt on the High Holidays, when
women wear their latest outfits to services.* They know nothing of the lavish bar mitzvah parties that so many Jews, born
or converted, find an impediment to religiosity.

At the same time, Jacob and Rena have no experience of the
pleasures afforded by a thicker, more layered Judaism, one that
poses all those nettlesome questions. Nobody in Lake Charles
refrains from shopping or driving on Shabbos; nobody, including the rabbi, lays tefillin; nobody sits through a full
Shabbos service with the entire Torah reading—and nobody
wonders if he should. When Reform Judaism is so reformed,
there are fewer places to find intellectual traction, fewer of the
challenges that can keep people engaged. Jacob and Rena, being smart and enthusiastic, will quickly reach the end of their
Lake Charles Jewish learning curve.

They will always be able to get more proficient in Hebrew,

---

*And when cell phones go off during High Holiday services, as happened at
one suburban New York synagogue I visited.

and there will always be more Torah stories to learn. (Was David the father of Jesse, or the other way around? Where was Daniel when he saw the handwriting on the wall?) But the sense that Judaism is a quicksand surface, that Jewish learning spirals out of control, and that even if one mastered Torah, there would be Talmud, and after Talmud the legal codes, and after that the mystical tracts, right down to the eternal significance of each piece of the aleph-bet—that sense is absent. At BEKI in New Haven and Kol Ami in Tampa, everybody knew the learned congregants in their midst and spoke of them with a quiet reverence. In Tampa, it was Morty, the retired rabbi from Philadelphia. In New Haven, it was, besides their leader Rabbi Tilsen, the married Rabbis Brodie, and Rabbi Lina, and all the Judaica professors. It's not that all the other members were striving to achieve the same Jewish knowledge, but there was an abiding sense, hanging in the air, of "If only I had the time . . ."

With three days until the festivities on Friday night, I decided to call on as many Lake Charles Jews as I could find.

First, I met David and Anne Reinauer, whose realty company, Reinauer Real Estate Corporation, had signs all over town. We sat on their porch on Shell Beach Road, which runs along the lake. They live well. Inside their big Victorian house is a mammoth kitchen where they prepare gourmet meals, except in the summer, when they relocate to their house in Provence and host week-long classes in French cooking for eight paying guests at a time. As we talked, we sipped red wine and ate cheddar Goldfish crackers and broken matzohs with a homemade olive spread. I asked David to tell me about his family, and he answered slowly and laconically, occasionally smoothing his white hair over his bald spot. Anne, who listened and occasionally added her own memories, had short blond hair and an upturned nose. She looked perkier, and it turned out that she was.

"My family came in the nineteenth century to the 'German coast,' south and a little west of New Orleans," David said. "My great-grandfather disembarked in New Orleans, then went to Berwick, Louisiana. His obituary says he went into business in Berwick, then moved here in 1888. Why, I don't know. I have a suspicion he might have known someone. Maybe he heard the lake is pretty."

"They lived in Alsace," Anne suggested, "and maybe when Germany took over Alsace, they left and came to the United States. They felt more French."

David continued, "Isaac, my great-grandfather, had a general merchandise store called I. Reinauer and Sons. My grandfather, Solomon, continued in that somehow or other. He ended up selling his store to a Mr. Love, Meyer Love, a Jewish guy. And Love's was the main men's store during my whole growing up until about 1970. My dad came back here after college. On my mother's side, Pearl Jacobs married Morris Muller, and Morris and my grandmother Dora were brother and sister."

This meant that David was a cousin of the Mullers, and of the redoubtable Pearl Jacobs Muller, the recently deceased Lake Charles doyenne about whom I had heard much. She died in 1994 at over one hundred years old, and everybody I met had an opinion of her. Even the kindly lady at the library who had told me, "Oh, Lake Charles has some wonderful Jews!" did not seem to think much of the late Pearl Jacobs Muller. Me, I wondered if Pearl Jacobs Muller had been a cousin of my grandmother Eleanor Jacobs.

"Morris's mother, Julia, had arrived in town," David said, "a widow with two children, and had started making hats in the back of her house and selling them in the front of the house. And that became Muller's."

"It became the first department store in town," Anne said. "It had the first escalator. It was very exciting."

"Morris ended up running it," David said. "My dad, a nephew, after college worked there for twelve years as a buyer, and he left there and got into the real estate business. And I bought that. Adolf Marx, a half brother of Morris's from when Julia remarried, continued running Muller's, even after they sold it to Federated Department Stores, until it closed about twenty years ago."

I had seen the Muller's building at the corner of Ryan and Division Streets, still empty.

"They're always coming up with some plan for what to do with that building," Anne said with a sigh.

I asked about being Jewish in Lake Charles.

"Anne converted to Judaism after we got married," David said. Her family was also German, they had also been in real estate, and David and Anne had been childhood friends for years before courting. They have four grown children, and the three who have married have all married Gentiles. One son has married two Gentiles.

"Growing up here, we were more oddities than anything else," he said. "There was an open house of old houses on Palm Sunday, and the temple was included on the tour. I was there to answer questions. It was remarkable: 'Do you celebrate Easter?' Growing up here, there was no prejudice I was aware of, other than when it came to religion I was a curious oddity, not a spiteful oddity."

Anne thought about this for a moment.

"I'm not sure I knew you were Jewish," she said. "Except you weren't in Sunday school, so I knew you weren't Presbyterian."

"As an adult now, I'm not aware of any overt anti-Semitism," David said. "As a businessperson, I honestly believe there is prejudice in the Christian community, people who might do business with me but won't because I am Jewish. But I haven't seen it. It's a leap." Some years ago, a swastika appeared on the synagogue, and a group of Catholics scrubbed it off as soon as it was discovered. "They were embarrassed anyone would do that," David said.

After high school, David left Lake Charles for the University of Pennsylvania, where he joined the campus chapter of Zeta Beta Tau, a national Jewish fraternity.

"At Penn, I was around more Jews than I had ever seen before," David said. "I found the camaraderie and warmth very comforting. My pledge class are still some of my best friends. I did have some Jewish friends growing up, and we still have strangely warm feelings, even though I don't see them anymore. And even though they have nothing to do with religion anymore."

It was getting late in the day. The ducks had finished their daily swim and were gathering on the banks of the lake. Anne said something about her son's divorce, and I heard in her voice that it was a painful topic. But then she added a hopeful note: her grandson, being raised by his Catholic mother, had just asked his father if he could start going to temple.

"He said, 'Dad, who decided I should be Catholic?' " David said.

We talked some more, discussing Jewish pride, Jewish generations.

"The old generation," Anne said, "they would say, 'Bagel? What's a bagel?' They were reacting so strongly against the Old World's view of Jews, so they were determined to be assimilated." Anne, the Presbyterian, had evidently seen this in David's family.

"My grandfather was president of the congregation, my mother was, and I was," David said. "I don't know why my father never was. I worked with the youth group when I first moved back here. Anne was principal of the Sunday school for ten years. With all that, our children aren't particularly interested. I don't know. But as Anne says, the last chapter is not written yet." He was talking about his grandson.

Just then, a car pulled into the Reinauers' driveway, and out bounded a white-haired woman with a smile comically wide, like a crescent moon. It was Brenda Bachrack, another Lake Charles Jew on my list of people to see. I had first heard of Brenda in Fayetteville, where her daughter Ruthie taught at Jacob Newman's religious school at Temple Shalom. I had not met Ruthie, but people in Fayetteville had told me to look up Ruthie's mother, Brenda, in Lake Charles. Jewish Geography, they call this game, the Hebrews' version of "six degrees of separation."

Brenda was returning Passover Haggadot—books from which the story of Passover is read—that she had borrowed from the Reinauers. She had only a few minutes to chat—she was on her way to a Temple Sinai board meeting—but she was excited to meet me, and she launched into stories about the Kushners, the Mullers, and Rabbi Peter Schaktman, an old interim rabbi who now lives in New York.

"I would love to stay!" Brenda said. "This is much more interesting conversation than what I am going to get at the synagogue!"

Brenda and I made plans to meet at her house the next day, and then she was off. I stood and stretched my legs. Why would a Jew like David, with an Ivy League degree, return to Lake Charles? This view from the porch, for one thing. As I was about to start for my car, Anne Reinauer touched my shoulder, and she said that if I needed anything during my visit—"even conversation"—I should stop by any night at this time. They were always there, she said, having a drink and watching the sunset reflected in the water. She seemed happy to have one more Jew in town.

The next afternoon, Brenda Bachrack had me over for tea. She lived in a one-story yellow house on Audubon Street with a pool in the back. It's the house that she and her husband, Harold, who died in 2001, built in 1955, six years after they married. Brenda was raised in Boston and attended Syracuse University, where she met Hal, a Brooklynite who was majoring in forestry because a high school teacher had told him that a forester would always have a job. "There will always be trees," the teacher had said. After Syracuse, Hal moved to Lake Charles to work for Davidson Sash and Door, a subsidiary of Houston Sash and Door. Months after settling in Lake Charles, Hal proposed to Brenda, still at Syracuse, through the mail. She wrote back to accept, and he sent back a ring, which the mailman "made a very big deal of presenting to me," Brenda said. Hal and Brenda moved to Audubon Street, which proved a wonderful place to raise their five children.

"On this street, there were fourteen houses and sixty-three children," Brenda said. "We had our own community right on this street. Lots of Catholics, and one sexy Jewish lady."

Hal and Brenda had both been raised in secular households. Brenda had had no Jewish education at all. After several years in Texas, Hal's family had returned to Brooklyn when he was twelve, and his grandfather had given him an intensive Hebrew course in time for him to become a bar mitzvah. But neither Hal nor Brenda felt out of place in Lake Charles, where the temple put a premium on friendship, not Jewish learning.

"When we first moved to town, our whole social life centered around the temple," Brenda said. "Our social, business, travel life was all together with people from the temple. It was the tightest community. When we got here, within a year, we'd been appointed superintendents of the Sunday school. I don't know how or why. We didn't have any children yet, but we'd been going to temple regularly, so it didn't matter. We loved kids, so we said sure. I'm still doing it, off and on, since 1950."

I asked Brenda what had changed most about the Lake Charles Jewish community in the past fifty years.

"What's changed most are the conversions—I don't think there were any mixed couples for at least the first thirty years. I've never been able to figure out why, other than the whole idea of outreach in Reform Judaism, bringing people in. My kids all married outside the church, but all their kids are being brought up Jewish. I think it's because of my husband, because we always kept Hanukkah, Passover, Purim. And also the three younger ones who went to Camp Jacobs are all intent on their Judaism. The older two didn't go, and they're less so." I had heard this from other parents in Lake Charles: Henry S. Jacobs Camp, a Reform summer camp in Utica, Mississippi, had been instrumental in giving their children a Jewish identity.

I asked Brenda to tell me a little more about her children, and I was surprised to hear that two still lived in Louisiana: Jonathan was in Covington and Ellen was in Mandeville. David lived in Grand Rapids, Michigan; Ruthie, I knew, lived in Fayetteville; and Emily lived with her husband and two daughters in Cherbourg, France, where, Brenda said sadly, the nearest synagogue is in Cannes, an hour and a half away.

"I'm very interested in keeping the religious school going," Brenda said. "I guess it's selfish, because I've invested so much in it myself. But also I think it's important because of what's going on in the world." She meant in Israel and in Louisiana too: the previous year, she said, a local schoolteacher had mentioned to her class how Jesus was killed by the Jews. "And one of our Sunday school children stood up—a nine-year-old boy—to say that wasn't so. And he was sent to the principal. Another one of our students told me that he hears that sometimes, and he just tells people, 'You can believe what you want, but if you want to know the proper chronology, I'll be happy to tell you'—and this is from a ten-year-old!

"I helped get *The Diary of Anne Frank* on the statewide required reading list. Now Elie Wiesel's *Night* is required reading too. I didn't do it, but I had something to do with it. There's a group in DeQuincy that are Holocaust deniers, and the gifted-class teacher called me in tears. I went up there to talk to the class—which included children who were from these families. I didn't attack anyone, just positively told them the story, what I knew and had seen."

Brenda's kitchen was grandmotherly. It was brightly lit, and there were family photographs on the refrigerator, sections of last Sunday's *New York Times* neatly piled on one corner of the kitchen table, and a cookbook called *Everyday and Challah-day Cooking* on top of the TV. I asked Brenda what she most liked to watch. "*West Wing* is my family," she said. "I love that show." When Brenda moved to Lake Charles, it would have been Ralph and Alice Kramden. The next year would be her fifty-fourth year with the religious school, which would have eighteen children.

"There are *six* newly moved-in young families," she said, with obvious pleasure.

Somehow, it all persisted. Temple Sinai had about the same membership in 2003 as it had had in 1953 and 1903. They endured. Like Lake Charles itself, and like all Louisiana, as muggy now as ever, poor as ever, as corrupt as in the days

of Huey Long. While taking a lunch break one day in Lake
Charles, I remembered back to my senior year of high school,
when we read *All the King's Men*, Robert Penn Warren's fic-
tional account of Long. His narrator, I remembered, was Jack
Burden, a newspaperman. Like *me*, I thought, and for a moment I felt a romantic charge, as if I were a character out of
literature. Then I realized I was eating a double hamburger
from Wendy's, and I felt less romantic. Still, I thought, I am
tracking Louisiana Jewry.

The day before, I had seen the name Sydney Ira Horn
on an attorney's shingle outside a building on Ryan Street.
Thinking Sydney Ira Horn sounded like a Jewish movie character, I had written the name down in my notebook. A Jew
named Sydney Ira is like a black man named Tyrone Jamal, or
a redneck named Billy Bob—scriptwriter's overkill. I decided I
had to find this fellow, so I went to the library and searched in
the yellow pages for Sydney Ira Horn's phone number. I
called, and a man with a swampy nasal accent answered the
phone, "Syd Horn." I told him about my project. He doubted
he could help much, he said, but he'd be happy to talk tomorrow: "Come by anytime from 10 a.m. to 4 p.m. I take lunch
in the office."

The next morning, I dressed in a clean, collared shirt. I arrived at 10:30 a.m. and parked in front of the Horn Building,
a low-slung, single-story white building set down in a parking
lot much too big for it. Several businesses had offices inside,
and I found my way to Sydney Horn's door. I knocked and
entered. In the reception area, answering the phones, sat a
squat man with a manageable paunch. He was wearing a blue
dress shirt, black pants, black socks, and black loafers. His
hair, too, was black, going a little bald in back. He looked a
little like Tom Bosley, Mr. Cunningham from *Happy Days*. He
was, in fact, the typical burgher we all know from our home-

towns, the insurance salesman or hardware man. But when he spoke, there was that accent I'd heard on the phone, pure country Acadiana, the accent of the boy who had served me at the Cajun diner, an accent close to Ross Perot's, emphatically not the accent of the town librarian or Jacob Ecker or David Reinauer.

"Come on into my office and sit down," he said.

He waved me into a small square room, lined on three sides with shelves and desks, three chairs crowded together in the middle. He invited me to take one, then asked me again about my project. I told him, and he reiterated that he doubted he could help much—especially since, he said, he was a Christian. But he would tell me what he remembered of Temple Sinai.

Sydney was born in 1939. When he was a child, his family went to temple on High Holidays and on very occasional Fridays. He never liked it much. "As far as I was concerned," he said, "I didn't care to ever go. I only went because my parents made me.

"What did I believe as a Jew? That there was a God. That there was a heaven and hell. I figured everyone went to heaven if they were a good person. I don't believe that anymore. It would be nice if it were true.

"The only part of the temple I ever liked was the reading of the Torah in Hebrew, and then it being translated into English. That was the only part that interested me. I didn't care about any of the holidays. The prayers didn't mean anything to me. I used to go to Sunday school, but only because my parents made me go. When I went to Tulane, I never went to temple.

"I married a Jewish girl, she was from an Orthodox family. I was brought up only to marry a Jewish girl. She didn't get much fulfillment from being Jewish. She started going to

Christian churches and ended up at Heritage Baptist. I didn't go at first, and she would come back and say what the preacher had said, and she would explain it."

From time to time, Sydney had thought about Christianity, but it had always been just thoughts. When he was seventeen, a man came to his family's door and offered him a New Testament. "I don't want it," Sydney told him. "I'm Jewish." Sydney asked the man if he believed that Moses had parted the Red Sea. Yes, the missionary said. Then Sydney asked him if he believed that Jesus walked on water and raised people from the dead. Yes, the man said. And that Jonah was eaten by the whale and spit back out? Yes. And that two of all the world's animals had been fit on Noah's ark? Of course.

Sydney was dumbfounded. "How," he asked the man at his door, "can any human being believe all those tall stories?"

But then the man asked Sydney a question: "Do you believe that God created the heavens and the earth?"

Sydney said yes, he reckoned that God had.

"If God can do a little thing like that," the man replied, "how hard would it be for him to part the Red Sea?"

Well, Sydney admitted, the missionary had him there.

"It was the first time I got inquisitive," Sydney told me. "But I never followed it up."

For several years, Sydney was a lapsed Jew with a wife who had found Jesus. Until one Sunday in 1977.

"I was working at home, and everything was going wrong. I had busted a finger, the lawn mower had broken. Nothing was going right. So I put all that down and went inside and watched TV. When my wife came home, I said, 'God was telling me I shouldn't be working today. I'm gonna go to church next Sunday.' She never pressured me.

"So I went to church the next Sunday and sat in the way back, because any talk of Jesus made my hair stand up. The

preacher read from the Bible and he explained it. I understood. It was the first time I understood anything in the Bible.
He explained that Jesus said this, that, and the other, and if
you don't believe it, you're not going to heaven. And I
thought, What if he was right? I'd better listen. But pretty
soon I was on the side where I believed everything he was saying. Are these tall stories? Not when you consider what God
did. God can do anything."

Sydney's conversion took some time. He pondered for a
while, asked some rabbis what they thought of Jesus. They
told him Jesus was a great teacher, but they couldn't see that
Jesus might be the Messiah. Did they think Jesus was a liar?
Sydney asked. No, they said. Well, then why didn't they believe him when he said he was the Messiah?

Being Christian has done good things for Sydney. He has
more of a conscience now, he said. He worries more about
how his actions affect other people. He still considers himself
a Jew, just one who believes that Jesus is the Messiah.

His new community suits him too.

"I'm gonna get in trouble for saying this," Sydney said, "but
most Jewish people that I meet I don't care for. Mostly the
New York Jews. That's the kind of Jew that turns me off. Of
course, I meet Christians I don't like too. I'm not anti-Semitic.
I meet blacks I like and blacks I don't like. Most of my clients
are black. When one of them is talking about one he doesn't
like, he'll call him a nigger. That's the word they use.

"I'm proud of being Jewish. One thing I like about Israel—
they don't take anything off anybody. That's the way a country
should be. It's like they say: never again. Some people say the
Holocaust didn't happen. I know it happened. I've seen those
pictures of them bulldozing people. It's sickening. I would
never go that way. If I go, someone's going with me. You see
some movies, there's six hundred Jews and only five guards

with machine guns. They're there like dumb sheep. I just don't understand."

Much of the time that Sydney does not spend at home, at Heritage Baptist Church, or at his law office in the Horn Building, he devotes to his writing. He has written an unpublished novel, inspired by *Dirty Harry*, about a New Orleans lawyer, and a screenplay called *Wyatt Earp's Tombstone Vendetta*, based on a novel by his favorite writer, Glen Boyer, the world's leading expert on Wyatt Earp. Sydney is also an enthusiastic member of the Louisiana branch of the Single Action Shooting Society, the association of "cowboy action shooting" aficionados.

"It's the fastest-growing kind of shooting," Syd said. "You know what a single-action pistol is? You have to cock it before you can shoot it. They're six-shooters, what Wyatt Earp used. We use three kinds of guns: lever-action Winchesters, sawed-off shotguns like on *Stagecoach*, and single-action pistols. You have a timer and a stage with building props, like a movie set. And you shoot at targets. For every one you miss, they add five seconds to your time. Whoever shoots the fastest wins." In his age group, Sydney is one of the best in the state.

I asked Sydney what he remembered of his youth at Temple Sinai.

"I had to learn the Sh'ma, of course. I still know that. And I had to learn to read Hebrew. I could then, but I can't remember any of that. We had to write a speech too. I don't remember that at all. I went to Sunday school starting around when I was ten, and I was confirmed about thirteen. They did bar mitzvahs, but there wasn't many of us who wanted or were forced to do them."

Sydney's grandfather came from Germany to Corpus Christi, Texas, and his son, Sydney's father, came from Texas to Lake Charles in search of work. He sold shoes at first, then

went into the popcorn and candy business; at the peak of his
fortunes, he was selling concession products to 140 theaters.
When that business soured, he went into mortgages and loans.
The story is not unlike the Reinauer story, or the Muller
or Marx stories: from Germany to Louisiana by way of dry
goods, clothes, or lending.

"I have one sister, four years older. She is married to a Jewish Vietnam vet. He was raised Orthodox. They have two
daughters, live in Dallas. I can't talk to them about religion.

"The other thing I got to do was meet Roy Rogers," Sydney
added. "As a kid he was my idol."

Through a childhood friend who had become Rogers's doctor, Sydney met Roy when the actor was eighty-two, shortly
before his death.

"He made me feel bad. He had done so much for people.
He had one son, Dusty. And he adopted twelve other children, who all had something wrong with them. He and his
wife took care of them. They were big Christians. His son,
Dusty, is a member of the Single Action Shooting Society."

I asked Sydney how old he was, then did a little math. Sydney Ira Horn, I realized, had been in the Temple Sinai confirmation class of 1952, along with a young David Reinauer.
Their Sunday school teacher was Brenda Bachrack.

For those of you who are counting—and Jews count things
like this—the balance sheet is in the red. In the minus column: three Reinauer children intermarried, five Bachrack children intermarried, one Sydney Ira Horn gone to Jesus. Every
old Jewish family in Lake Charles told this story, one way or
another. Some had stayed, others had fallen away. Susan Bat-
testin, one of Pearl Jacobs Muller's granddaughters, warmly
welcomed me and talked about her enduring affection for Ju-

daism, and about her daughter's summers at Camp Jacobs; Susan's sister, now Catholic, did not return my call to arrange an interview.

But in the plus column, Anne Reinauer had converted, and now two other converts were becoming b'nai mitzvah—I had come to Lake Charles for their simcha. I arrived at Temple Sinai on Friday afternoon to find the kitchen full of good smells and astir with activity. Betsy Ecker, Jacob's wife, was spooning hummus into a large dish. Francine Cohen, a local dance teacher, was mixing her sangria—one-third Sprite, one-third orange juice, one-third wine, plus a little Cointreau and triple sec. Faye Barnhart, the temple administrator, walked in and gave Betsy a kiss: "Well, if it isn't the wife of the bar mitzvah boy!" Faye walked out into the social hall to turn on the yahrzeit board, with illuminated bulbs for members of Temple Sinai who had died during that week in the Jewish calendar. She was quickly replaced in the kitchen by Rena LeJeune, who sashayed in wearing a bright red dress with gold embroidery across the bodice, the outfit topped off by a red and blue yarmulke.

Usually, the temple was entered through the garden and the door to the social hall, but tonight, the sanctuary double doors were open to the street. At the front, the narthex, were two sign-in books, one for Jacob and one for "Rinah," with a Hebrew spelling. After they're born, Jews are given Hebrew names that include the Hebrew names of their parents; for example, a boy named David whose parents are Sam and Abby might be named David ben Shmuel v'Avigail. Converts take for their parental names Abraham and Sarah, after the patriarch and matriarch of the Jewish people. Written at the top of Rena's book, in Hebrew script, was "Rinah bat Avraham v'Sarah," and at the top of Jacob's book, "Yaakov ben Avraham v'Sarah." Jacob and Rena already had Hebrew names, given at birth, as if their parents had known something ahead of time. It lent the evening a whiff of fate.

If, as Judi Gannon says, God wants you to make one mistake, Rena and Jacob obliged, and then some. Pronunciations were not perfect. Rena made the same mistakes as in rehearsal; "lay-more" was still "law-more." They both looked terrifically proud. Jacob was in a sharp blue suit, a red tie, and a white yarmulke, and Rena, in her red and gold, looked like Annie Oakleystein, Jew of the Old West. In the front pew, Rena's husband, Wendell, and Jacob's wife, Betsy, smiled as they surveyed the audience, looking left and right and behind them, then down the pews, at assorted children and grandchildren, children's spouses, and grandchildren's boyfriends and girlfriends.

Farther back in the sanctuary, wearing his ring from the Texas A&M class of 1948, Simon "Si" Davidson, former proprietor of Davidson Sash and Door, the first employer of Hal Bachrack, listened in. In 1940 Si became the first-ever bar mitzvah in Lake Charles. His father was a Louisianan, but his mother, a Polish Jew from Boston, would have none of this confirmation nonsense, and Si was sent to nearby Beaumont, Louisiana, every Saturday to study with the rabbi.

Sitting behind Si in the pews was Nathan Dondis, the vice president of Temple Sinai. Later, while presenting certificates to Jacob and Rena, he would say, "Who knows? Now that I've seen that y'all can do it, maybe I can do it!"

Across the aisle from Nathan sat Bruce Katz, Si Davidson's son-in-law, who had grown up in Galveston, Texas. For his bar mitzvah, he led the entire Friday night and Saturday morning services, with no English. At his party afterward, at the Flagship Hotel, he got drunk for the first time.

On the podium stood Rabbi Leo, who said, "What would a

bar or bat mitzvah be without a bar or bat mitzvah speech? Tonight we're privileged to have two!"

In her speech, Rena spoke about her decision to become a bat mitzvah: "9/11/2001 caused me to make a 360-degree turn in my life. I came to a Thursday night candlelight prayer service here, at the temple. The lady who sat next to me was Helen Wolkow, our rabbi's wife. Fear, worry, and concern for what lay ahead ruled my hours. I committed to the temple and attended services. That Saturday, I attended the Hebrew and Torah study group . . ."

Jacob spoke about his path to conversion and about his parashah, but it's his conclusion I remember best:

> And a final word to the many others who would like to do your own bar/bat mitzvah ceremony. You may not even know that you want to do it, but Rabbi Wolkow will help you to understand that you really want to do it. It will take you about a year of study, followed by a week or two of panic, so you need to start soon, very soon. There are people here to help you. And after you have done all of that hard work, you will realize that you still don't know enough, so that is when the real work will begin. So come to the Hebrew and Torah classes (next Saturday, not tomorrow) and Schmooze on Thursdays when the rabbi is here. And I think we can expect another absolute beginners' Hebrew class to start in the fall. The current beginners' Hebrew class will meet tomorrow at the regular times.

The Hebrew beginners' class, Jacob might have mentioned, was taught by one Jacob Ecker.

After the speeches, Rabbi Leo returned to the pulpit

and looked up at the organist in the balcony: "I didn't give you any warning, Sharon, but can we give a priestly benediction?"

Sharon struck a dramatic major chord on the organ, and Rabbi Leo motioned for Jacob and Rena to stand up, with their backs to the Torah ark. Facing Jacob and Rena, with his back to the congregation, Rabbi Leo raised his hands to bless them with the Hebrew of Numbers 6:24–26, the words of Aaron to the children of Israel, which by tradition are given by Jewish fathers to their children on Shabbos eve, or by rabbis to b'nai mitzvah or to couples about to marry.* The blessing may be given on any occasion you wish. After the Hebrew, the rabbi gave the blessing in English: "The Lord bless and protect you. The Lord deal kindly and graciously with you. The Lord bestow His favor upon you and grant you peace."

At the party afterward, people drank Francine's sangria and ate raw vegetables, hummus, challah, and bagels. The Reinauers were there, and also the Davidsons, Katzes, Eckers, LeJeunes—several minyans' worth of Lake Charles Jews and fellow travelers. After I had eaten my fill and made small talk, I wandered down a corridor toward the rabbi's study. In a small hallway, poorly lit, there was a wall of black-and-white photographs showing confirmation classes going back a century. I found Sydney Ira Horn, now a Baptist. I found Tony Kushner and David Reinauer. At the far lower left corner of the wall, a faded picture in a simple black frame showed the Lake Charles confirmation class of 1923, nine teenage Jews in

---

*In more traditional synagogues, the priestly blessing is conferred not by the rabbi but by the congregation's Kohanim, men (and sometimes women) descended of the priestly caste. Their families often have names like Kohn, Cohen, or Kagan—though not all Kohanim have names like Cohen, and not all Jews named Cohen are Kohanim.

their Saturday (or Sunday) finery. In the front row, at the far
left and far right ends, were two young girls, perhaps eight
years old, wearing white dresses and holding small wicker bas-
kets. These were the flower girls. The left-end flower girl had
short blond hair and narrow eyes; beneath her on the matting,
in black ink, was written the name "Elinore Jacobs." My
grandmother, with her first name misspelled.

The last person I interviewed in Lake Charles, and my favorite, was Faye Barnhart, the temple administrator. Rabbi
Leo insisted I talk to her. She was the keeper of the lore, he
said; she knew the stories. We talked late in the evening, after
the sun had set, as she was locking up the building. She was
hurrying about, her gray curls bouncing merrily on her head,
snapping back into position like Slinkys. Every couple of minutes I would catch her pausing, trying to decide what needed
doing next, and in one of those moments, I was able to look
her up and down: I saw that she had big blue eyes and a smile
so big it was almost bawdy. She wore a chai, a golden pendant
of the Hebrew letters chet and yud, which spell the word for
"life."

Faye was born in 1928 in Creole, Louisiana, to a Jewish
father and a Catholic mother who had started observing Judaism after her marriage. Her mother had had a confirmation
ceremony when she was in her fifties and considered that her
conversion. When Faye was little, her daddy had a sister in
Lake Charles, so Faye's family would come to Temple Sinai,
but only rarely, as for High Holidays, because back then it was
an all-day trip. Faye had been at Temple Sinai for Si Davidson's bar mitzvah in 1940; she had been around for every bar
mitzvah ever held in Lake Charles.

"We were the only Jewish family in Creole," Faye told me.

"Daddy taught us from the Bible and the prayer books. We really didn't know much about Judaism. We went to Mass with Mother's relatives in Grandpa's house. But Daddy always taught us we were Jewish. We moved here in 1941 to Lake Charles. I started going to religious school, and was confirmed in 1946, and started teaching religious school right after. I was married in 1951. My husband wasn't Jewish, but we were married by Rabbi Abraham Cronbach from Cincinnati."

By that time, Faye had already lost all three of her brothers to Duchesne's muscular dystrophy, which is carried by women but affects only men. Two of her brothers had been sent to live with Catholic relatives, but one, her brother David, had stayed at home and been raised Jewish. It was to honor him that Faye and her husband named their only son David—and he died in 1970, when he was sixteen.

"He was my one son," Faye said. "My son died two weeks before he was to be confirmed."

I said that I had noticed the beautiful sculpture in his honor out by the garden. Faye said that there had originally been a fountain by the sculpture too, "but it kept clogging."

Faye asked me if I knew Berwick, "on Route 10, on the way to New Orleans?"

I said that I remembered passing the exit.

"My cousin was the last one to be buried in the Jewish cemetery there. She was Catholic, but she married a Jewish man and kept a Jewish home. I went to her funeral and said Kaddish for her. She was Catholic, but she asked me to say Kaddish for her."

I thanked Faye for talking with me, and for showing me the temple's treasures, its *Angels in America* poster signed by Tony Kushner and its *Driving Miss Daisy* poster signed by Alfred Uhry: "For Temple Sinai on the occasion of their hundredth anniversary." I had had a wonderful time, I said. I was sorry to be leaving town so soon.

Faye asked what I was planning to do with my remaining time in Lake Charles.

I was planning, I thought to myself, to sit in the town library, right by the desk of the lady who had told me that Lake Charles had some wonderful Jews, and to figure out what I thought of all this. In this town where many of the Jews were not even officially Jewish, were descended from Gentile mothers, had intermarried, and wouldn't know how to keep kosher even if they'd wanted to, there was still an insistent passion about keeping Judaism alive—whatever that meant. That night, the town had come out to honor two converts making a commitment to Judaism—but the man and woman the rabbi blessed that night had better Hebrew than most of the lifelong Jews watching them. A year earlier, when Rabbi Leo had announced his year-long course for adult b'nai mitzvah, six men and women had signed up. Now only the two converts had made it across the finish line.

I was, I wanted to tell Faye, going to figure out some way that Lake Charles could nurture the energy these two converts had inside them and make it spread. I was going to raise money to bring Annie Bass or Judi Gannon or Mendy Greenberg to town one Friday night to chant the entire Torah portion. The visiting scholar would walk to shul, wearing a yarmulke, and chant every line of Pinchas or Vayelech. Then for twenty minutes he or she would deliver a dazzling drashah, explicating the parashah in light of the teachings of Rashi, the latest quarrels in the pages of *Tikkun* or *Commentary*, and a favorite Bernard Malamud or Isaac Babel short story. And it would all be done in such a way that people would feel not judged, not inadequate, but grateful and humble.

I wanted to promise Faye that I would hire for Lake Charles a permanent rabbi, because even atheists need a rabbi nearby, if not to learn from, then to abuse.

Instead, what I finally said was: "I'm going to look for the graves of dead relatives."

She was delighted.

"Are you going to the cemetery tomorrow? My husband is buried there. He was Methodist and didn't believe in organized religion. But we kept a Jewish home—he was very emphatic about that. And the rabbi buried him. My husband, son, brother-in-law, and nephew are buried there."

"I'll say Kaddish for them," I said.

"That would be nice."

So I did. On a hazy, stillborn Saturday, I pulled off the road that leads out of town and stopped at the graveyard. I found the small Jewish section and looked around for graves marked "Jacobs," but I couldn't find any that seemed to belong to me. None of my kin had stayed in Lake Charles long enough to die. So I went looking for Barnhart graves, and I found those. I said Kaddish for them: for Faye Barnhart's Methodist husband and her quarter-Jewish son, and for all the other dead Jews around them, lying still in pine boxes topped by weeds.

7

We're All Jews Now

*I*n 1908, the Hebrew Publishing Company, at 632–34 Broadway, New York City, published *Bar-Mitzva Speeches: A Collection of Various Bar-Mitzva Speeches in English, Hebrew, and Yiddish, Compiled by Famous Jewish Scholars and Orators,* edited by Professor G. Zelikowitch. It is a chrestomathy of short talks, about six hundred words each, for use by a bar mitzvah (or in some cases the father of a bar mitzvah speaking to his son) who does not have the time or the inclination to write his own. Most of them are generic discourses on the themes of Jewish nationhood, the covenant with God, and the importance of tefillin. A speech written by one S. Balk is titled, in a clumsy translation, "For an Orphan to His Bar-Mitzva." It begins, "Friends and Congregation: A child who was not punished by Providence, by the Almighty, to be an orphan, commences to perform the commandment of putting on phylacteries"—tefillin—"when he becomes thirteen years of age. But an orphan, like I am, has to perform this act at the age of twelve. A child who has a father can romp and jump and enjoy himself one more year: a father's shoulders carry him. But I must become wiser earlier and understand that I have to carry the burden of responsibilities to my twelfth birthday." I had never heard of this rule, and in a collection of canned speeches, this one stood out like a wound. I thought of the boy who had no father to sit down and write a speech with him, a boy who, maybe, was helped by this book.

I found two other collections of bar mitzvah speeches: a trilingual volume like the first, from 1921, and one entirely in Yiddish, from 1932, a little late in the day for Yiddish in America—the boy who was given that book probably smirked and rolled his eyes: Didn't the old rabbi know that everybody spoke English now? Like the 1908 book, both of these had been printed in downtown Manhattan, the 1932 book on Canal Street, and the other, the 1921 book, at 176 Park Row, near the approach to the Brooklyn Bridge.

I don't think they make collections like these anymore. I bought them from the National Yiddish Book Center in Amherst, Massachusetts, which rescues and preserves out-of-print Yiddish books. Not long ago, one of them fell off my coffee table, and the old glue, aged to the point of disintegration, failed to hold the sewn binding to the cloth cover; the pages all fell out in a coherent clump, and I had to stuff them back in and secure the book with a rubber band. These books are old. They are of a time when books for Jewish boys were published in Yiddish, Hebrew, and English, a time when some boys read all three.

But in another sense the books are amazingly contemporary. Canned speeches, like canned term papers! Curious, I went on the Internet and discovered that, today as ever, you can buy bar mitzvah speeches (which seems relatively less horrifying than the eulogies that the same Web site sells for parents to give at their dead babies' funerals). The speeches online would seem like a sure sign of civilizational decline if I didn't have on my desk these books that are decades old, proving that it was always so.

In addition to being charming nostalgia pieces, these books

are a somber reminder that the bar mitzvah was never pure. The money changers were always in the temple. There was always a bar mitzvah business. B'nai mitzvah are not quite men, just boys struggling to become young men, and where there have been boys, there have always been bored, lazy boys, happy to take help where they could get it. And these boys, whose rabbis have always known that they lack the maturity of men, have nonetheless always gone on with their bar mitzvah ceremonies and parties. Sid Klevens from Alaska, Hank Kaminsky from Arkansas, all the men I met who said things like "I left Judaism the day after my bar mitzvah"—even if they were flunking Hebrew school and getting their bar mitzvah speeches straight from books, they still had their day in shul.

It might make us a little uncomfortable that there has always been an element of make-believe in the bar mitzvah tradition; it may be tempting to think that somehow the tradition is tainted, perhaps beyond redemption. But I think that the fiction of adulthood has been present in *all* b'nai mitzvah, even of the best boys, and even in the olden days, a thousand years ago, when men and women married in their teens and had been helping on the farm or in the family business since earliest childhood. Even then, there was a little fiction involved in saying that the bar mitzvah was the beginning of manhood. After all, the boy wasn't *quite* ready to marry, and he was not yet big enough to live on his own or to win a fist-fight. He still needed the protection of a real man, a father or an older brother. Someone to help him write his speech, or to buy it for him.

But that element of fiction is, I think, intrinsic in a rite of passage. When medical students graduate and are awarded the M.D., that does not mean they are full doctors. They enter residency programs, honing their diagnostic skills and work-

ing under master teachers until they can perform the most difficult procedures on their own. Catholic priests are generally
ordained well before they take control of parish churches.
These apprenticeships allow time for the fiction of accomplishment slowly to become reality. You spend three years calling yourself a doctor and practicing what it's like to be a
doctor, and then one day the white coat actually fits, and
you're a doctor, in name and in feeling. The passage into
adulthood is like that. First comes a period of trial adulthood.

That is why the bar mitzvah ceremony began as a recitation
of the *Baruch shepatarani* prayer, the father's thanking God for
releasing him from responsibility for his son's transgressions.
A thirteen-year-old, the medievals decided, is old enough to
know right from wrong. That was the first step. And the
prayer was, in time, traditionally yoked to the boy's first Torah
or haftarah reading, then to a big party, so the boy was now
expected to be old enough to speak in public and to show social niceties as a host. To know right from wrong, to read Hebrew in front of a large crowd, and to greet the crowd and
accept their gifts afterward—all good skills for a budding man
to have.

But he is hardly old enough to take a bride. He is not ready
to go to war. We would be horrified if our thirteen-year-olds
decided they were ready to quit school, marry, and have children. If the bar or bat mitzvah were really meant to be the
beginning of adulthood, then it would be a perennial joke.
Thirteen-year-old children are not adults, and in the history
of Judaism they never were. Aviva Shane, an Israeli immigrant
I met in Marin County, California, told me that her granddaughter had become a bit of a terror after becoming a bat
mitzvah. "She kept saying, 'You have to let me do this, I'm a
woman now!' So her mother had to put a stop to *that*."

The last thing we need is for b'nai mitzvah to signal the beginning of all adult prerogatives; the bar mitzvah evolved to mark the beginning of the beginning of adulthood, the moment when a child accepts moral responsibility for his actions and so begins to claim more freedoms. "Now that I am a bar mitzvah," said Graham Maso, on an April morning when I visited Temple Sinai in Brookline, Massachusetts, "I have more responsibilities as a Jewish adult. I also have more privileges, such as being able to stay up later and be out longer, because my parents now trust me more than when I was younger. However, having all these responsibilities means that I have to act more thoughtfully toward others, and to not put myself before others."

His Torah passage that morning had been Leviticus 19, which famously includes the line "Love your neighbor as yourself: I am the Lord." "From my Torah and haftarah portions," Graham said, "I have learned something very important: the Golden Rule, to treat others the way you wish to be treated. Also, it helped me to recognize that my friends treat me better than I think, and they do help me when I need it. I truly believe that this has been a great experience, becoming a bar mitzvah."

As one who has full rights in the religious sphere, the bar or bat mitzvah is ready to conduct a religious ceremony in front of adults and can now participate in the eternal debate about what it is to serve God and behave rightly. As Annie and Mendy and Graham all realized, Judaism, traditional Judaism, is not about prerogatives; it's about obligations. If the bar or bat mitzvah ritual is seen in that light, as a humbling rather than an exalting experience, there is no reason that today's children cannot, at twelve or thirteen, become religious adults of a sort. They can (and do) begin to fast on Yom Kippur. When they start working summer jobs, they can give tzedakah, or charity. They can begin praying as adults.

And even by the most contemporary standards, thirteen remains a sensible age for children to begin the beginnings of their adulthood. They are not old enough to drive, but they are probably tall enough to see over the steering wheel. They are not old enough to be parents, but they are old enough to get pregnant. They should not drop out of school, but they are at an age when the truant officers probably won't come looking. Character is a muscle: it needs to be flexed in childhood, but the real training comes at the age when you're more to blame for your choices than your parents are. In that light, the bar and bat mitzvah come at the right time. The medievals knew what they were doing.

Most Jewish adults, I am sure, don't spend a lot of time thinking about their own b'nai mitzvah. Several old men told versions of the same story, one in which the bar mitzvah was a fond but hardly profound memory. For months they were crammed with just enough Hebrew to get through the haftarah. Then, on a Shabbos morning, they did the reading, were given a shot of schnapps and a little herring for lunch, and that was it. For poor Jewish boys in the early part of the twentieth century, from families that may have been ostensibly Orthodox but whose observance had lapsed severely in America, the bar mitzvah was often a little nod to tradition that had no moral heft as long as one's days were consumed with worries about rent money. When my grandfather, for instance, talks about his childhood, he never talks about his bar mitzvah, but he often mentions being ashamed to wear hand-me-downs to school and being roughed up by Protestant boys in Roxborough, the Gentile section of Philadelphia where he, his parents, and his seven brothers and sisters lived.

Stan Kaplan, a retired pharmaceutical scientist from the

Bronx who now lives in northern California, could not recall for me what haftarah he read at his bar mitzvah in 1951, but he remembered being terrified of tasting liquor for the first time.

"My biggest trepidation going into my bar mitzvah day was the drinking of schnapps," he said. "During the week prior to the bar mitzvah I attempted to taste schnapps by putting my lips or tongue to a glass of schnapps, and the burning sensation was more than I could stand.

"At the end of the service all the congregation and invited guests went down to the basement social hall for a kiddush consisting of kosher wine, challah, and pickled herring. We were a very poor family, and this kiddush was the extent of the celebrating after the service. An interesting story about the challah is that it was four to five feet long and two to three feet wide and was made by my uncle, who was a baker. I had to get the challah to the shul before sundown on Friday, and I carried it on my outstretched arms on a city bus to bring it from the bakery to the shul.

"The moment of truth had arrived. Everyone had left the sanctuary for the social hall except the old men at the back table, and I was dillydallying on the bimah trying to avoid the inevitable. Well, I proceeded to the table and joined the circle of men. Shot glasses of schnapps were handed out. It was typical for the old men to tilt their heads back and swallow the entire contents of the shot glass in one gulp. Some said 'L'chaim!' and as all the heads went back I immediately threw my schnapps over my shoulder. This was something I had not planned or even thought of until the moment it happened. To this day I have never had a drink of straight whiskey."

Fifty-two years later, Stan could not remember anything about the religious service, but he remembered the old men of the shul who wanted to toast him with schnapps, and he remembered how he had weaseled out of having his first taste of alcohol without embarrassing himself or hurting the oldsters' feelings. Many times I heard that kind of folksy, mundane, affectionate memory. Several men told me that they had received fountain pens for their b'nai mitzvah, a common gift at mid-century, and they all followed that revelation by telling the joke about the bar mitzvah speech that begins not "Today, I am a man!" but "Today, I am a fountain pen!" Many times I heard the story of how difficult it was to remember which elderly aunt was which. Twice I heard about the uncle or cousin who took the boy out back for his first cigarette. Everyone I interviewed from Long Island told me about Leonard's of Great Neck, the legendary kosher catering hall that had so many weddings and b'nai mitzvah that as soon as your group left the hors d'oeuvres room for the party room, they cycled the next party in behind you, keeping all the rooms going at the same time. Many times, more than I want to remember, I heard the urban legend, popular in the 1990s, about how bored Jewish girls, attending their thirtieth bar or bat mitzvah of the season, ducked out to provide the bored boys with oral sex in the bathrooms. (I have yet to hear an urban legend about the boys' reciprocating.)

I liked these stories, these small, homely dramas of b'nai mitzvah—the shot glass, the cigarette, the fountain pen—and I did not worry that they weren't more profound. Nor did I worry about the children I met, the very few, who seemed most interested in their parties. At its best, the party is a communal celebration of one child's personal accomplishment. The family honors its son or daughter, and the community honors the family. Friends from school, synagogue, and neighborhood honor one of their own. Gentiles celebrate Jews. But even at its worst, the party is a useful precaution, for it ensures that if the day has no spiritual meaning for the child—or even if, as I saw several times, the acrimony between divorced parents overshadows everything else—the day will not be a total waste. The day will at least be a memorable marker of time and effort. Just as it is worthwhile to have a birthday party even after a bad year—in fact, a bad year makes the party even more important, as a reminder that you got through it—bad b'nai mitzvah, like bad years, still deserve a party.

And even if you hate studying, even if you think that Judaism is stupid, it's nice to hear the rabbi and your parents give speeches about how proud they are of you. A lot of the gifts, you want to return (last season's Old Navy T-shirt, the latest Michael Jackson CD), but some of them you keep. The money, you save. Maybe it will take you to Europe the summer after freshman year of college. Maybe it will help you, like John Newman in Arkansas, to buy your first plot of land. Better a bad bar mitzvah with a good party than a bad bar mitzvah with a bad party.

Whatever gives the bar mitzvah its slightly malodorous whiff, whatever makes it an embarrassment, a *problem*, even for proud Jews, is not the straightforward reality, but reality refracted through our imagination, or our lack of it. So that we take true stories of gala parties and imagine that no spiritual light could possibly have shone on them; we take young, inarticulate adolescents and suppose that they are incapable of profound religiosity, even though they will soon be teenagers, more capable of infatuation and heartbreak than their parents have been for twenty-five years. Or we simply allow our discomfort with being Jews, our fear that the Gentiles are watching and laughing, to focus our attention on the failed bar mitzvah, the one that truly is just an excuse for a party, and to blind us to the hard work of children who—learning a dead language, reading from ancient texts, and being celebrated for it—do inch closer to being Jewish men and women. We fail to see what their accomplishments mean, not just for them, but for the Jews, and even the Gentiles, who surround them.

The renaissance of b'nai mitzvah, and their increasing frequency and increasing rigor, suggest that Jews hunger for this ritual. They have different reasons. The converts, like Jacob Ecker and Rena LeJeune, want to affirm their commitment to a new faith. The grown women want to claim an honorific rite denied them as girls. The boys and girls want to please their parents, have a party for their friends, and, often, do the best job they can. Some children are excited about being admitted to the minyan, with all the rights and responsibilities of adult prayer. All these motivations bespeak a general urge to belong, but more specifically an urge to ask, in a public, visible way, to be counted as one of the Jews.

Jews can look and act, to the rest of the world, like Christians, but being Jewish is not like being Christian, or at least not like being Protestant. It is more like being Catholic, Muslim, or Mormon. Most American Protestants do not see themselves as members of a worldwide religious tribe. Typical Presbyterians from Pittsburgh do not think that they have much in common with Presbyterians in Scotland; most Episcopalians are not terribly interested in the sister Anglican churches in Nigeria or India. Southern Baptists have a strong international missionary program, but they can also be obsessively patriotic, in a very parochial way. There are Lutherans who care deeply about their denominational identity, but how many of them would be upset if their children married outside the faith? How many Congregationalist parents hope desperately for Congregationalist sons-in-law?

But in its very theology, Judaism is corporate. The Jews are a chosen people—the covenant was not with Abraham alone, but with all his descendants. To say the prayers after a meal, three Jews must be present; to say the prayer for the dead, ten. As the Hasid in Anchorage said to me, one of the greatest compliments is to say of a man, "There's a minyan in him"— he has the souls of many in one. On becoming a bar or bat mitzvah, a child has joined the worldwide, international, extended-family minyan.

The popularity of b'nai mitzvah is not a result of their usefulness. There is no strong evidence that the bar or bat mitzvah will reverse Jews' low birthrates or counter religious indifference. While committed Jewish families see b'nai mitzvah as necessary to rearing a good Jewish child, that is no way to account for adult b'nai mitzvah—and what is more, it's no way to account for the enthusiasm of the children themselves, whose excitement has little to do with abstract notions of Jewish survival. B'nai mitzvah cannot be explained through Torah, which nowhere mentions the ceremony; Jews are not commanded to celebrate the bar mitzvah.

Rather, they are commanded to act like Jews: to pray, to tell the story of the Exodus every Passover, to reproduce young Jews, to circumcise the boys. But as rewarding as the Jewishly lived life can be, and as fun as reproduction is, they seem to express inadequately our religious peoplehood. What evangelical Christians express by being born again, or Mormons by going on a two-year mission, Jews express through the bar and bat mitzvah. They proclaim their commitment to Judaism every time they say their prayers, but this is the only time they make that commitment with an audience watching.

Performing one's religious devotion in front of people is a terrifically ennobling experience. When Pentecostals get struck by the spirit and fall on the floor and writhe, they are, in some sense, having *fun*. The Jewish liturgical mode is not, except among the Hasidim, quite so lively, but standing onstage as the cantor chants the hazzanut and the congregation intones the prayers, all in preparation for your Torah reading—you don't soon forget that. How often in the average life does one get to be onstage? For most of us, very seldom. Most of us are applauded three times: at birth, at graduation, and at marriage. The Jews had the genius—not at first, but after a couple thousand years of existence—to make a big to-do in honor of their sons' learning. No matter how little you learned, you still got to go onstage. Eventually, girls did too.

The early Reform movement abandoned the bar mitzvah, just as it abandoned other markers of Jewish distinctiveness— Saturday worship, dietary restrictions, head coverings—and just as it tried to emphasize the common heritage of Judaism and Christianity. By contrast, when Zionist fervor and Jewish pride peaked in the late 1960s—when a love of Jewish difference became okay—the future of the bar and bat mitzvah was secured. For most American Jews, daily prayer and strict observance of kashrut no longer seemed like meaningful ways to be Jewish, but the public celebration of Torah learning was a compelling idea. It was worth years of education, whose successful conclusion merited a party. The party would be an ecumenical affair: except for wedding rites, the bar mitzvah is the American religious event most often attended by members of other religions (Catholic schoolchildren, for example, seldom invite non-Catholic friends to their confirmations). And the gifts would include more responsibility, higher expectations, and more anxiety than seemed worthwhile. Another gift too: the congratulations of the old men in the back of the room, waiting to say "l'chaim" in your honor, waiting to give you a shot of schnapps.

As Jews' connections to those Old World traditions have faded, the bar and bat mitzvah have become more important. The United States is a warm home for religion, but it can be a solvent, dissolving cultural differences in favor of an undifferentiated piety. This is not only a Jewish problem, but an American one. Jewish communities have had to reclaim their Judaism, and by celebrating Judaism publicly, b'nai mitzvah advance that cause. The more opportunities Jews have to escape Judaism, the more b'nai mitzvah there seem to be.

The lesson there, that public celebration is good, is one that other religions seem to be learning. In the 1980s, St. Philip's, an Episcopal church in Durham, North Carolina, started Rite 13, a Christian ceremony for adolescents passing into adulthood. "We were looking at the Jewish tradition of bar and bat mitzvahs," Reverend Cathie Caimono told the *New York Times* in 2003. "We realized there were no established rites of passage for adolescents in our church and our culture. We thought we wanted to do something similar for our kids." Twelve hundred churches, mostly Episcopal but also Presbyterian, Methodist, Baptist, and Lutheran, have bought the curriculum, which, according to the *Times*, "includes religious training, social service and discussion of sex and relationships." After completing the program, a boy or girl graduates in a public ceremony in which he or she must read from Psalm 139 and answer questions from the minister, who then offers a blessing. Afterward, the child sits in the pews with other teenagers who have undergone the rite.

So maybe Rite 13 will take off, and all the Protestants will be doing it, and maybe it will begin to supplement the Catholic confirmation too, and then the Muslims will get in on the act. Someday maybe every American child born to a religion that honors the Old Testament will be expected to declaim a passage aloud. And they will greet each other in junior high school hallways, bump fists, ask each other what's up, and then tease each other about that night's homework: the Torah portion, the reading from the Prophets, the 139th psalm of King David. And that would be yet another Jewish gift to the world, another thing that some old bearded men figured out one night, ages ago, talking about their religion, which curiously lived on even though a lot of very smart people, rabbis and historians and sociologists, kept expecting it to die; another thing, like Hebrew itself, like the words of Moses on Sinai, that other religions saw was good, too good to leave to the Jews alone.

Acknowledgments

I have tried my best to avoid errors of history, philology, and theology. For their help in these and other editorial matters, I am grateful to Paul Elie, Rachel Goodman, Dara Horn, Sarah Larson, Betsy Lerner, Kathryn Lewis, Ivan Marcus, Jordana Schuster, Charlotte Strick, and, most of all, Cyd Fremmer. The Koret Foundation's Young Writer on Jewish Themes award helped support me while I wrote. And I hope this book is sufficient thanks to all the children, women, and men who patiently welcomed me into their religious lives.

5/05